HEY, James!

by Mark Tonra.

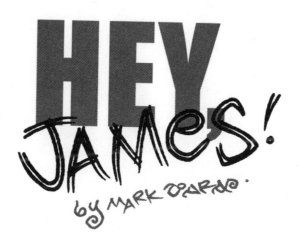

HEY, JAMES!

by Mark Tonra

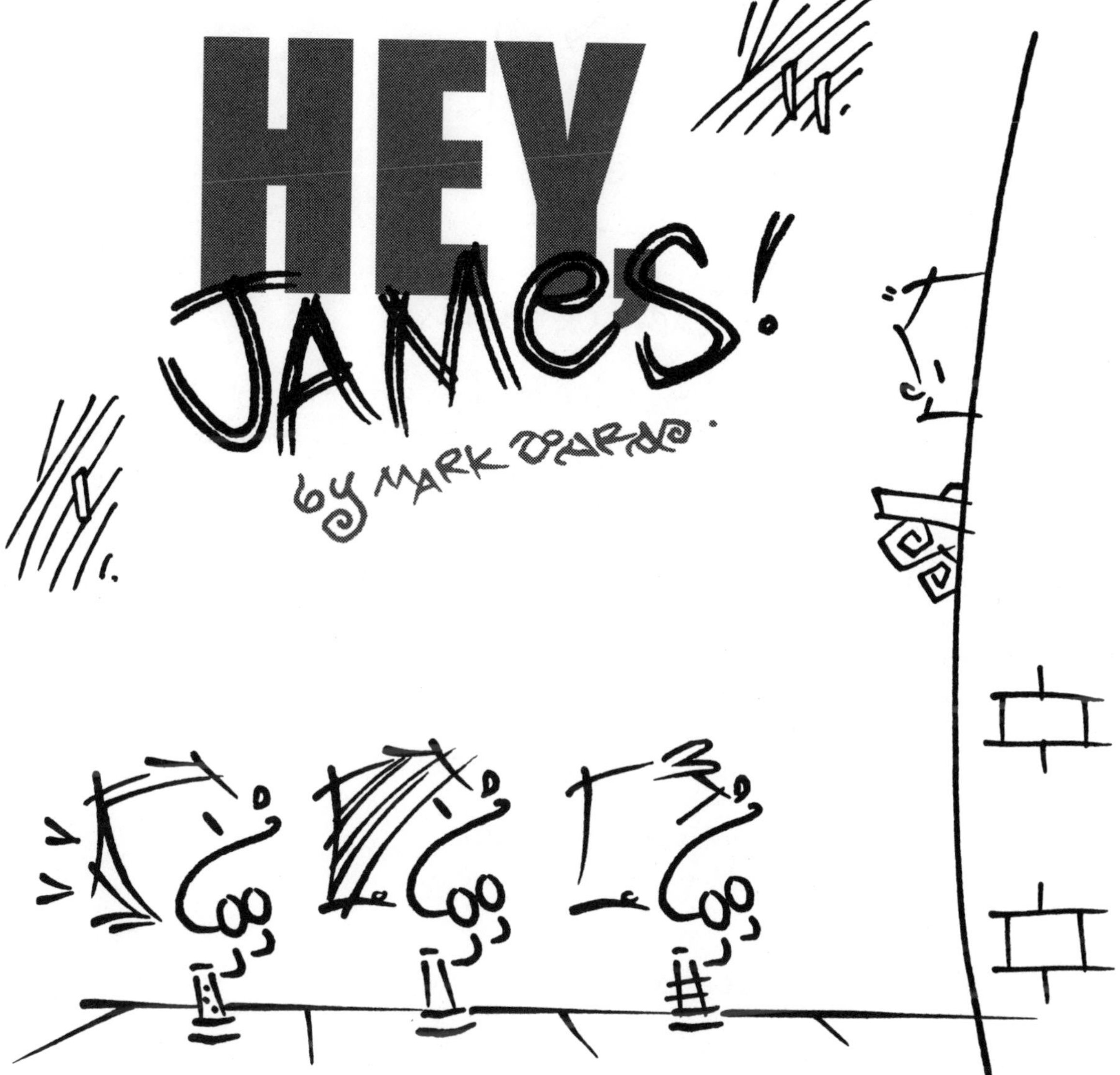

Andrews McMeel Publishing

Kansas City

FOR SARAH & JAMES!

Thanks to: Sparky, Segar, Herriman, Wilde, Seuss, Thoreau, Blyth, Sendak , and Picasso.
Without whom: Erin, Sue, Lee, Andrews McMeel, uclick, and Universal Press Syndicate.

www.JamesFans.com

www.uComics.com

ISBN: 0-7407-3308-7

Library of Congress Control Number: 2002113728

03 04 05 06 07 BBG 10 9 8 7 6 5 4 3 2 1

Foreword

It's true. It happens. Sometimes.

James Tonra
January 2003

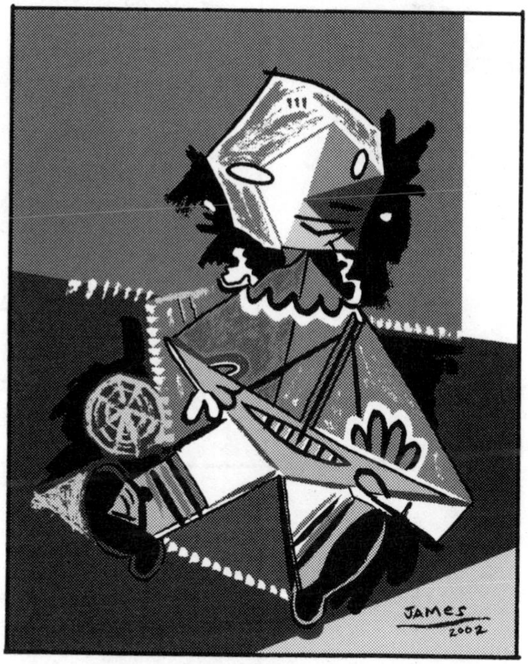
JAMES
2002

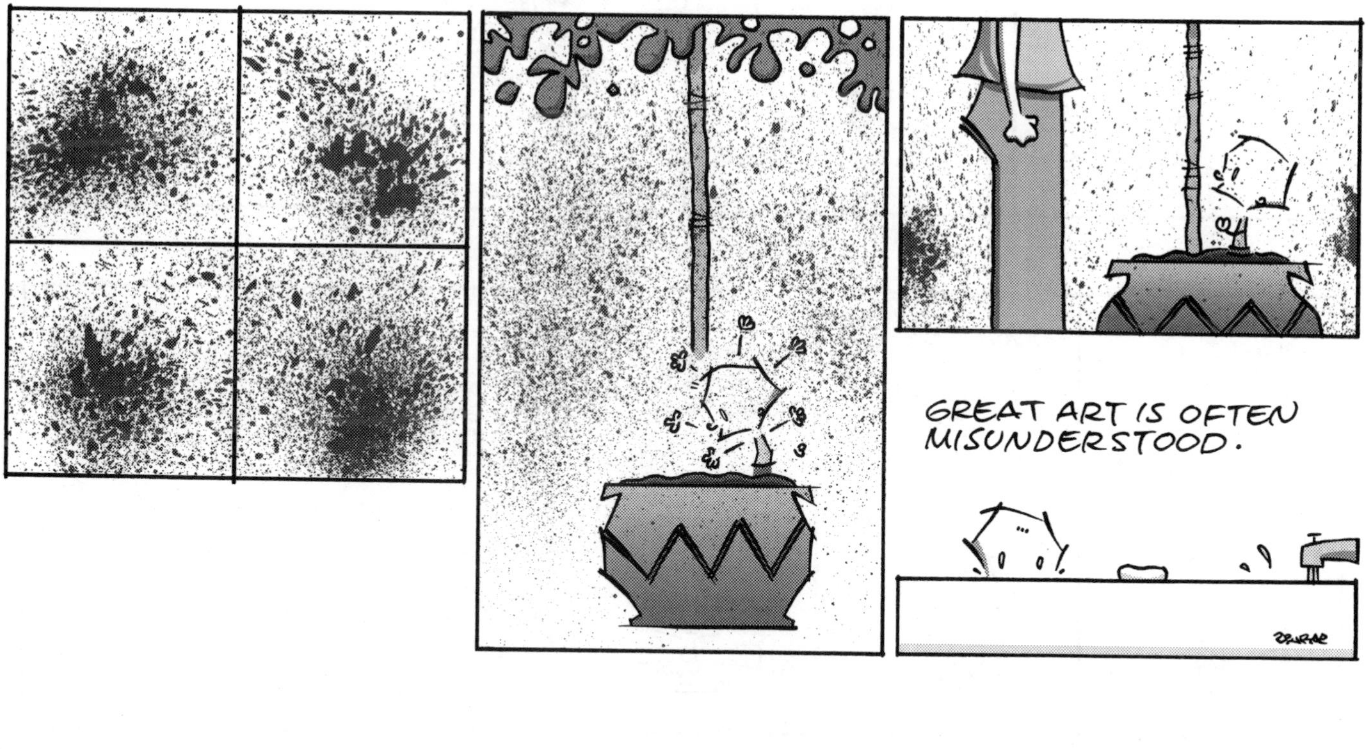
GREAT ART IS OFTEN
MISUNDERSTOOD.

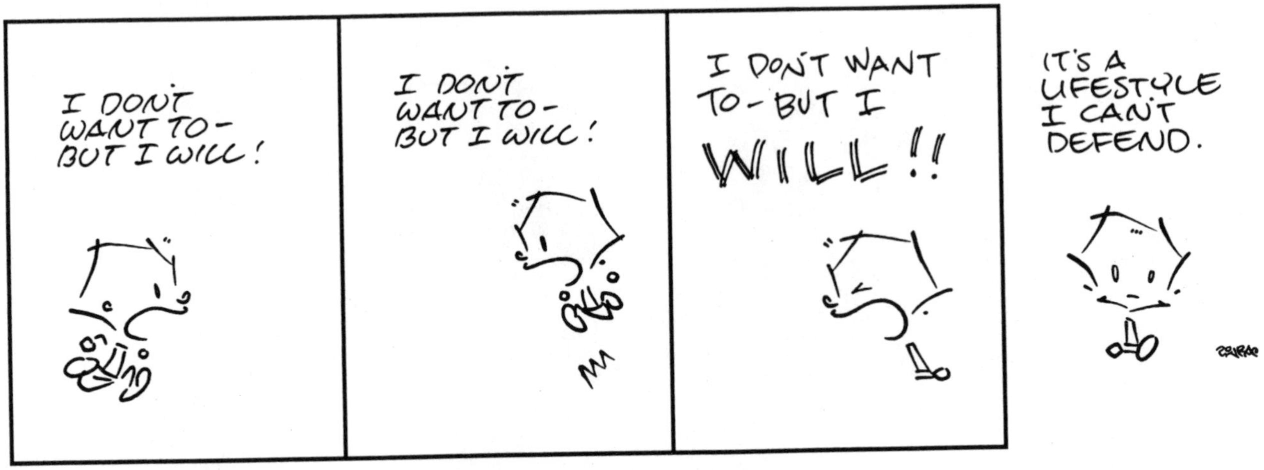
I DON'T WANT TO- BUT I WILL!
I DON'T WANT TO- BUT I WILL!
I DON'T WANT TO- BUT I WILL!!
IT'S A LIFESTYLE I CAN'T DEFEND.

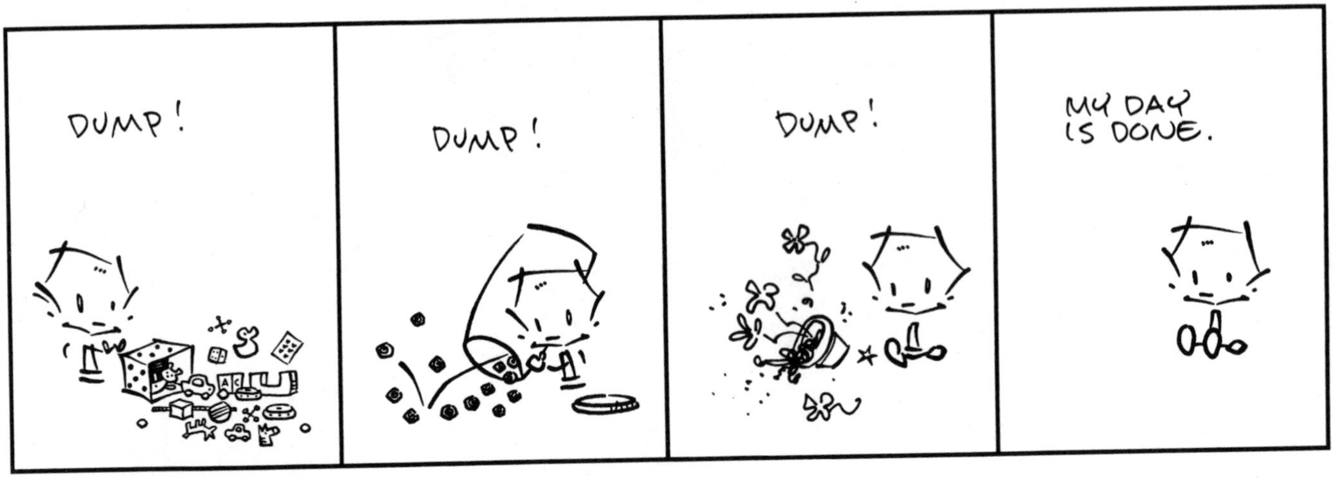
DUMP!
DUMP!
DUMP!
MY DAY IS DONE.

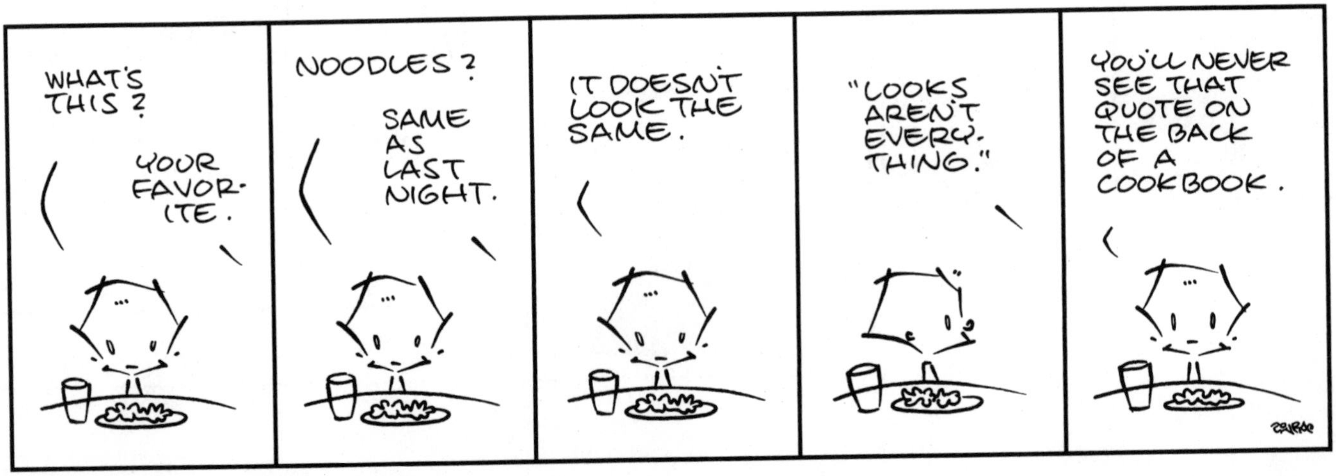
WHAT'S THIS?
YOUR FAVOR-ITE.
NOODLES?
SAME AS LAST NIGHT.
IT DOESN'T LOOK THE SAME.
"LOOKS AREN'T EVERY-THING."
YOU'LL NEVER SEE THAT QUOTE ON THE BACK OF A COOKBOOK.

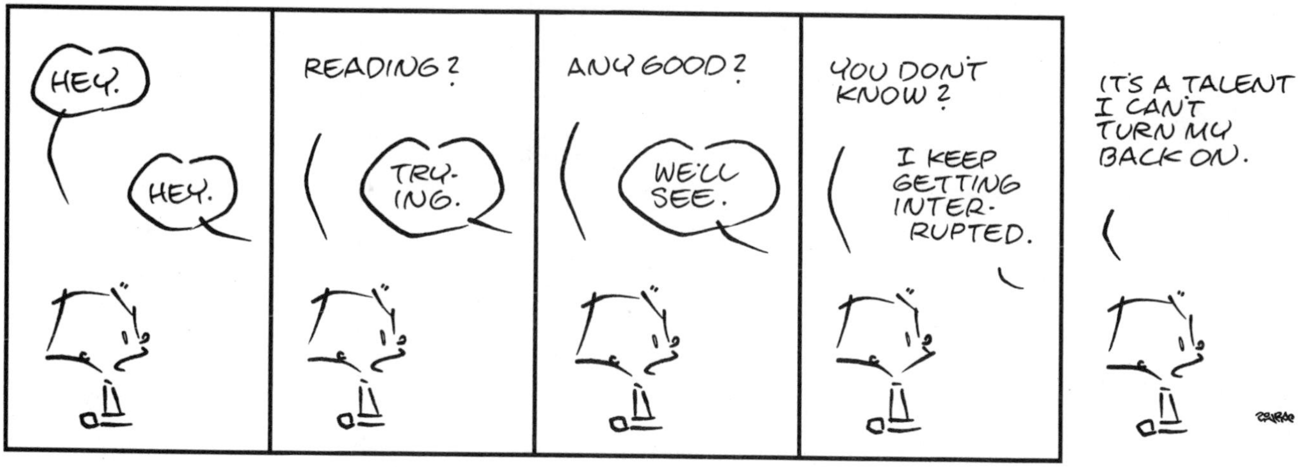
HEY.
HEY.
READING?
TRY-ING.
ANY GOOD?
WE'LL SEE.
YOU DON'T KNOW?
I KEEP GETTING INTER-RUPTED.
IT'S A TALENT I CAN'T TURN MY BACK ON.

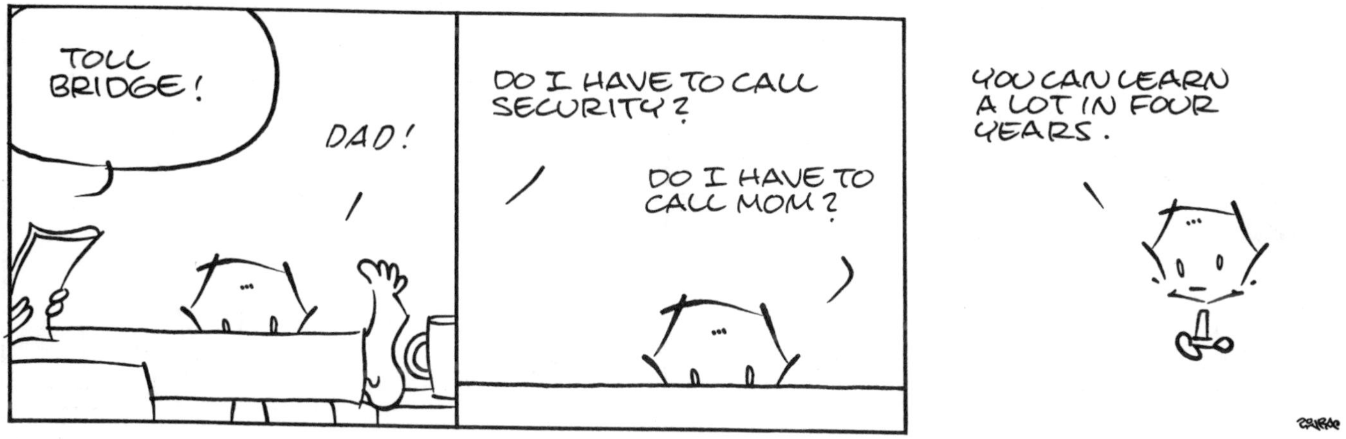
TOLL BRIDGE!
DAD!
DO I HAVE TO CALL SECURITY?
DO I HAVE TO CALL MOM?
YOU CAN LEARN A LOT IN FOUR YEARS.

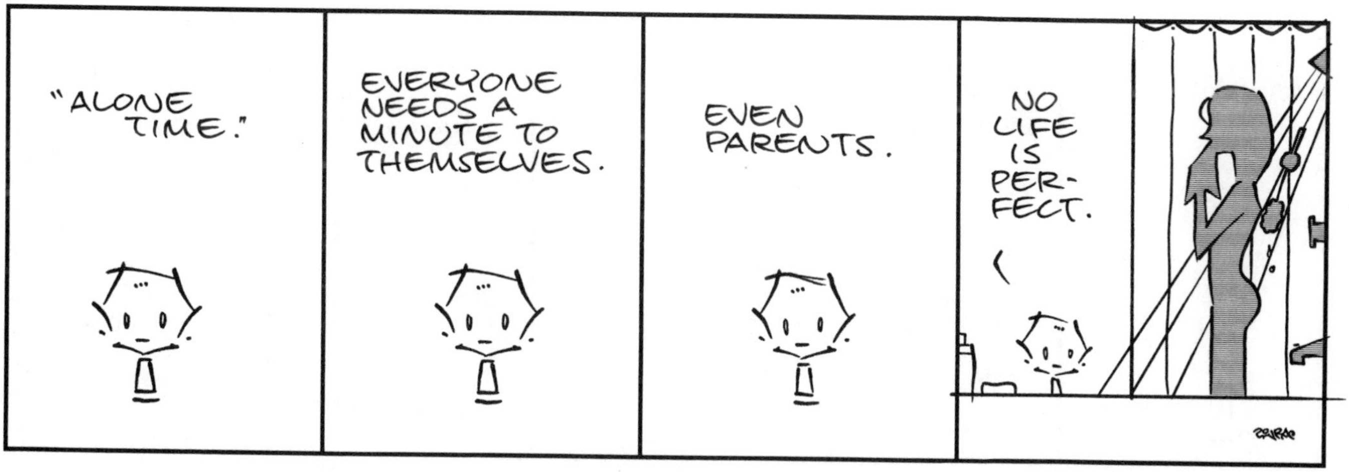
"ALONE TIME."
EVERYONE NEEDS A MINUTE TO THEMSELVES.
EVEN PARENTS.
NO LIFE IS PER-FECT.

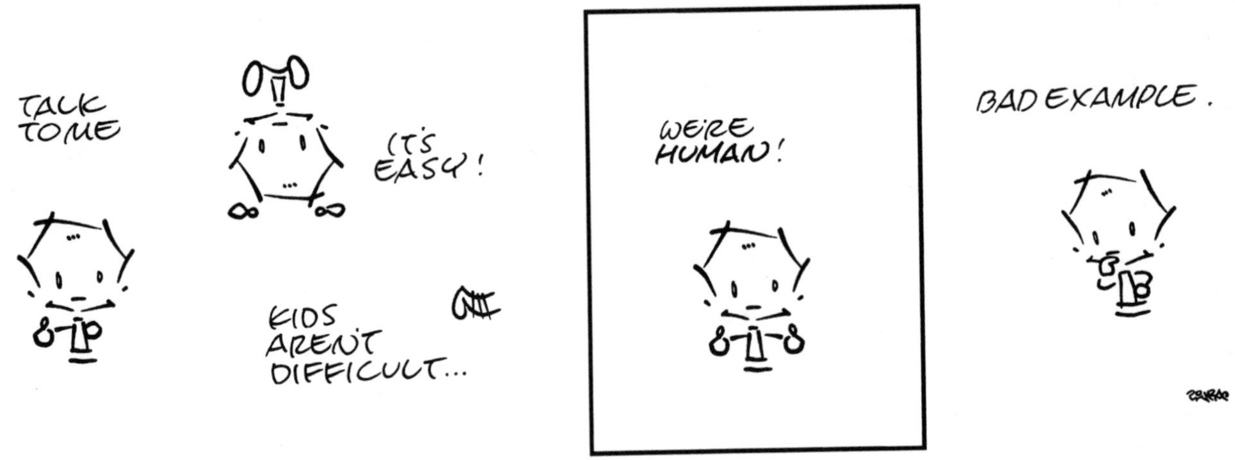
TALK TO ME
IT'S EASY!
KIDS AREN'T DIFFICULT...
WE'RE HUMAN!
BAD EXAMPLE.

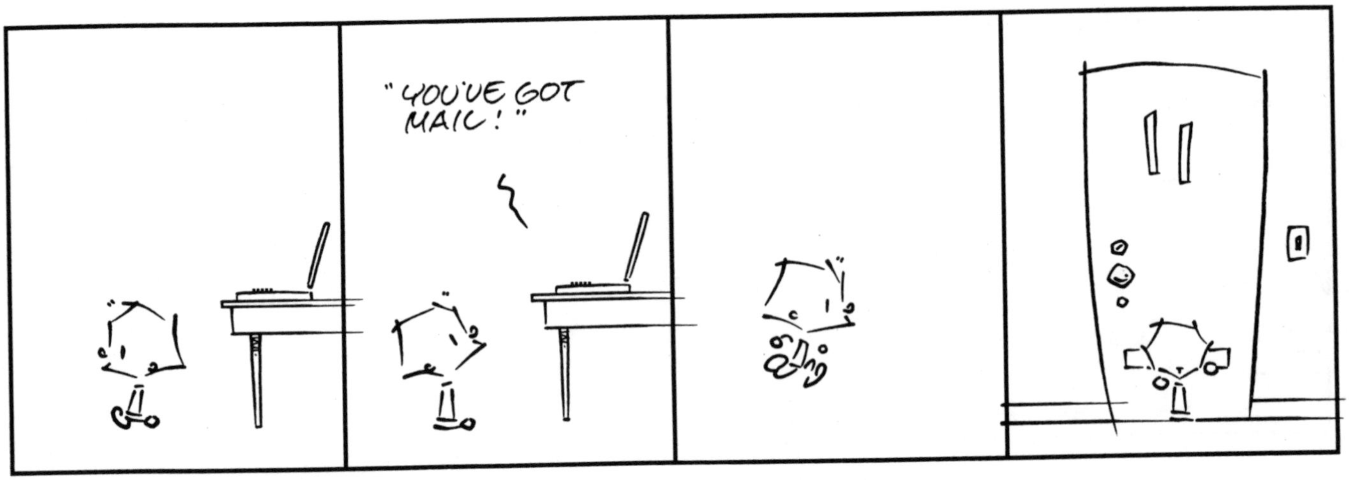
"YOU'VE GOT MAIL!"

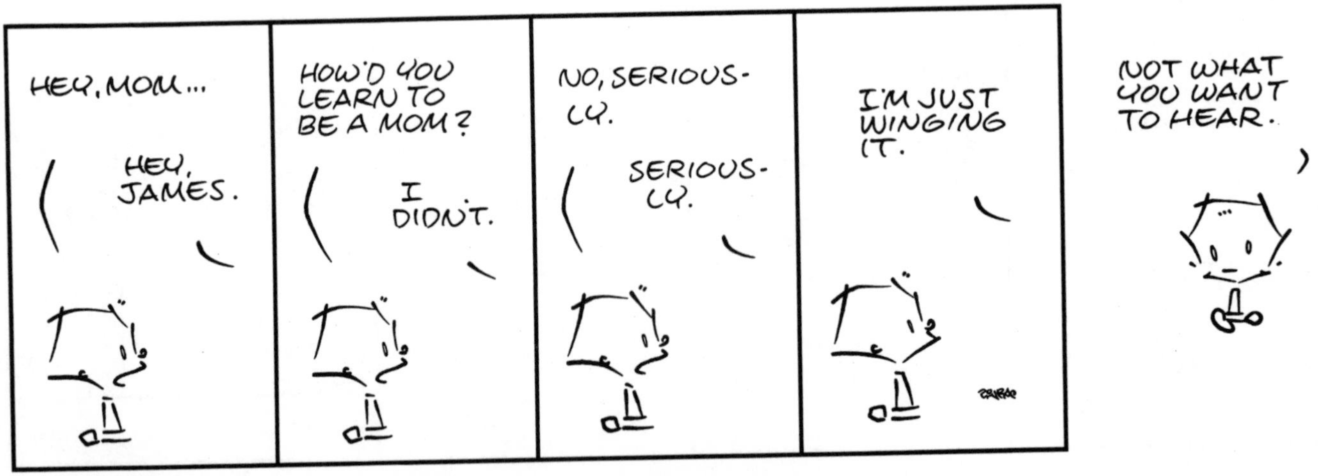
HEY, MOM...
HEY, JAMES.
HOW'D YOU LEARN TO BE A MOM?
I DIDN'T.
NO, SERIOUS-LY.
SERIOUS-LY.
I'M JUST WINGING IT.
NOT WHAT YOU WANT TO HEAR.

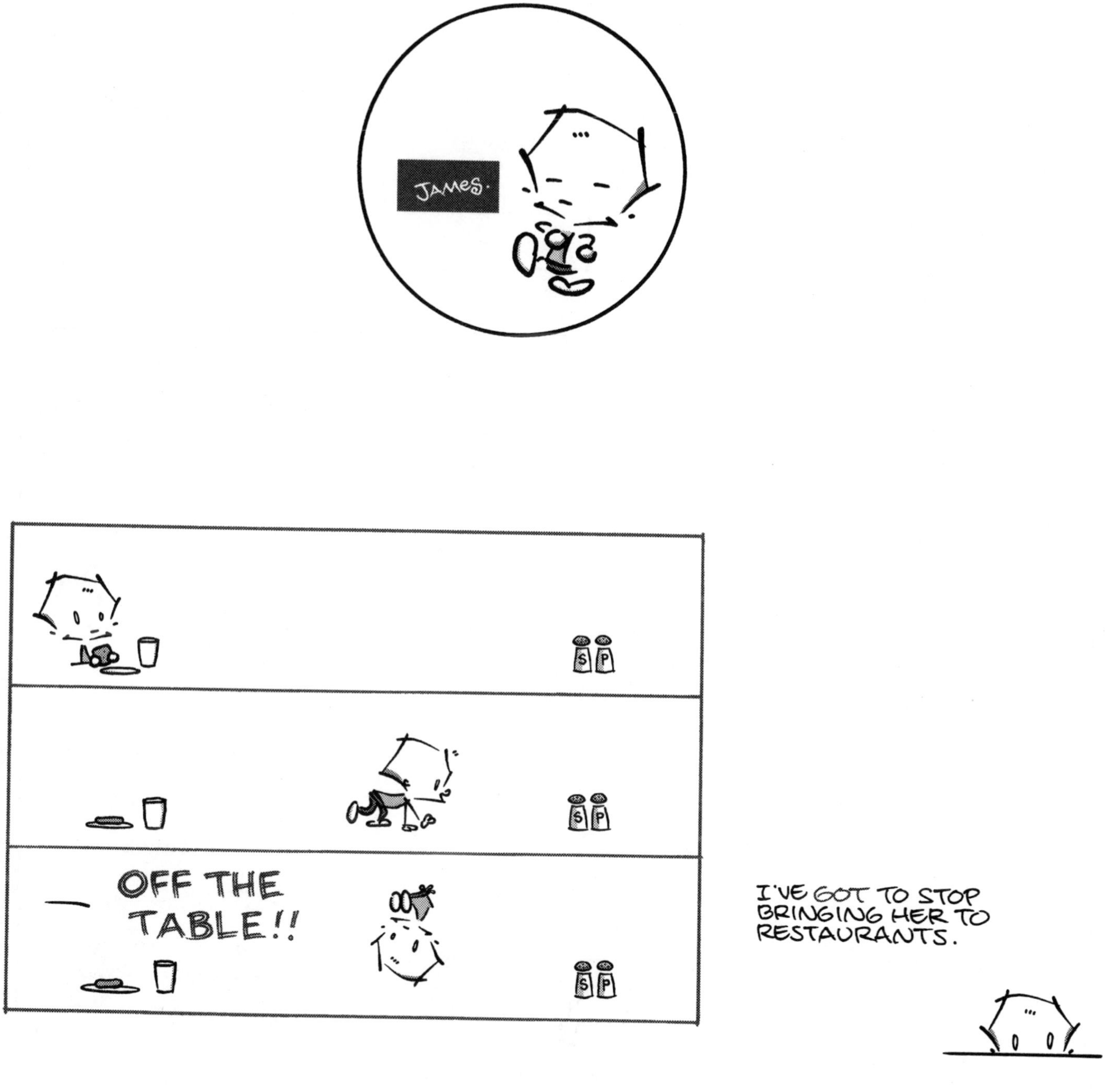
JAMES.
— OFF THE TABLE!!
I'VE GOT TO STOP BRINGING HER TO RESTAURANTS.

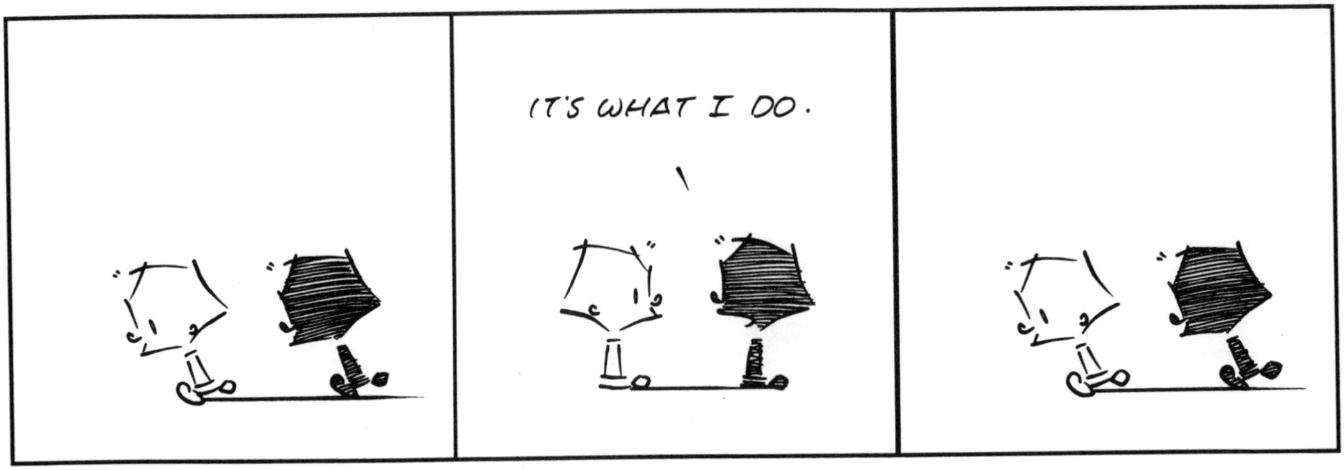
IT'S WHAT I DO.

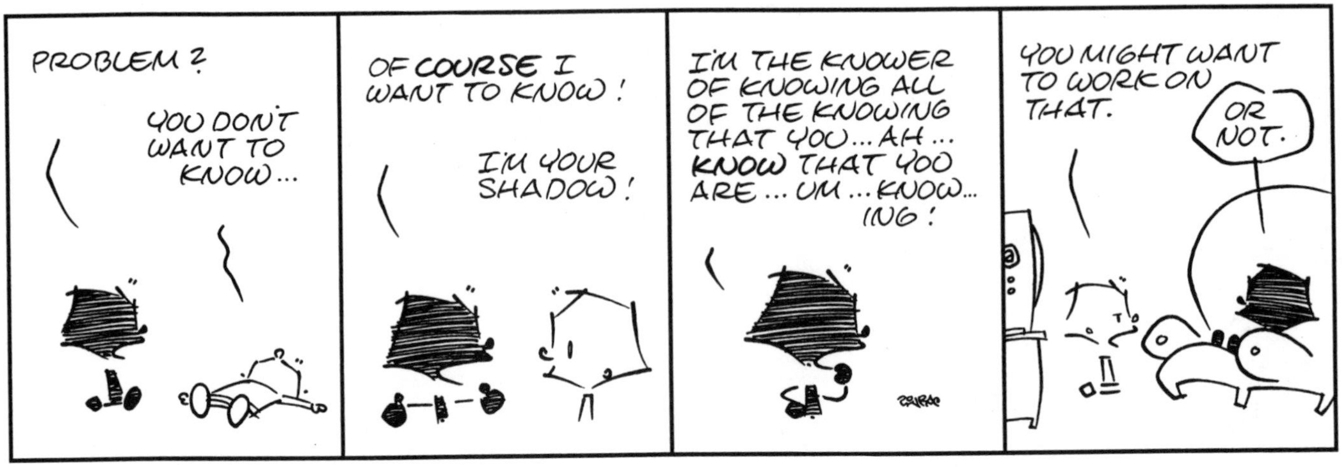
PROBLEM?
YOU DON'T WANT TO KNOW...
OF COURSE I WANT TO KNOW!
I'M YOUR SHADOW!
I'M THE KNOWER OF KNOWING ALL OF THE KNOWING THAT YOU... AH... KNOW THAT YOU ARE... UM... KNOW... ING!
YOU MIGHT WANT TO WORK ON THAT.
OR NOT.

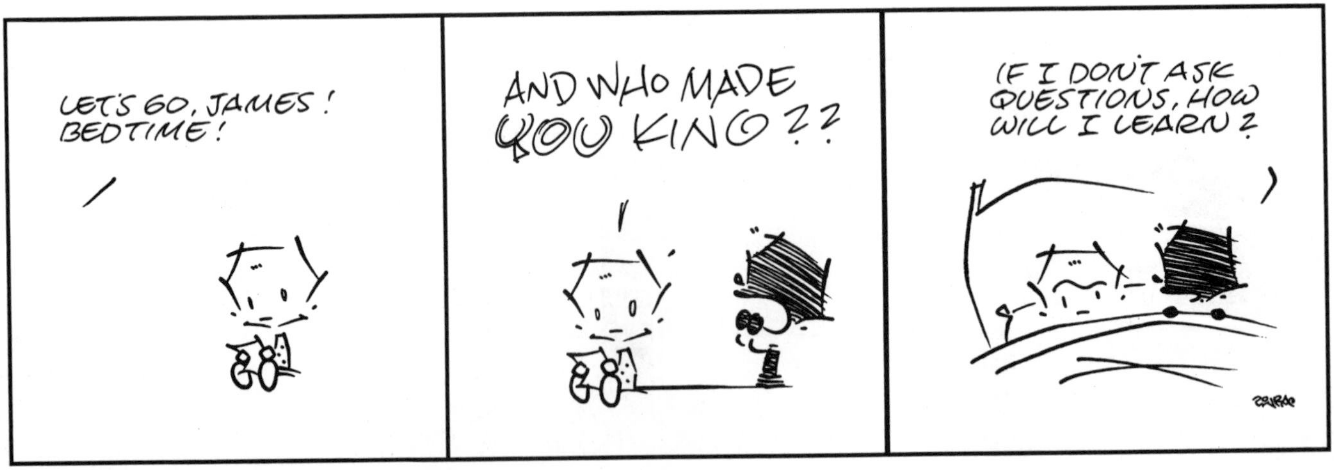
LET'S GO, JAMES! BEDTIME!
AND WHO MADE YOU KING??
IF I DON'T ASK QUESTIONS, HOW WILL I LEARN?

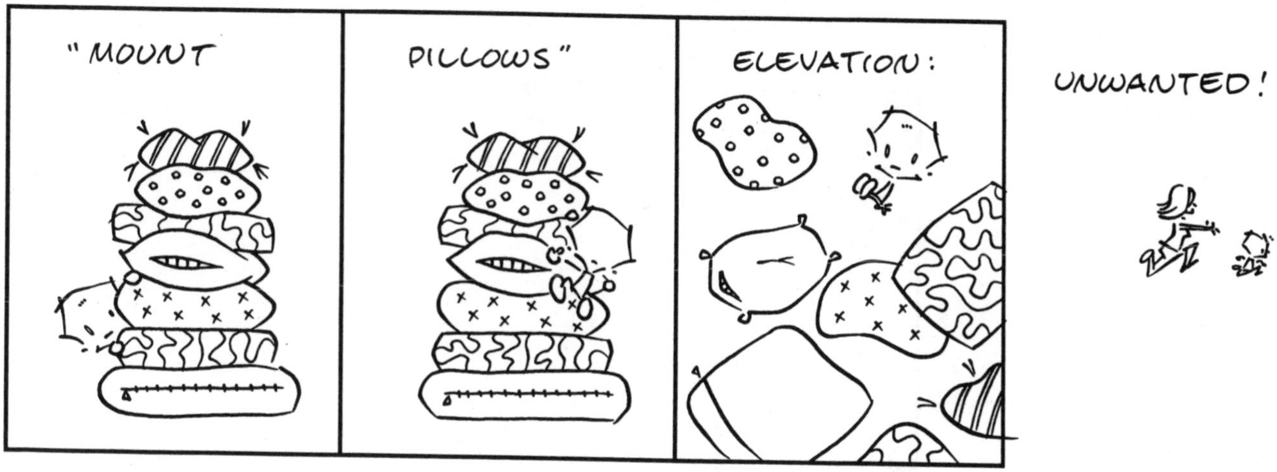
"MOUNT
PILLOWS"
ELEVATION:
UNWANTED!

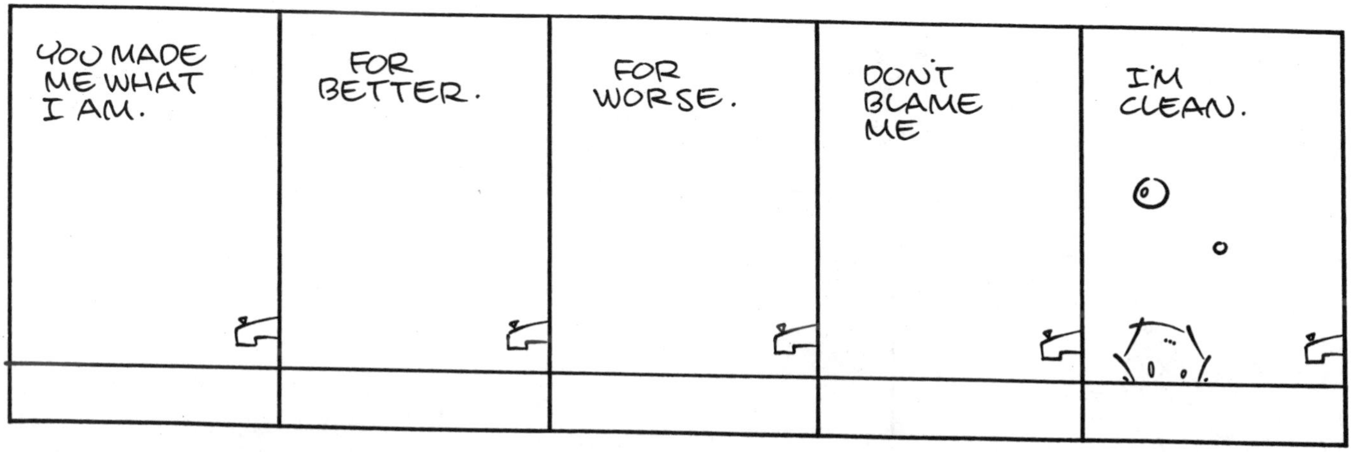
YOU MADE ME WHAT I AM.
FOR BETTER.
FOR WORSE.
DON'T BLAME ME
I'M CLEAN.

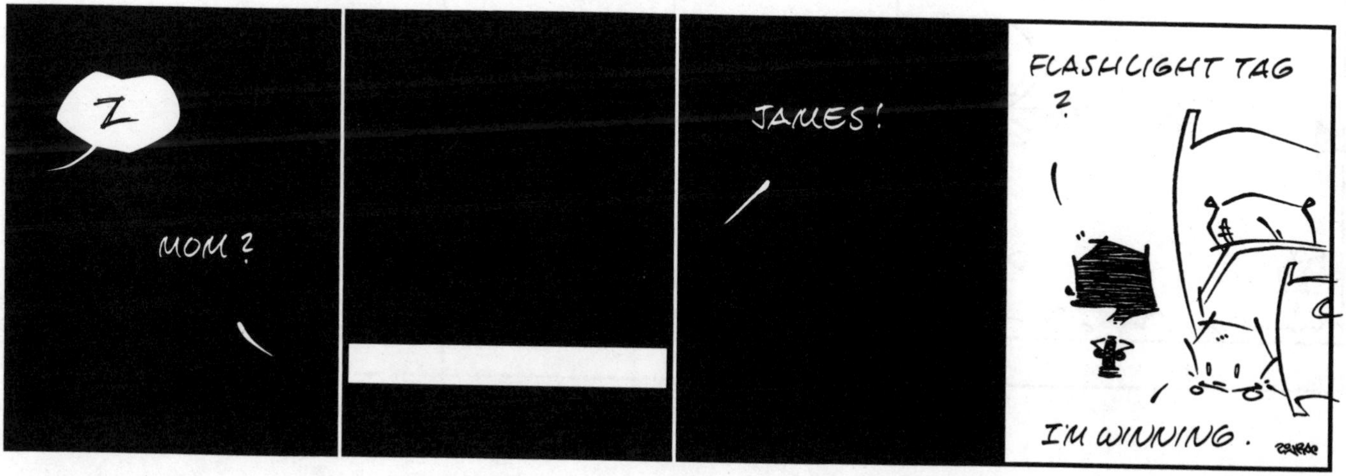
Z
MOM?
JAMES!
FLASHLIGHT TAG?
I'M WINNING.

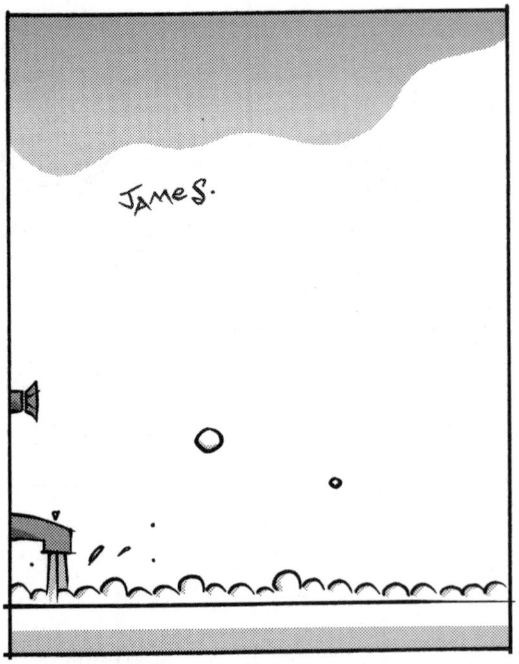
JAMES.

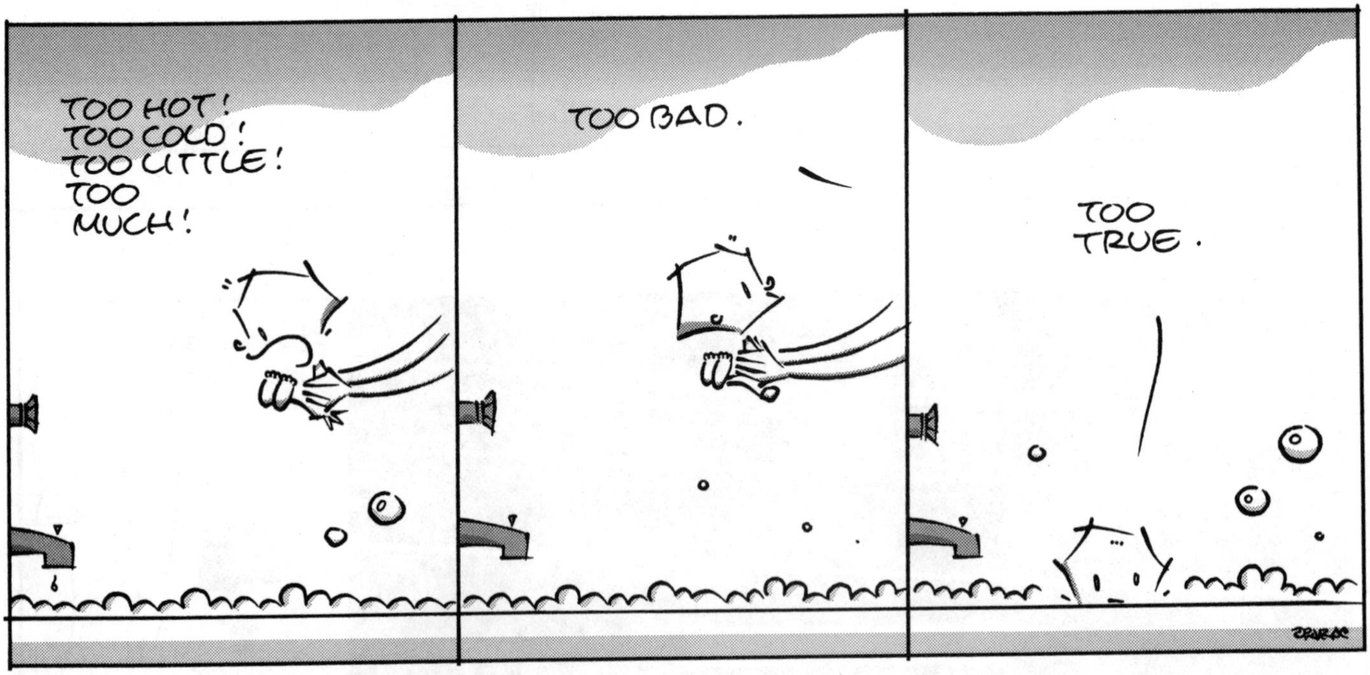
TOO HOT! TOO COLD! TOO LITTLE! TOO MUCH!
TOO BAD.
TOO TRUE.

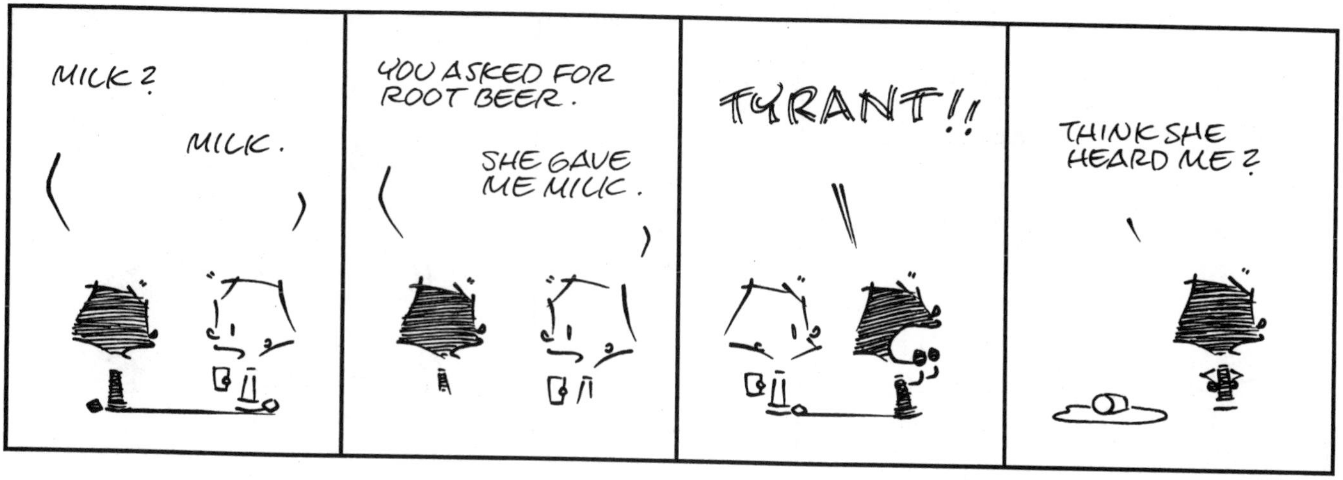
MILK?
MILK.
YOU ASKED FOR ROOT BEER.
SHE GAVE ME MILK.
TYRANT!!
THINK SHE HEARD ME?

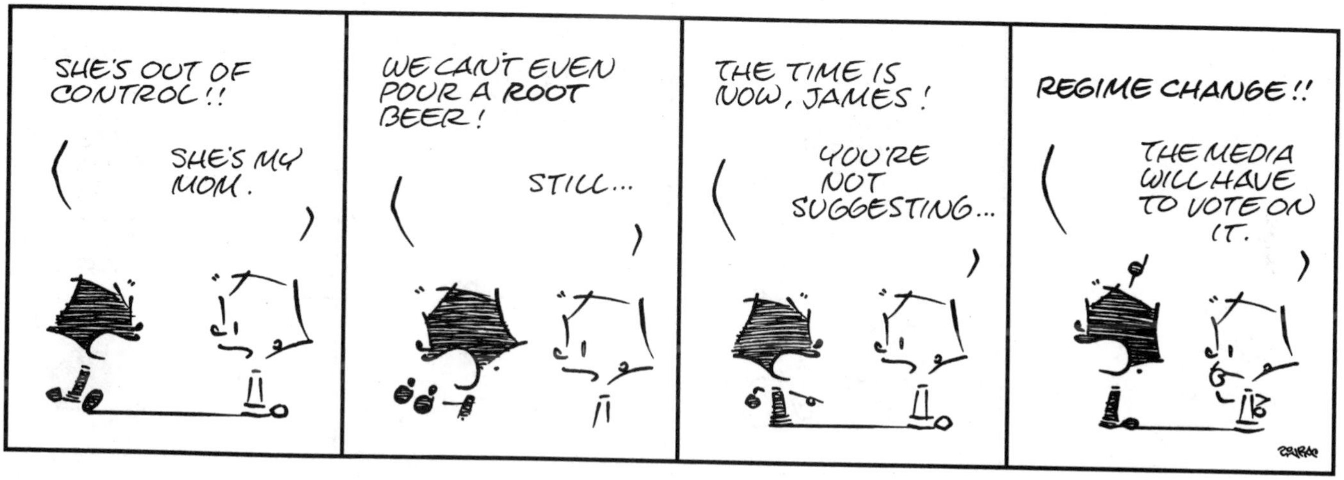
SHE'S OUT OF CONTROL!!
SHE'S MY MOM.
WE CAN'T EVEN POUR A **ROOT** BEER!
STILL...
THE TIME IS NOW, JAMES!
YOU'RE NOT SUGGESTING...
REGIME CHANGE!!
THE MEDIA WILL HAVE TO VOTE ON IT.

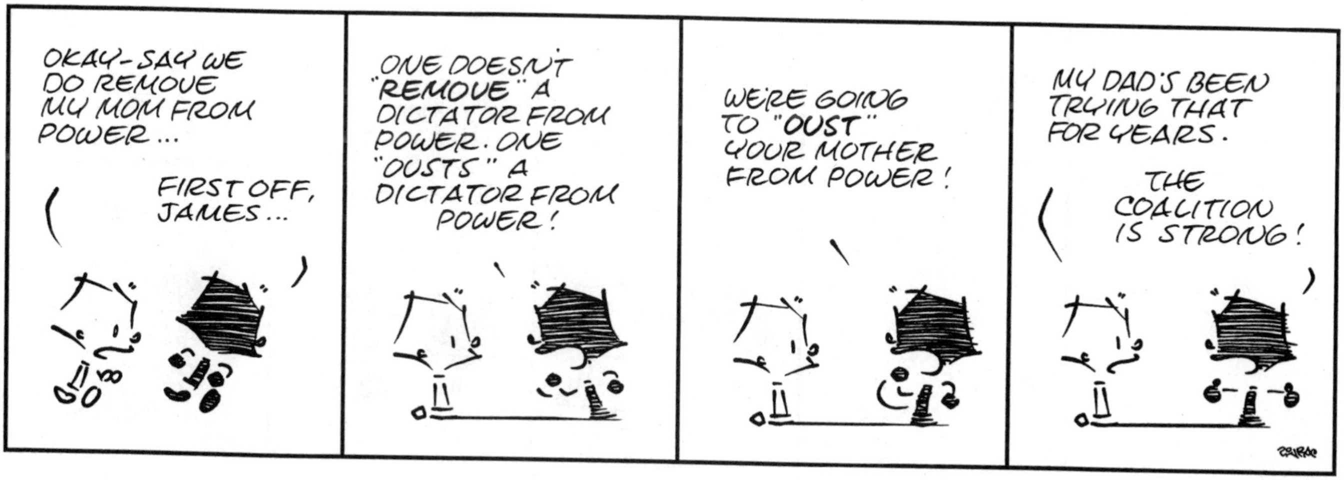
OKAY- SAY WE DO REMOVE MY MOM FROM POWER...
FIRST OFF, JAMES...
ONE DOESN'T "**REMOVE**" A DICTATOR FROM POWER. ONE "OUSTS" A DICTATOR FROM POWER!
WE'RE GOING TO "**OUST**" YOUR MOTHER FROM POWER!
MY DAD'S BEEN TRYING THAT FOR YEARS.
THE COALITION IS STRONG!

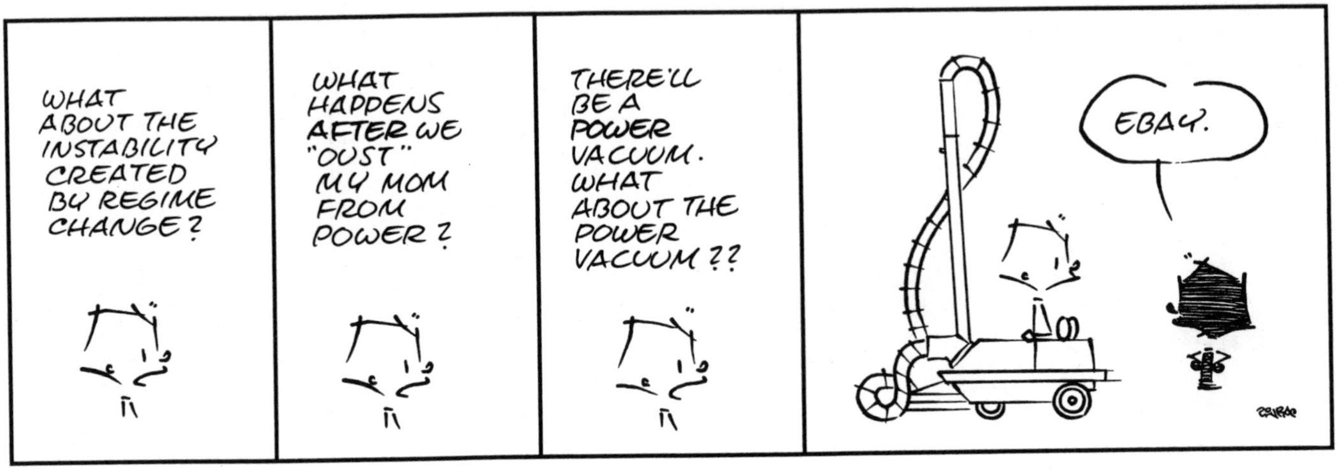
WHAT ABOUT THE INSTABILITY CREATED BY REGIME CHANGE?
WHAT HAPPENS AFTER WE "OUST" MY MOM FROM POWER?
THERE'LL BE A POWER VACUUM. WHAT ABOUT THE POWER VACUUM??
EBAY.

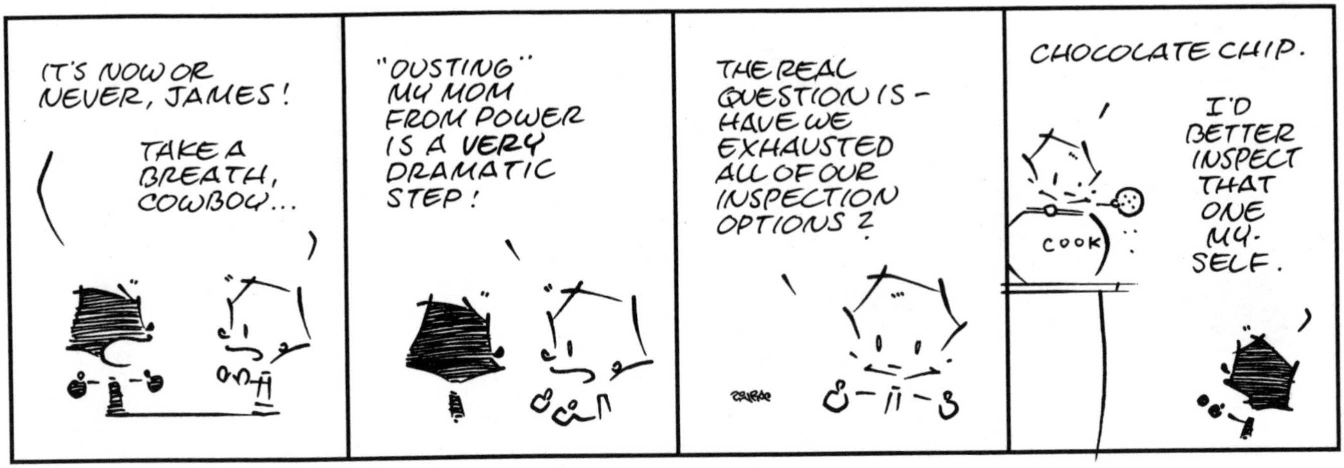
IT'S NOW OR NEVER, JAMES!
TAKE A BREATH, COWBOY...
"OUSTING" MY MOM FROM POWER IS A VERY DRAMATIC STEP!
THE REAL QUESTION IS - HAVE WE EXHAUSTED ALL OF OUR INSPECTION OPTIONS?
CHOCOLATE CHIP.
COOK
I'D BETTER INSPECT THAT ONE MYSELF.

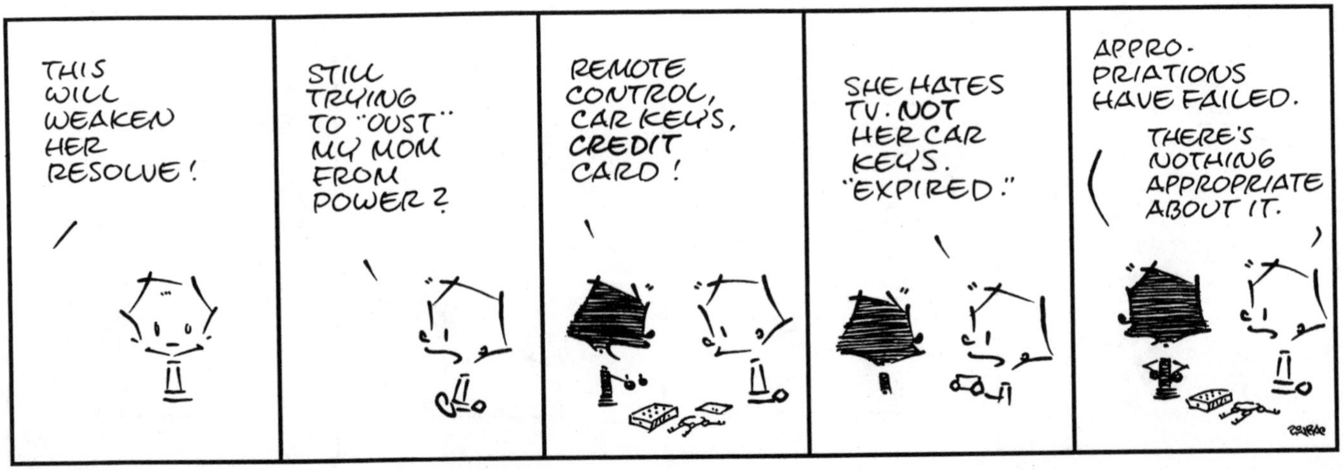
THIS WILL WEAKEN HER RESOLVE!
STILL TRYING TO "OUST" MY MOM FROM POWER?
REMOTE CONTROL, CAR KEYS, CREDIT CARD!
SHE HATES TV. NOT HER CAR KEYS. "EXPIRED."
APPROPRIATIONS HAVE FAILED.
THERE'S NOTHING APPROPRIATE ABOUT IT.

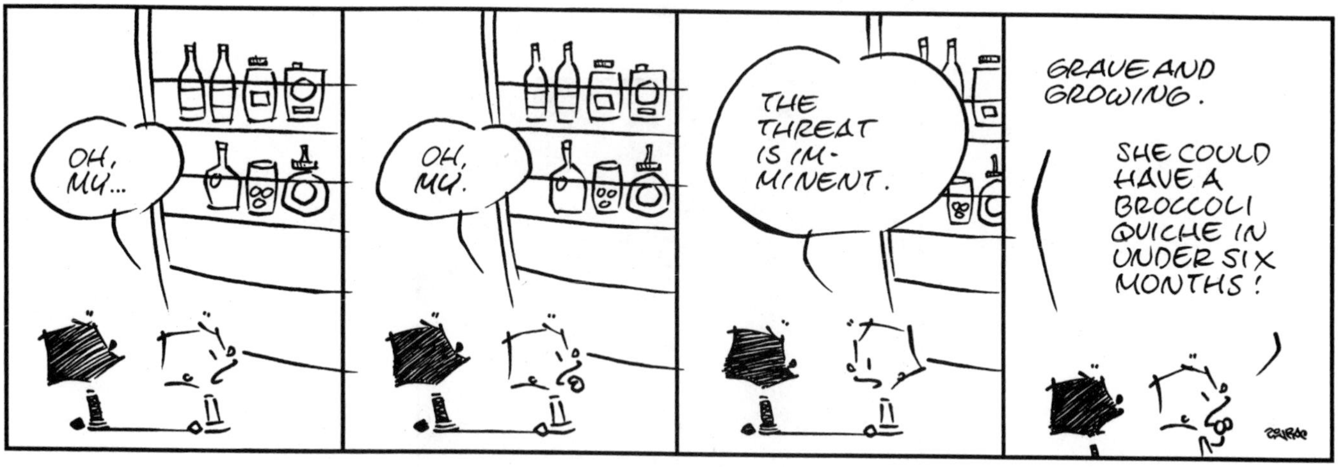
OH, MY...
OH, MY.
THE THREAT IS IM-MINENT.
GRAVE AND GROWING.
SHE COULD HAVE A BROCCOLI QUICHE IN UNDER SIX MONTHS!

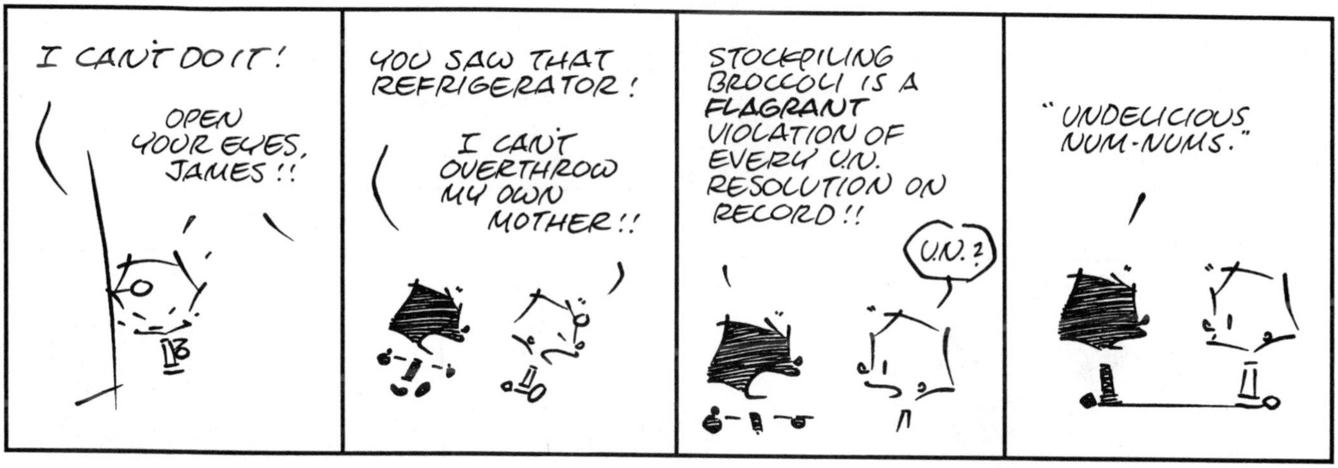
I CAN'T DO IT!
OPEN YOUR EYES, JAMES!!
YOU SAW THAT REFRIGERATOR!
I CAN'T OVERTHROW MY OWN MOTHER!!
STOCKPILING BROCCOLI IS A FLAGRANT VIOLATION OF EVERY U.N. RESOLUTION ON RECORD!!
U.N.?
"UNDELICIOUS NUM-NUMS."

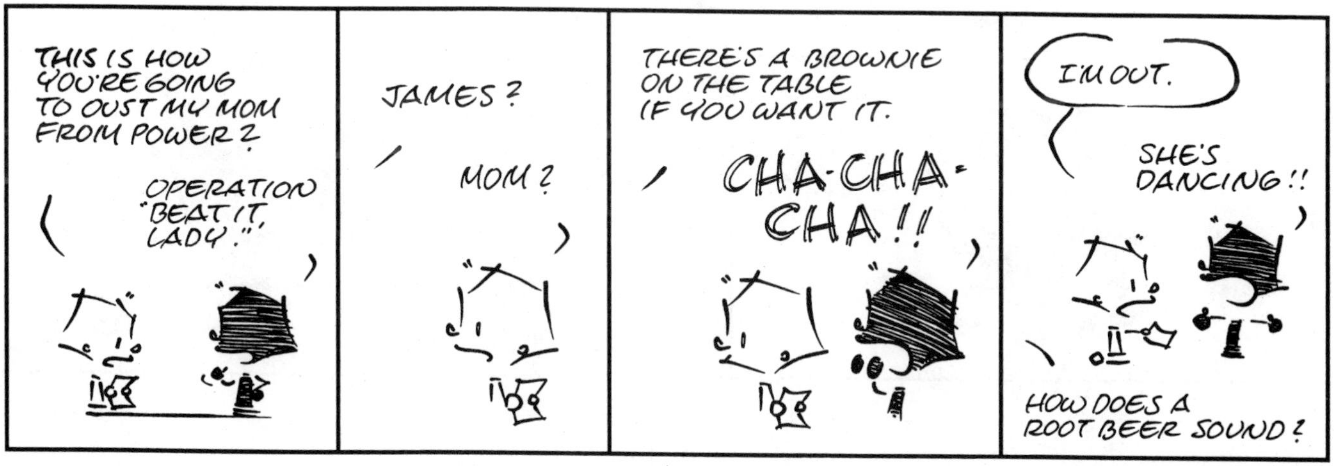
THIS IS HOW YOU'RE GOING TO OUST MY MOM FROM POWER?
OPERATION "BEAT IT, LADY."
JAMES?
MOM?
THERE'S A BROWNIE ON THE TABLE IF YOU WANT IT.
CHA-CHA-CHA!!
I'M OUT.
SHE'S DANCING!!
HOW DOES A ROOT BEER SOUND?

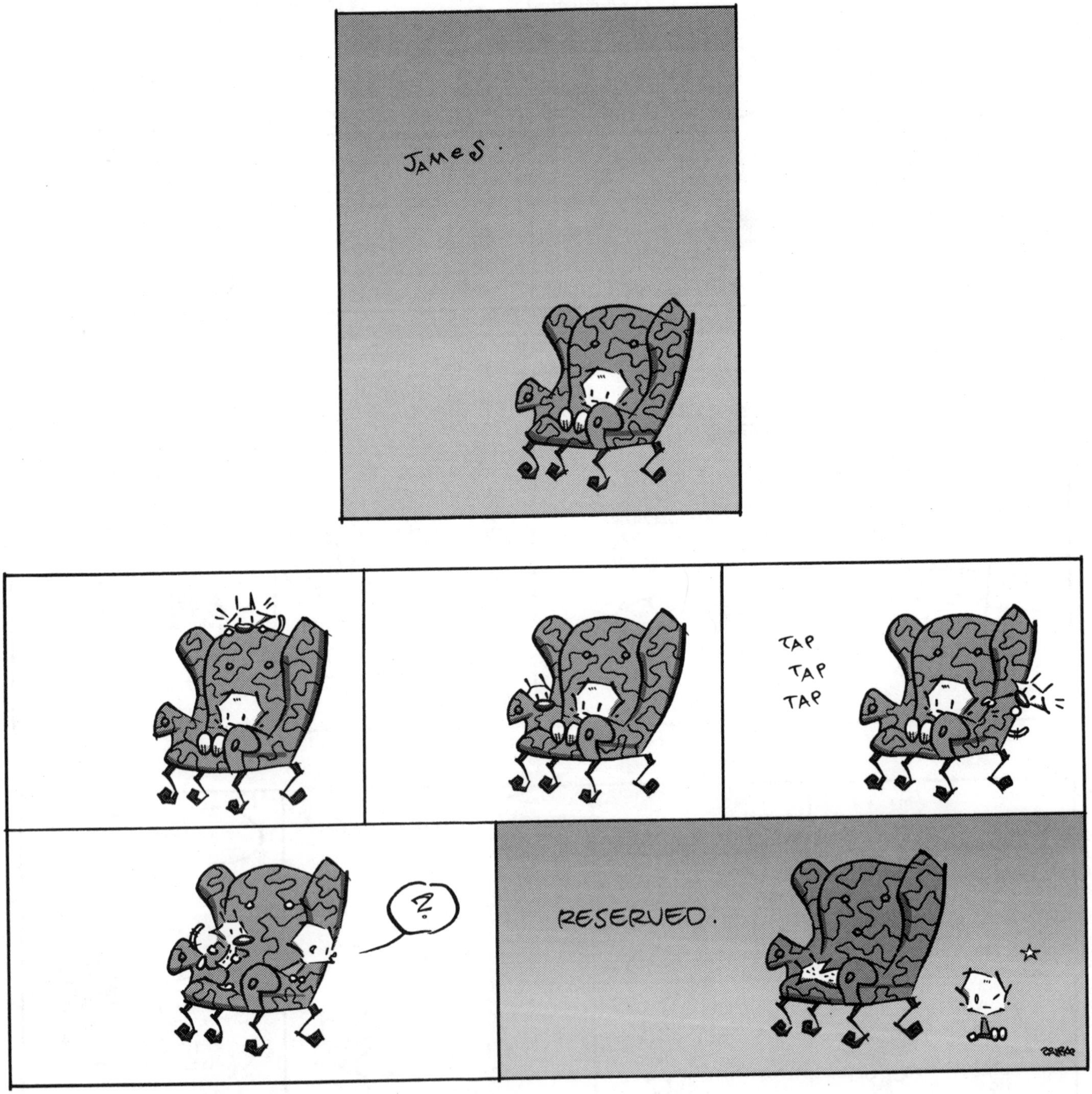
JAMES.
TAP
TAP
TAP
?
RESERVED.

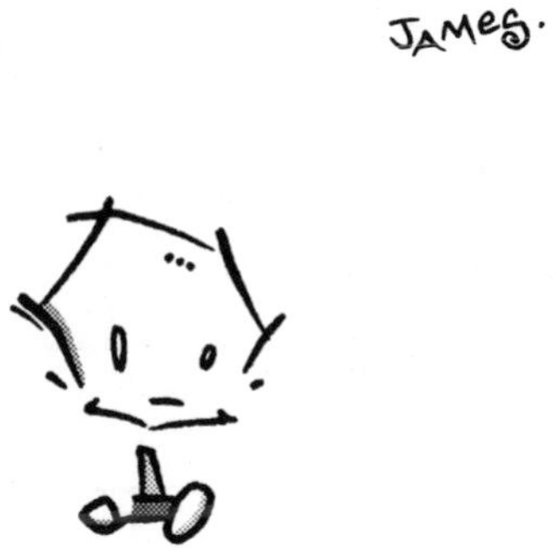
JAMES.

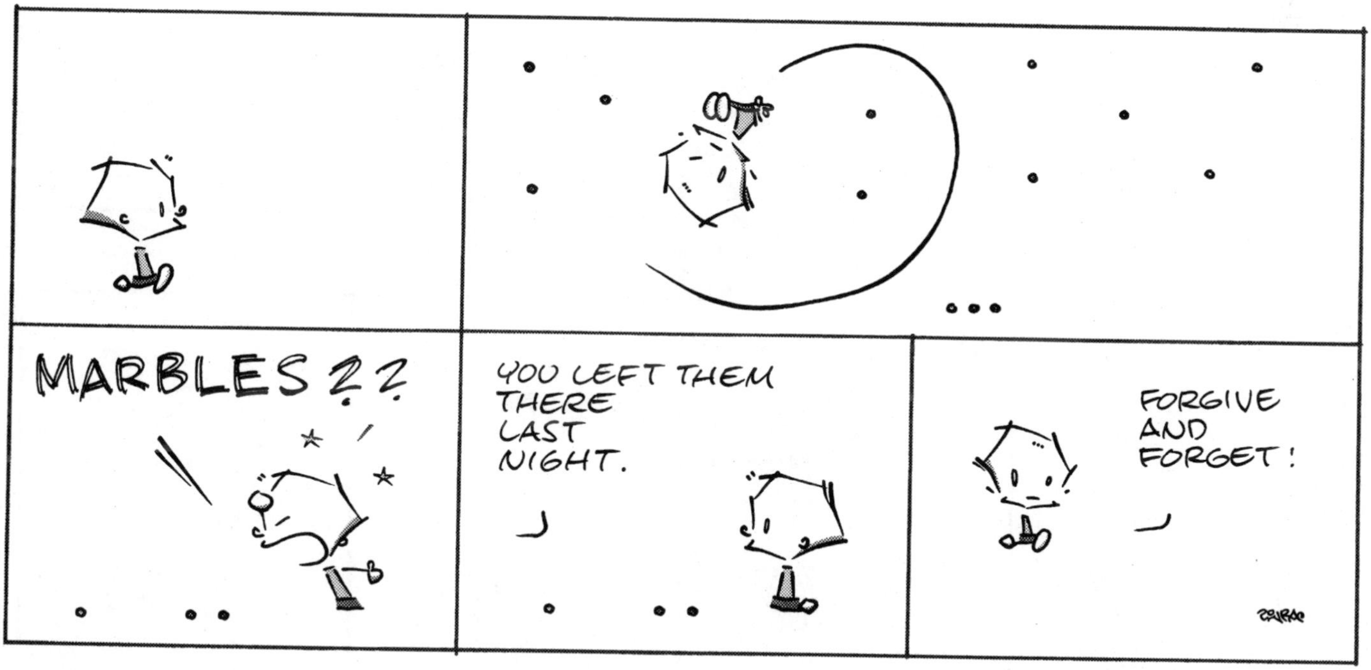
...
MARBLES ??
YOU LEFT THEM THERE LAST NIGHT.
FORGIVE AND FORGET!

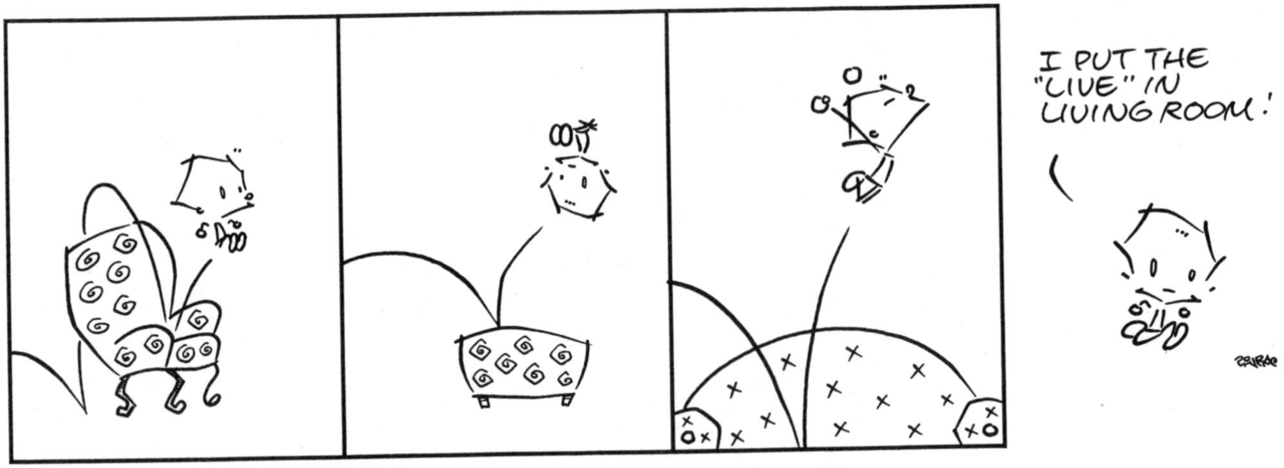
I PUT THE "LIVE" IN LIVING ROOM!

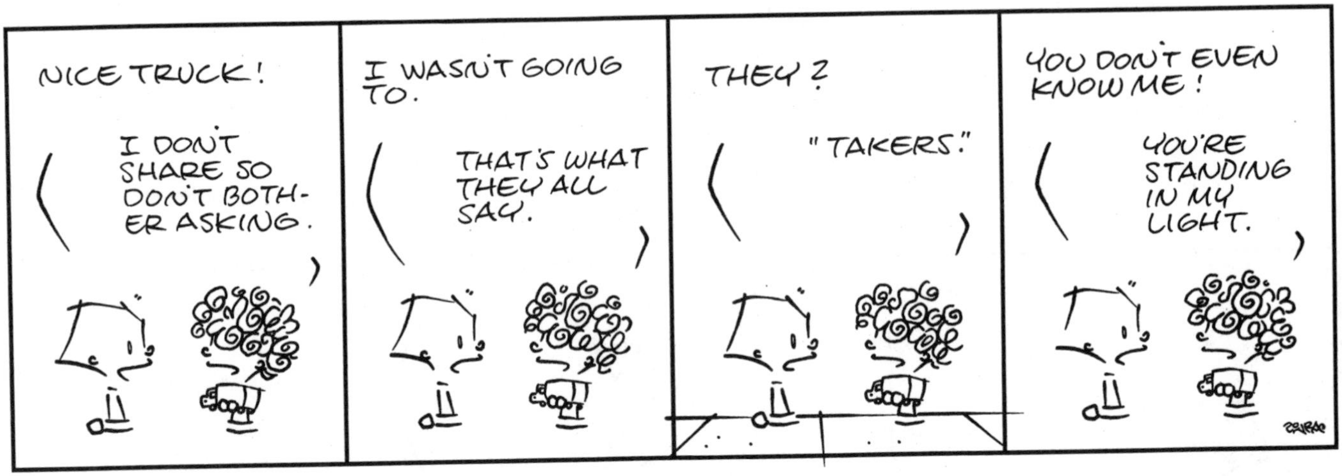
NICE TRUCK!
I DON'T SHARE SO DON'T BOTHER ASKING.
I WASN'T GOING TO.
THAT'S WHAT THEY ALL SAY.
THEY?
"TAKERS."
YOU DON'T EVEN KNOW ME!
YOU'RE STANDING IN MY LIGHT.

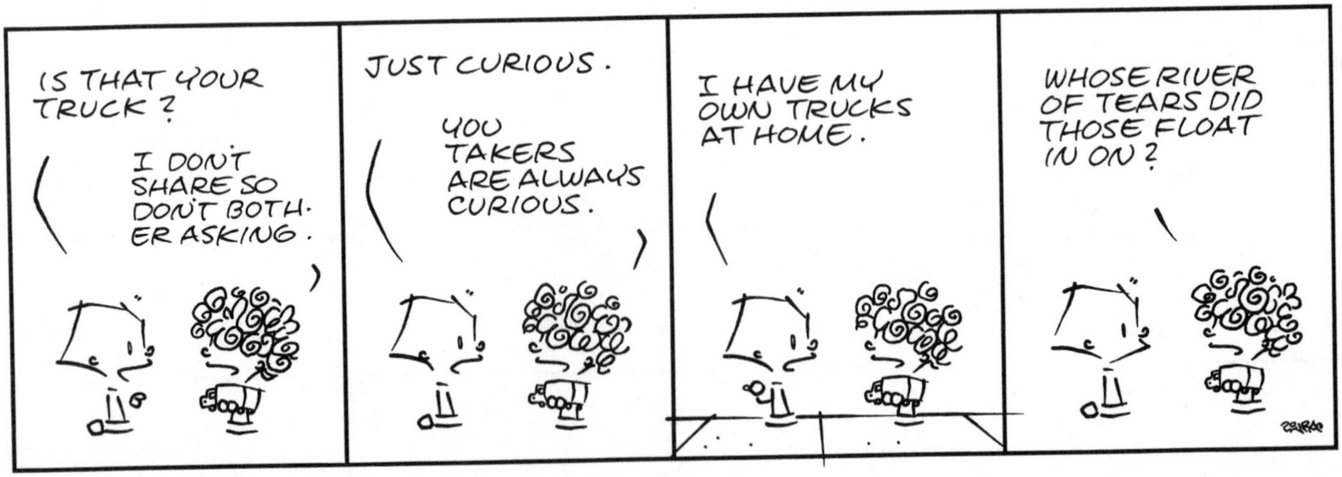
IS THAT YOUR TRUCK?
I DON'T SHARE SO DON'T BOTHER ASKING.
JUST CURIOUS.
YOU TAKERS ARE ALWAYS CURIOUS.
I HAVE MY OWN TRUCKS AT HOME.
WHOSE RIVER OF TEARS DID THOSE FLOAT IN ON?

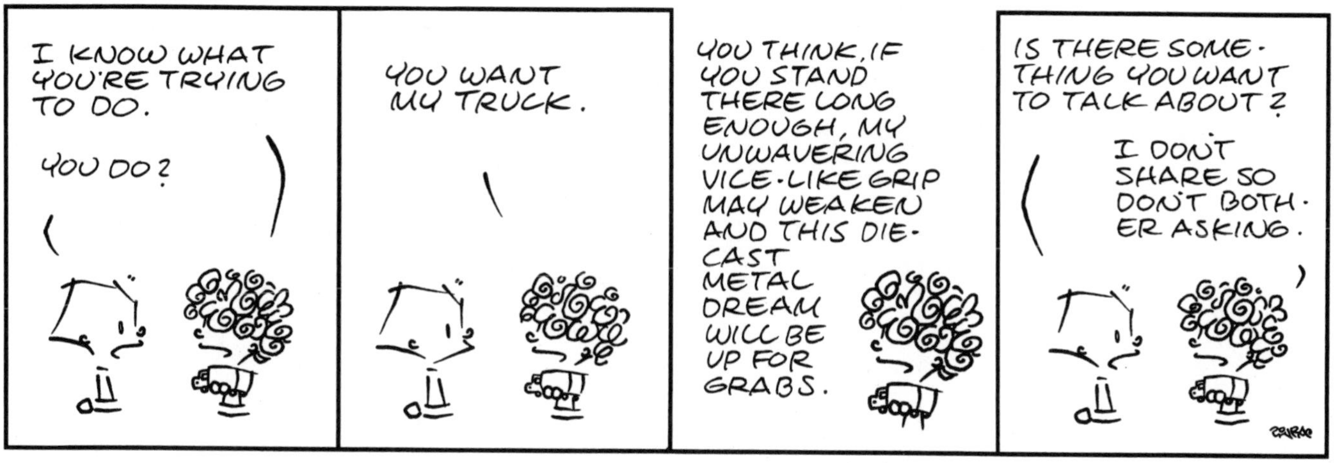
I KNOW WHAT YOU'RE TRYING TO DO.
YOU DO?
YOU WANT MY TRUCK.
YOU THINK, IF YOU STAND THERE LONG ENOUGH, MY UNWAVERING VICE-LIKE GRIP MAY WEAKEN AND THIS DIE-CAST METAL DREAM WILL BE UP FOR GRABS.
IS THERE SOME-THING YOU WANT TO TALK ABOUT?
I DON'T SHARE SO DON'T BOTH-ER ASKING.

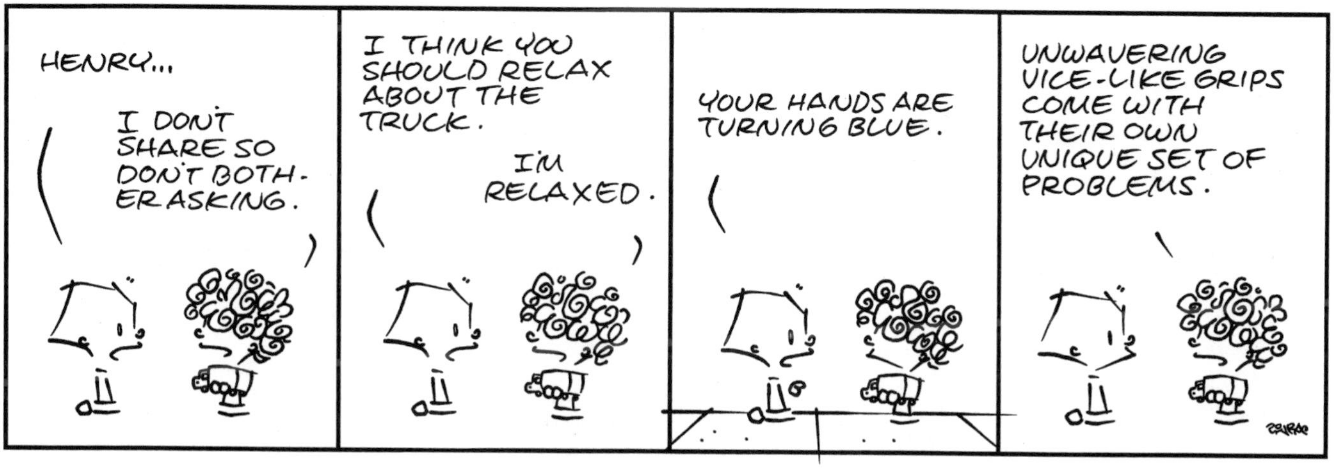
HENRY...
I DON'T SHARE SO DON'T BOTH-ER ASKING.
I THINK YOU SHOULD RELAX ABOUT THE TRUCK.
I'M RELAXED.
YOUR HANDS ARE TURNING BLUE.
UNWAVERING VICE-LIKE GRIPS COME WITH THEIR OWN UNIQUE SET OF PROBLEMS.

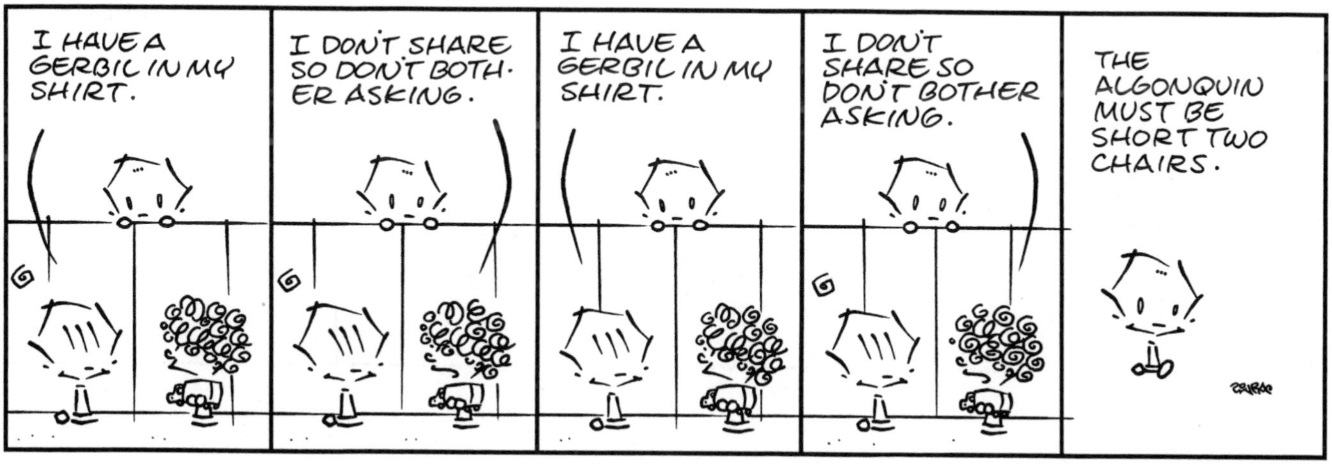
I HAVE A GERBIL IN MY SHIRT.
I DON'T SHARE SO DON'T BOTH-ER ASKING.
I HAVE A GERBIL IN MY SHIRT.
I DON'T SHARE SO DON'T BOTHER ASKING.
THE ALGONQUIN MUST BE SHORT TWO CHAIRS.

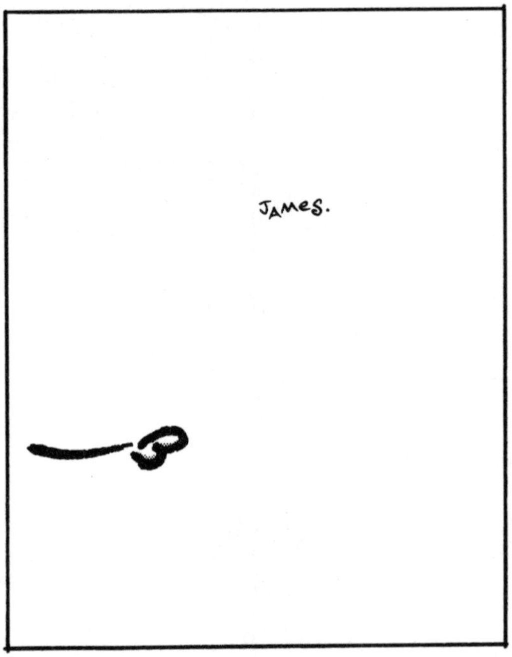
JAMES.

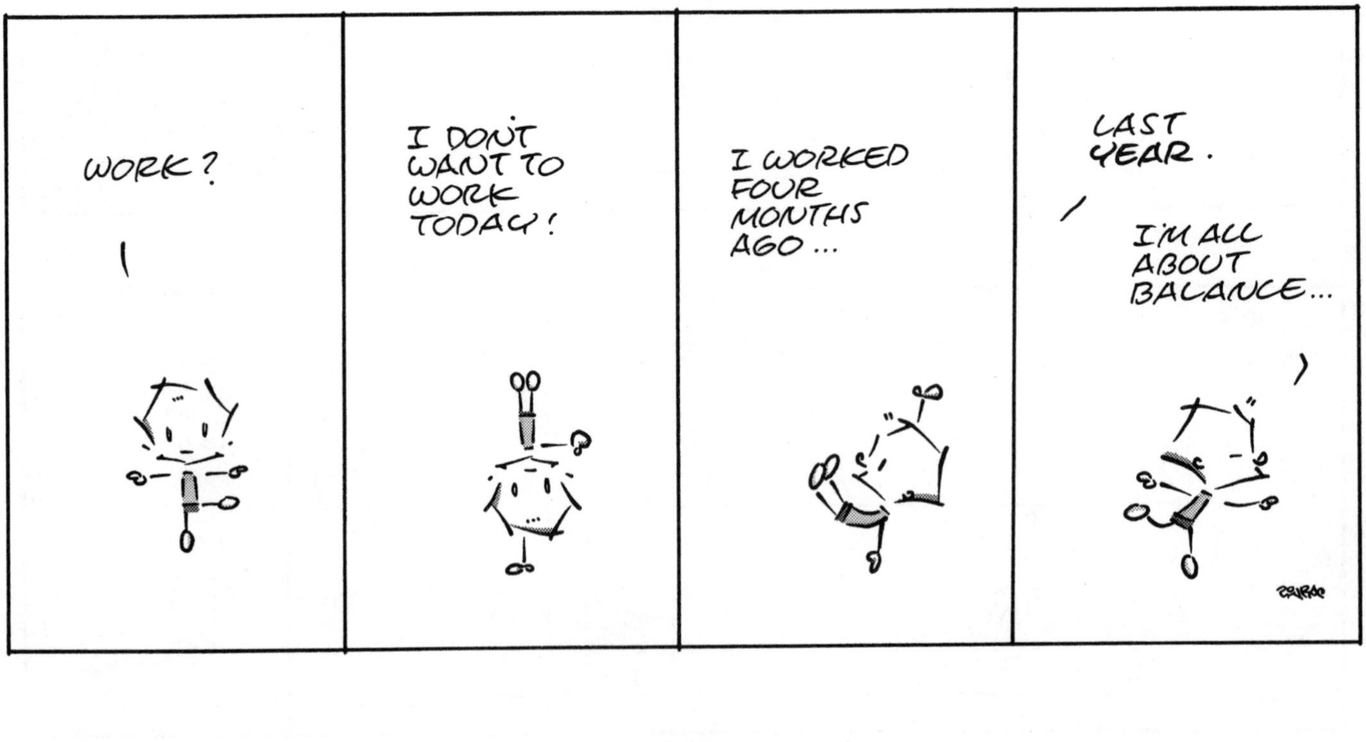
WORK?
I DON'T WANT TO WORK TODAY!
I WORKED FOUR MONTHS AGO...
LAST YEAR.
I'M ALL ABOUT BALANCE...

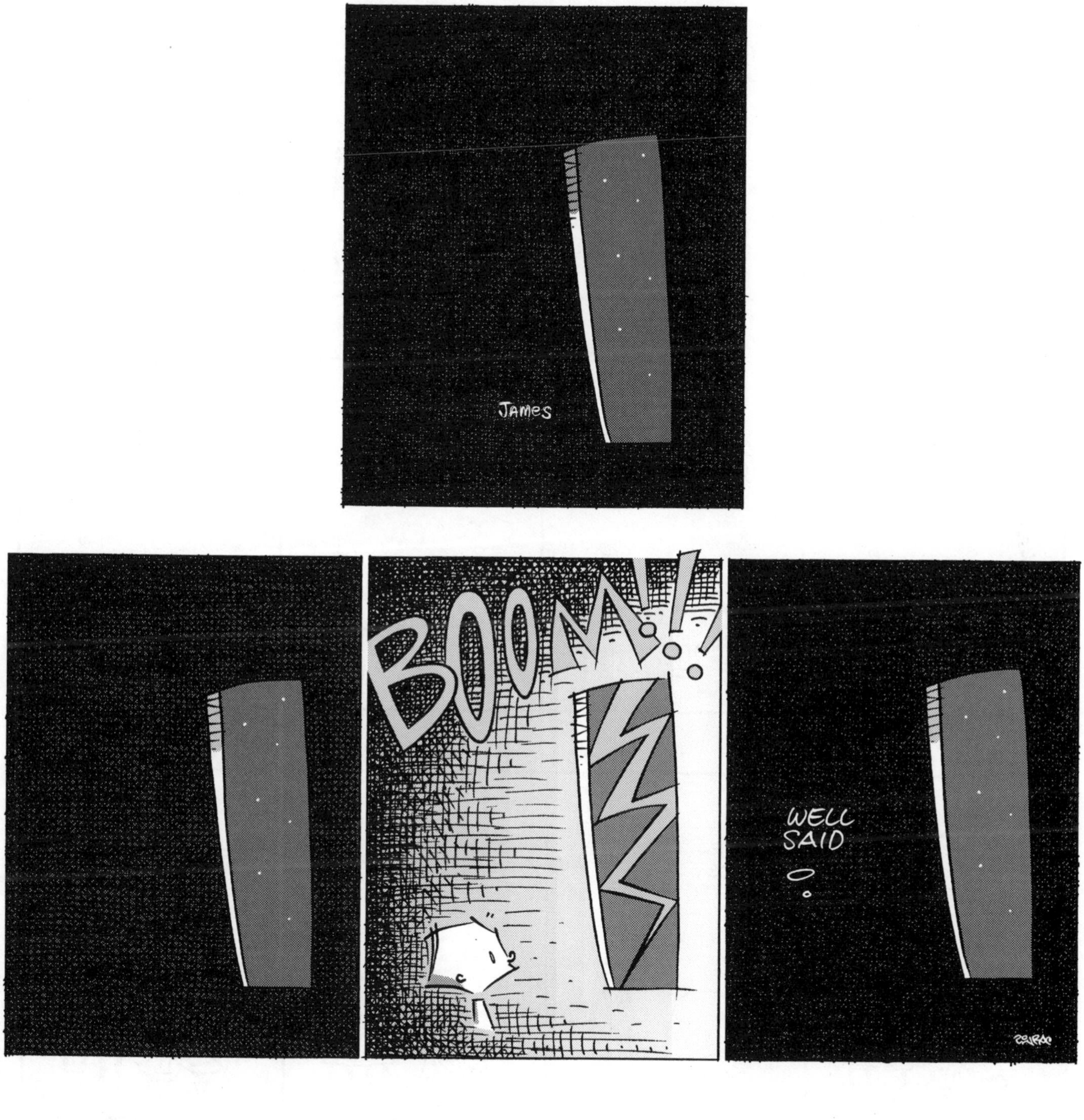
JAMES
BOOM!!!
WELL SAID

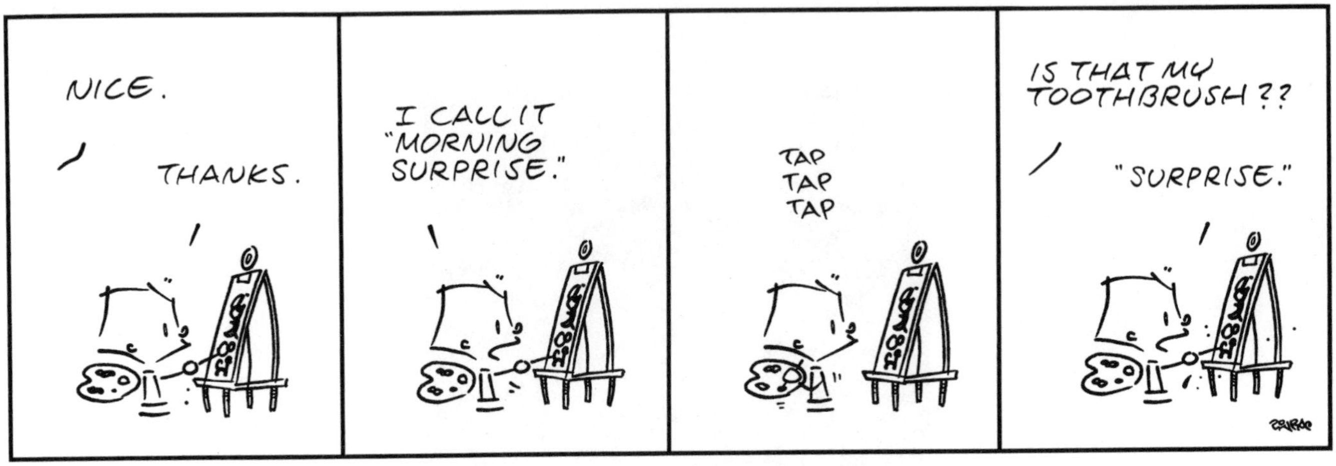
NICE.
THANKS.
I CALL IT "MORNING SURPRISE."
TAP TAP TAP
IS THAT MY TOOTHBRUSH ??
"SURPRISE."

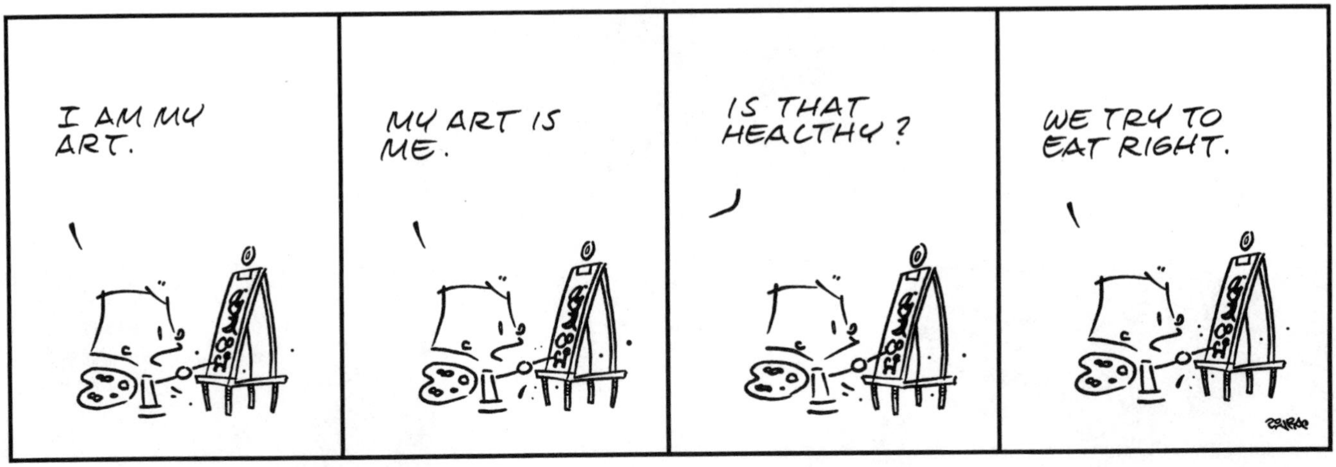
I AM MY ART.
MY ART IS ME.
IS THAT HEALTHY ?
WE TRY TO EAT RIGHT.

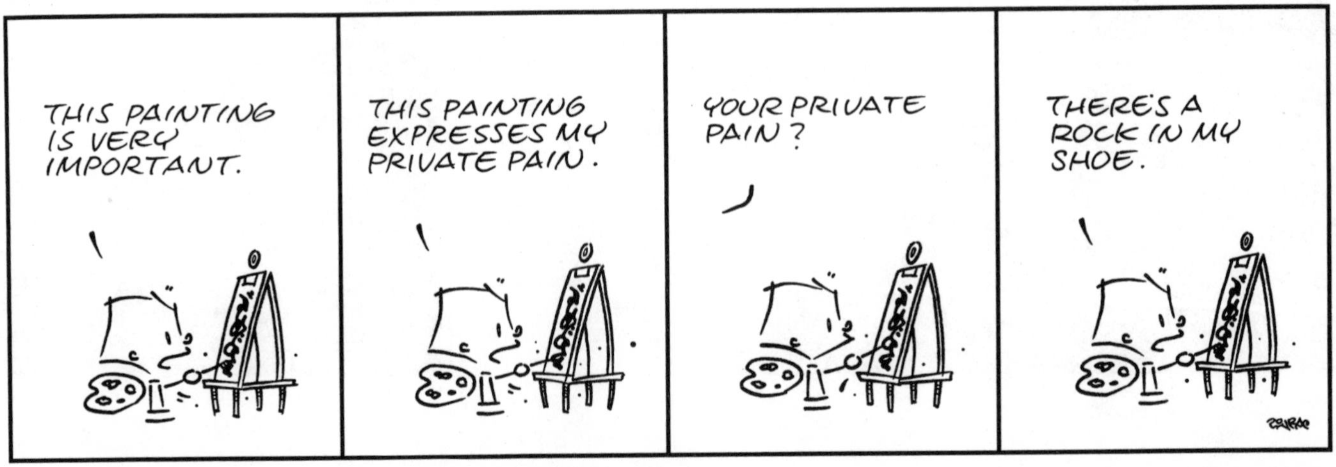
THIS PAINTING IS VERY IMPORTANT.
THIS PAINTING EXPRESSES MY PRIVATE PAIN.
YOUR PRIVATE PAIN ?
THERE'S A ROCK IN MY SHOE.

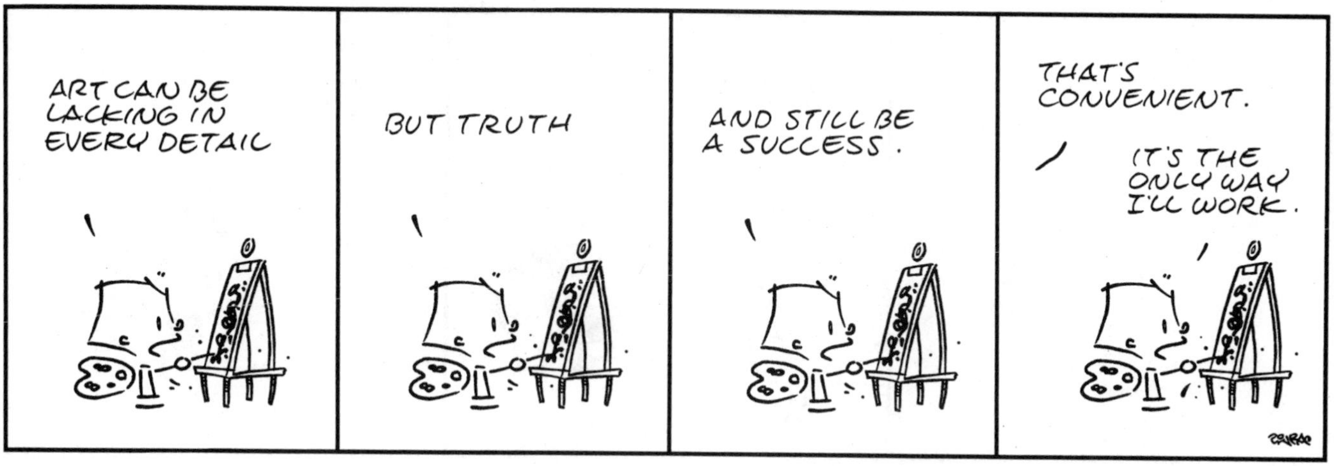
ART CAN BE LACKING IN EVERY DETAIL
BUT TRUTH
AND STILL BE A SUCCESS.
THAT'S CONVENIENT.
IT'S THE ONLY WAY I'LL WORK.

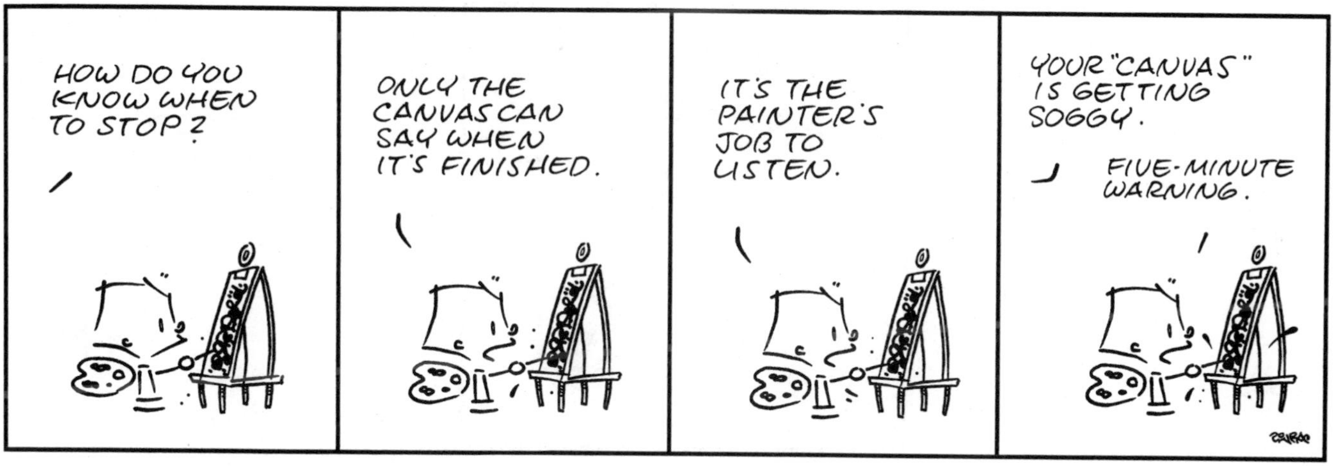
HOW DO YOU KNOW WHEN TO STOP?
ONLY THE CANVAS CAN SAY WHEN IT'S FINISHED.
IT'S THE PAINTER'S JOB TO LISTEN.
YOUR "CANVAS" IS GETTING SOGGY.
FIVE-MINUTE WARNING.

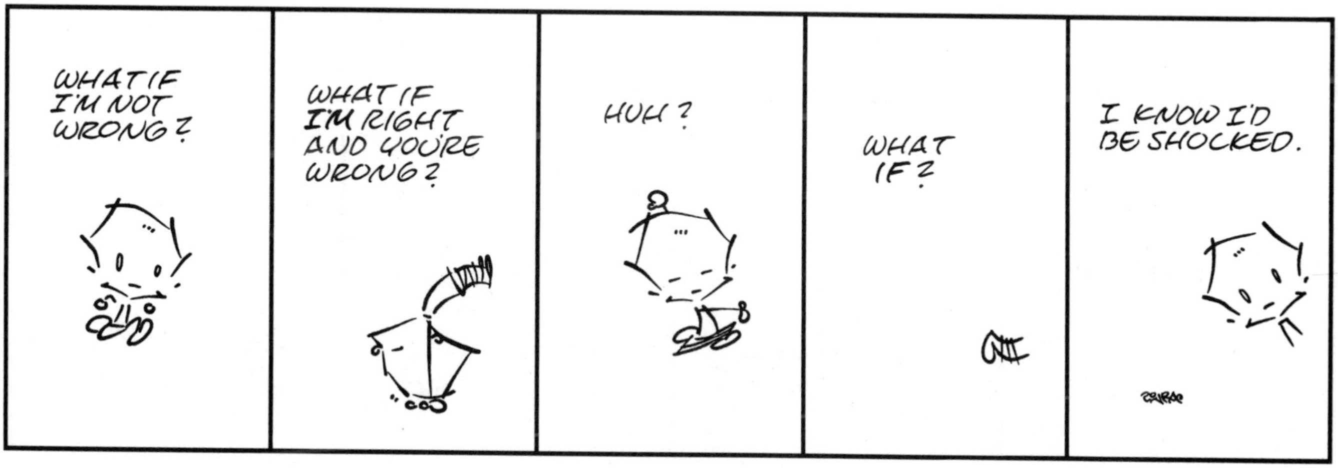
WHAT IF I'M NOT WRONG?
WHAT IF I'M RIGHT AND YOU'RE WRONG?
HUH?
WHAT IF?
I KNOW I'D BE SHOCKED.

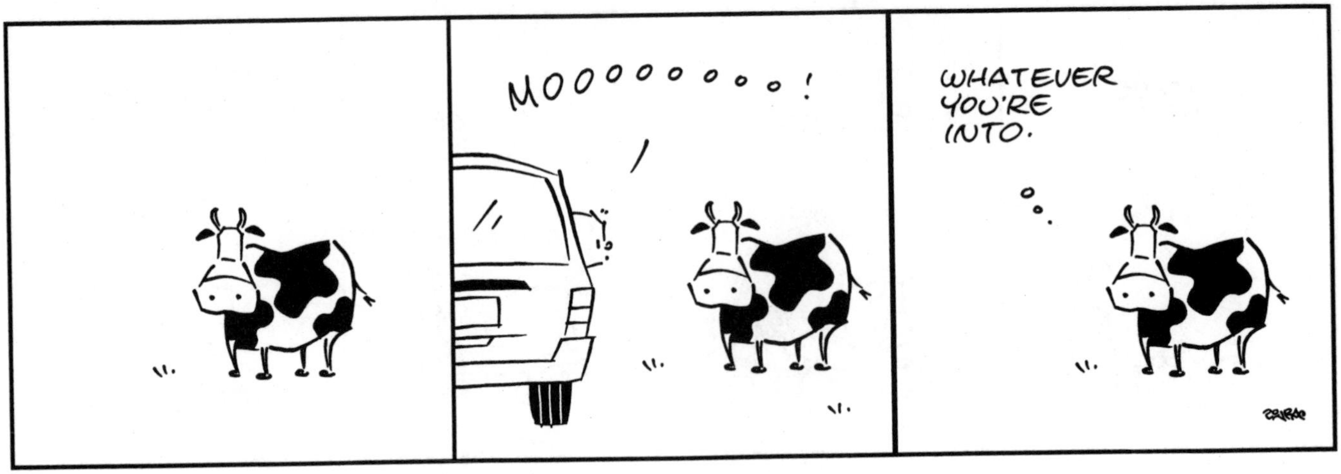
MOOOOOOOOO!
WHATEVER YOU'RE INTO.

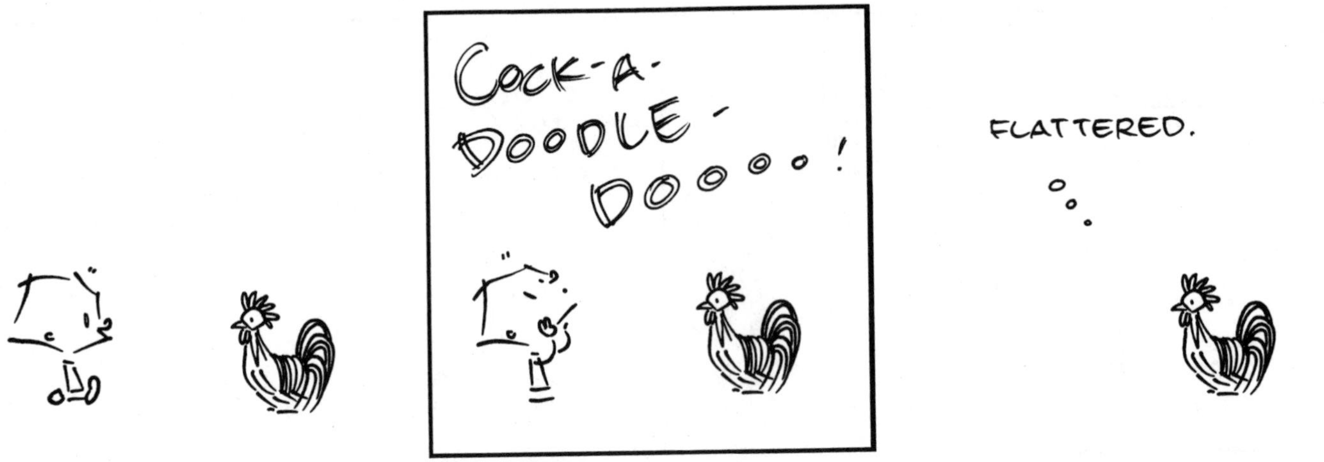
COCK-A-DOODLE-DOOOOO!
FLATTERED.

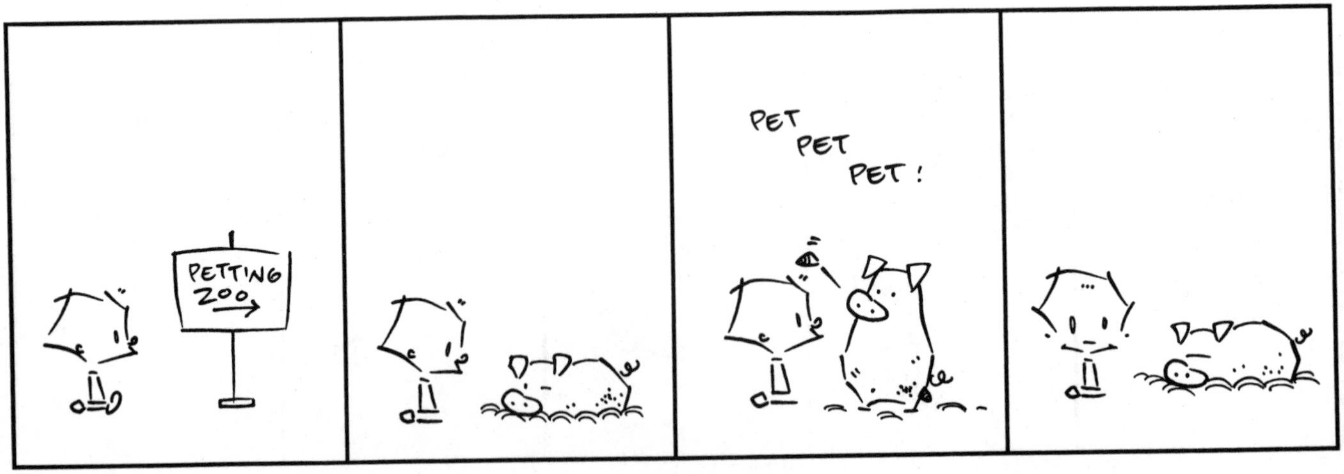
PETTING ZOO
PET PET PET!

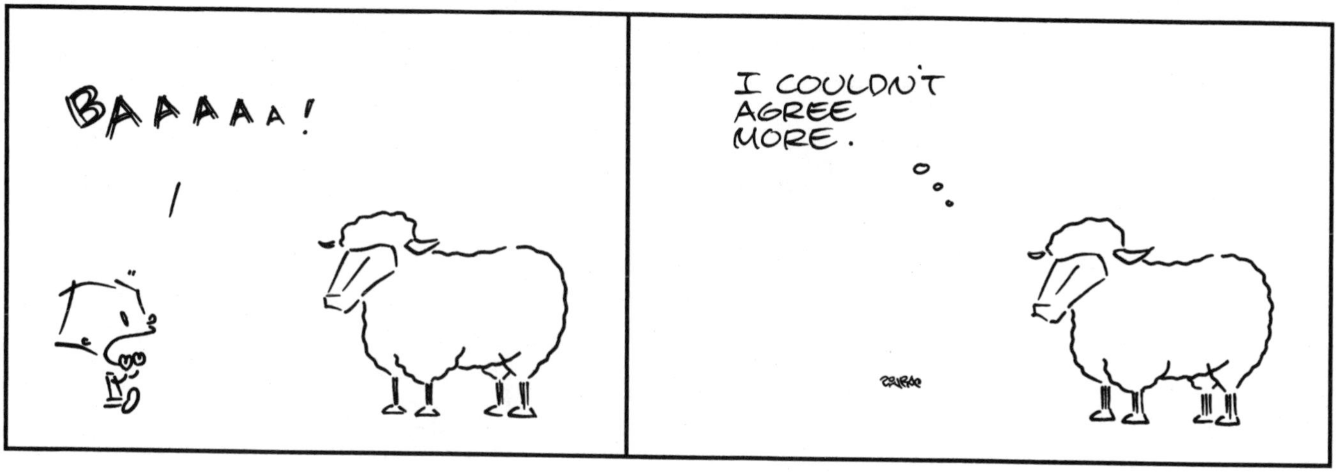
BAAAAA!
I COULDN'T AGREE MORE.

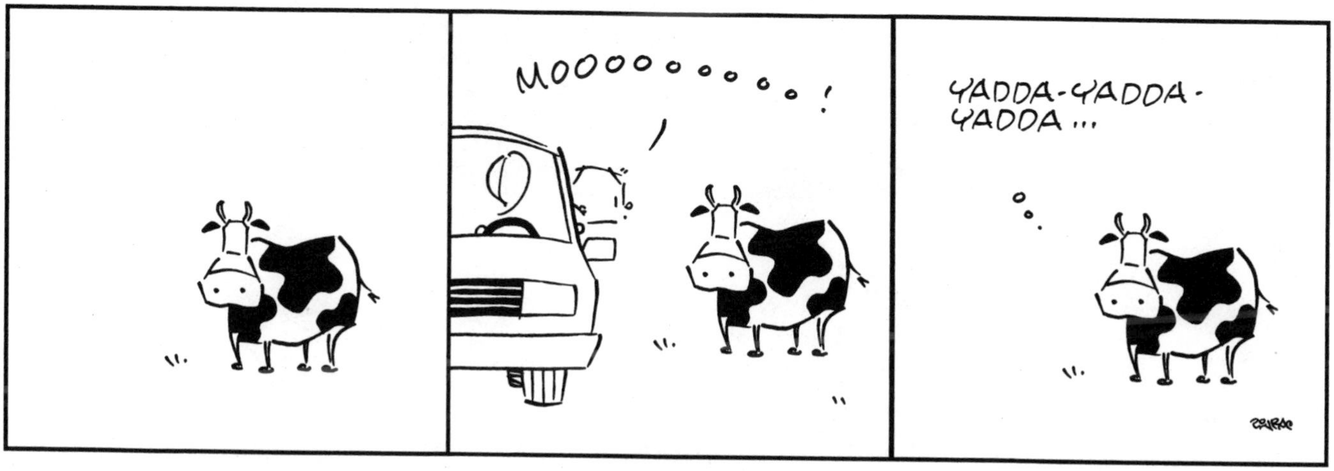
MOOOOOOOOOO!
YADDA-YADDA-YADDA...

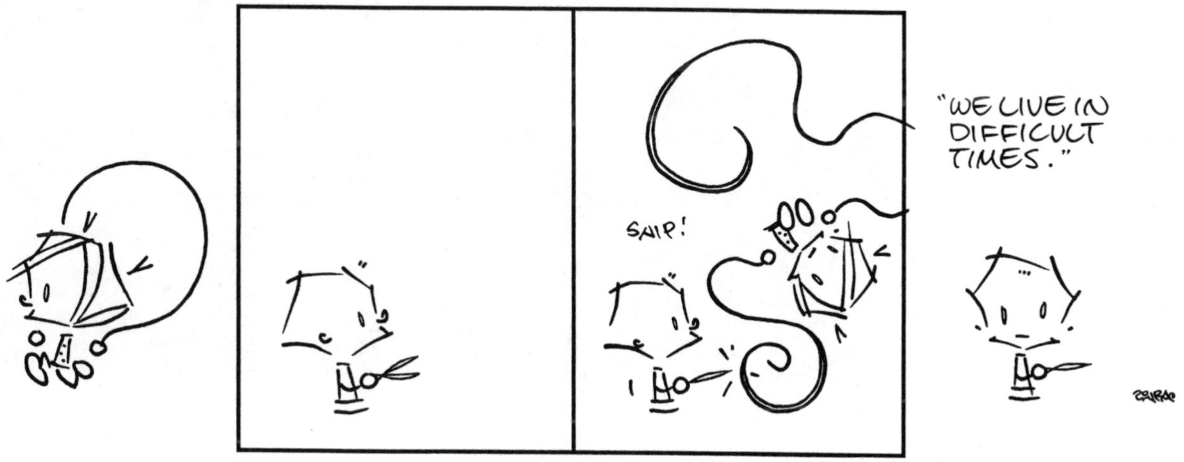
SNIP!
"WE LIVE IN DIFFICULT TIMES."

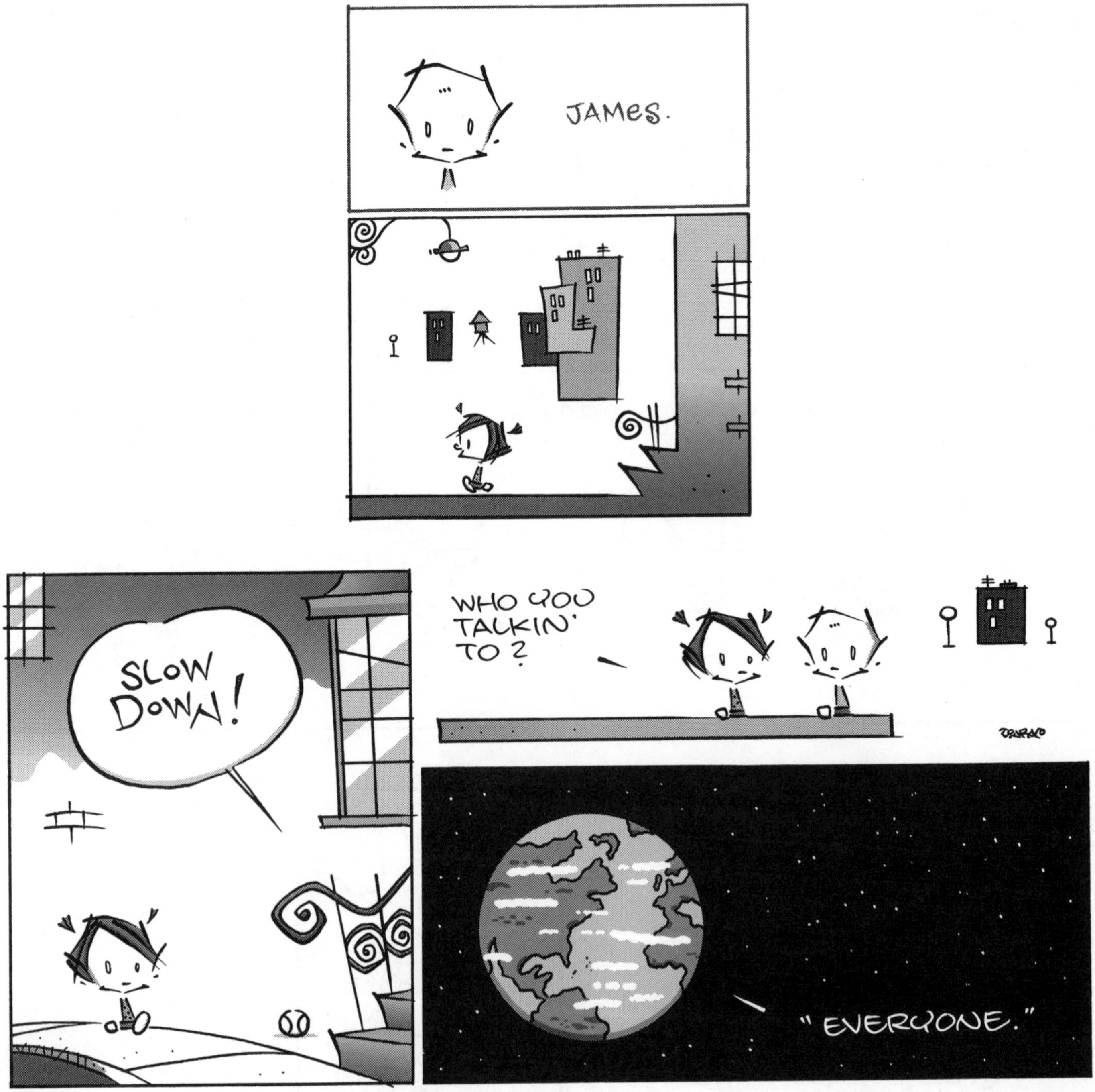
JAMES.
SLOW DOWN!
WHO YOU TALKIN' TO?
"EVERYONE."

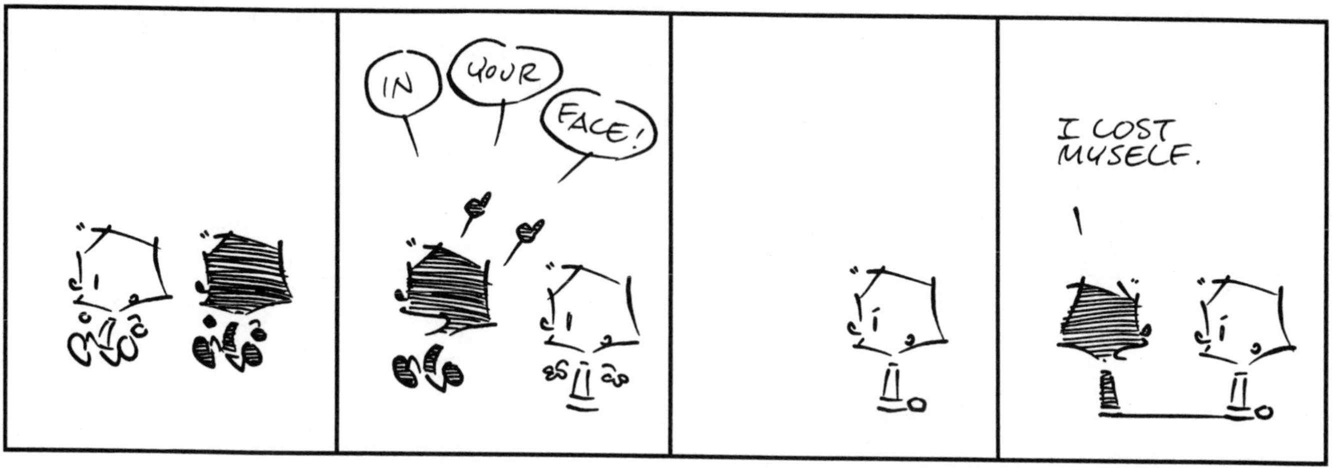
IN
YOUR
FACE!
I LOST MYSELF.

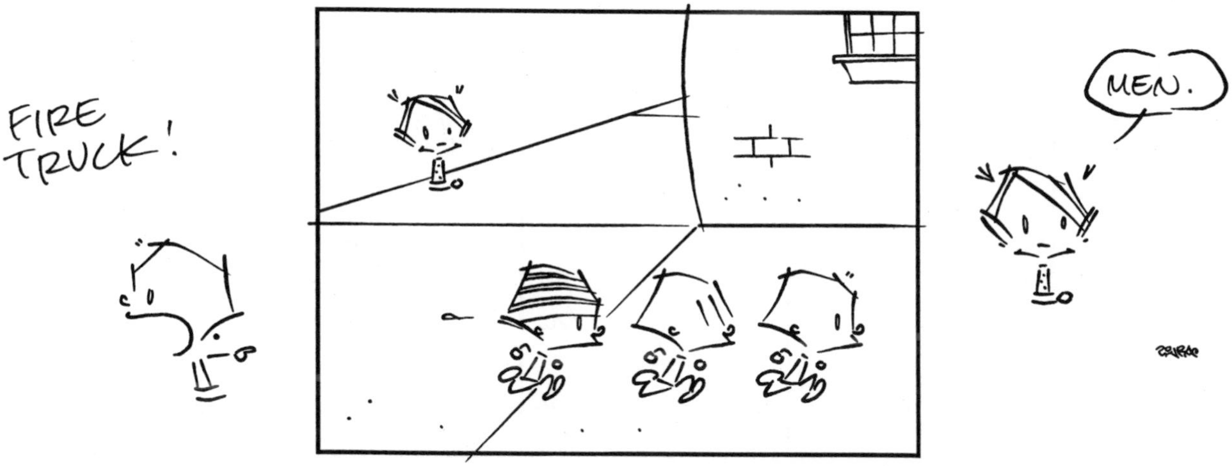
FIRE TRUCK!
MEN.

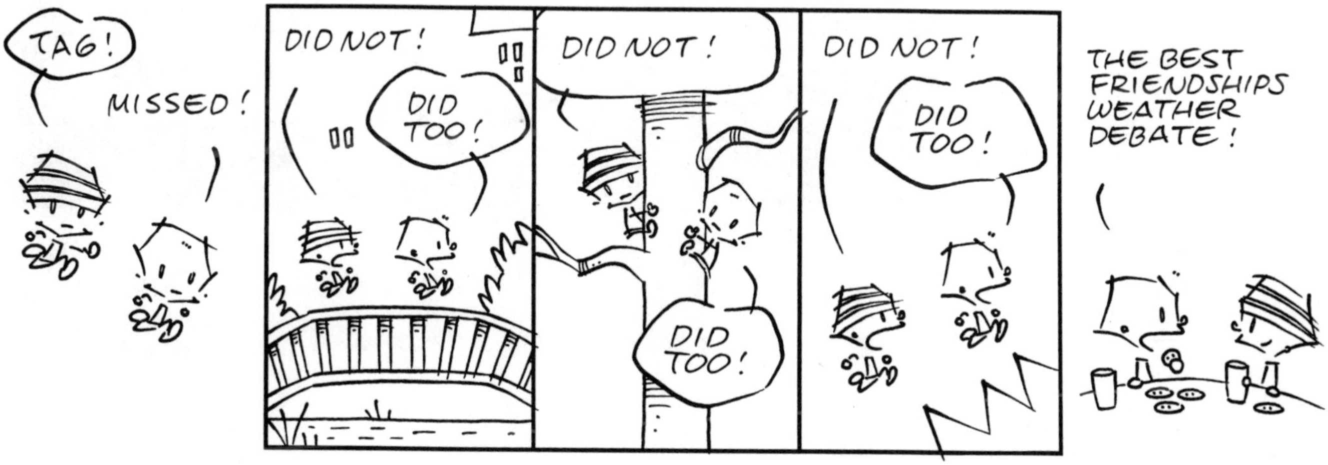
TAG!
MISSED!
DID NOT!
DID TOO!
DID NOT!
DID TOO!
DID NOT!
DID TOO!
THE BEST FRIENDSHIPS WEATHER DEBATE!

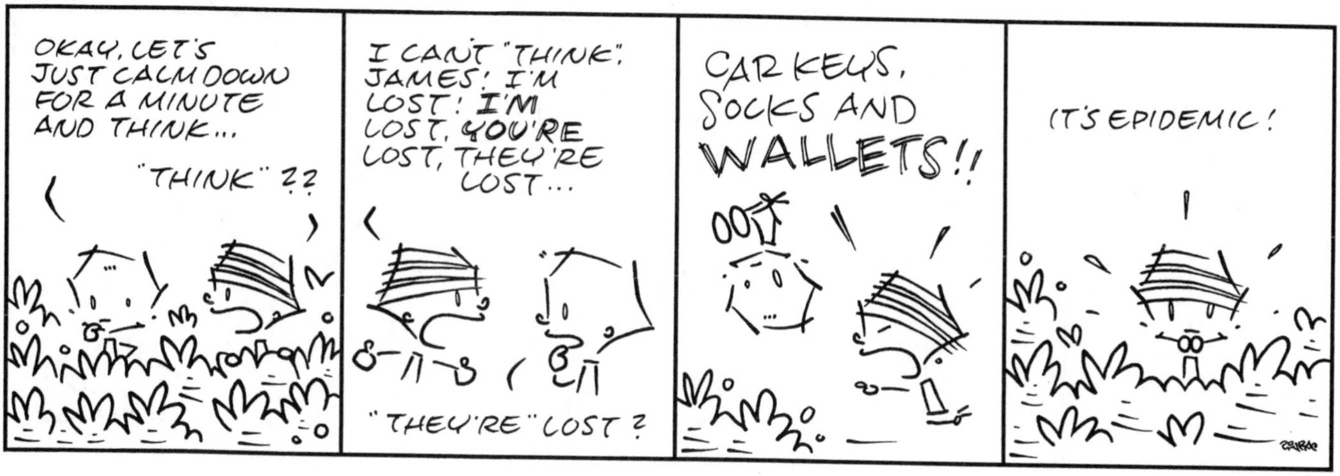
OKAY, LET'S JUST CALM DOWN FOR A MINUTE AND THINK...
"THINK" ??
I CAN'T "THINK", JAMES! I'M LOST! I'M LOST, YOU'RE LOST, THEY'RE LOST...
"THEY'RE" LOST?
CAR KEYS, SOCKS AND WALLETS!!
IT'S EPIDEMIC!

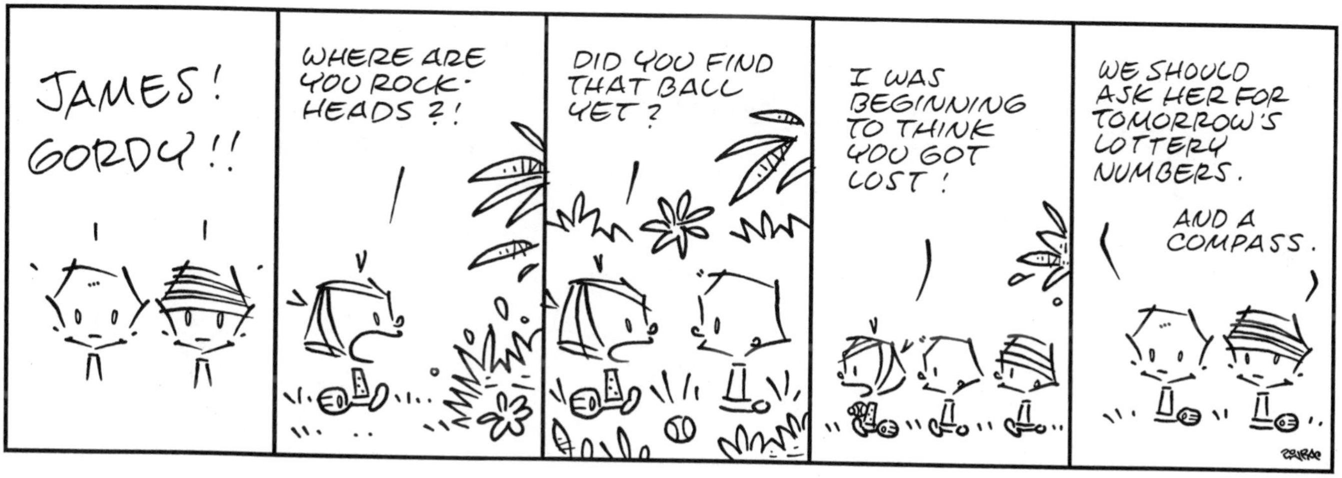
JAMES! GORDY!!
WHERE ARE YOU ROCK-HEADS?!
DID YOU FIND THAT BALL YET?
I WAS BEGINNING TO THINK YOU GOT LOST!
WE SHOULD ASK HER FOR TOMORROW'S LOTTERY NUMBERS.
AND A COMPASS.

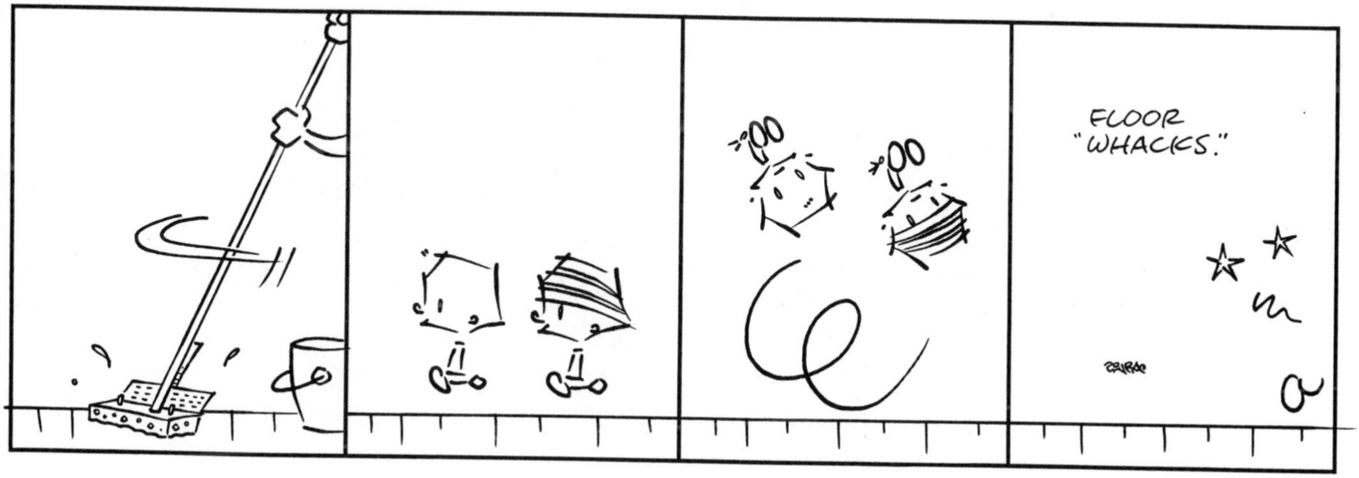
FLOOR "WHACKS."

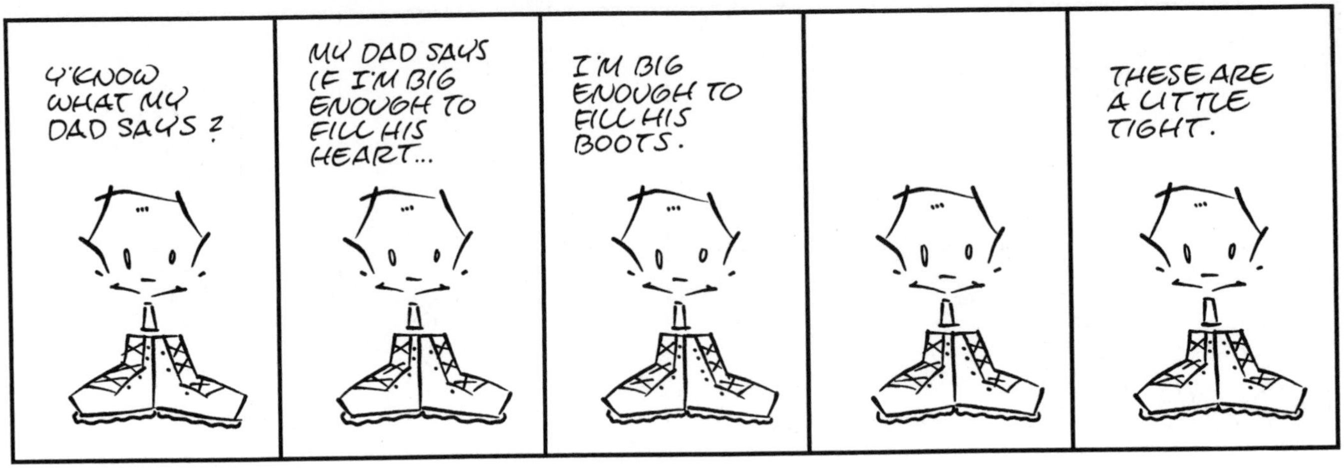
Y'KNOW WHAT MY DAD SAYS?
MY DAD SAYS IF I'M BIG ENOUGH TO FILL HIS HEART...
I'M BIG ENOUGH TO FILL HIS BOOTS.
THESE ARE A LITTLE TIGHT.

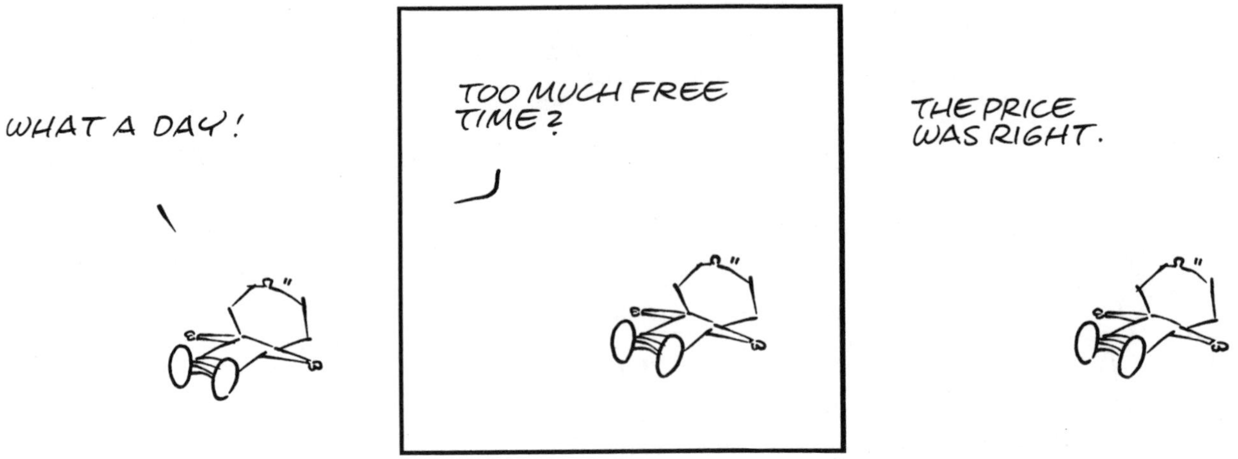
WHAT A DAY!
TOO MUCH FREE TIME?
THE PRICE WAS RIGHT.

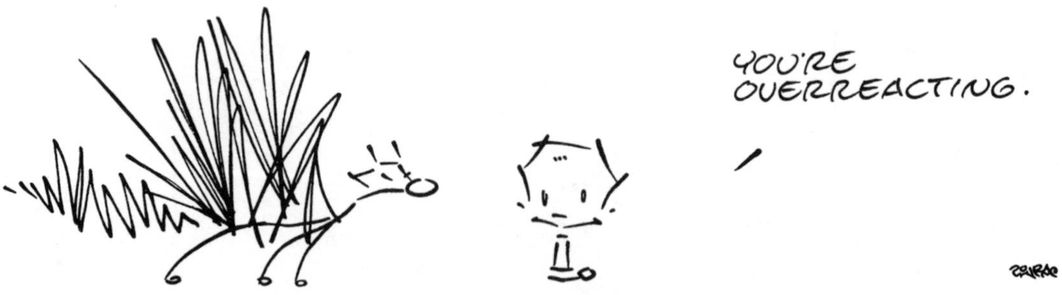
YOU'RE OVERREACTING.

JAMES
HEY.
HEY.
BAD DREAM?
DELIGHTFUL DROOLING GOOGALIE MONSTERS.
"DELIGHTFUL"?
THEIR WORDS, NOT MINE.

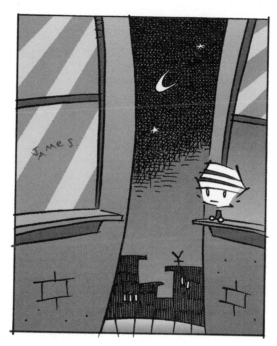

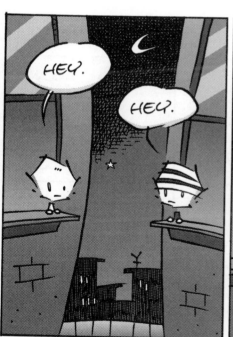

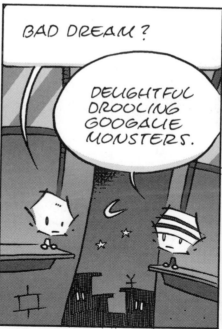

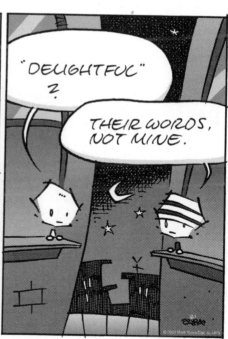

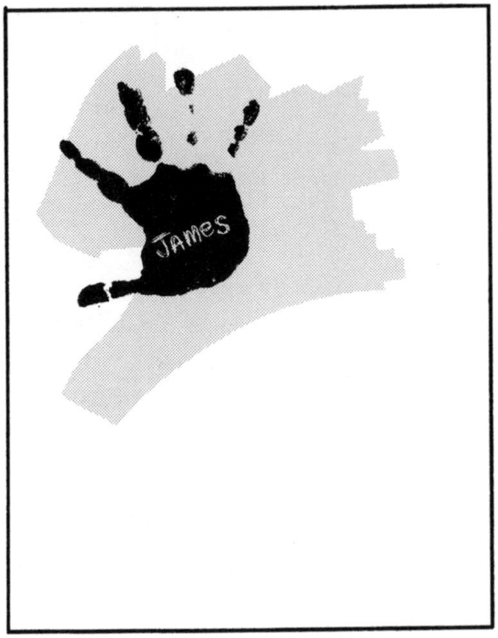
James

TRUE OR FALSE?

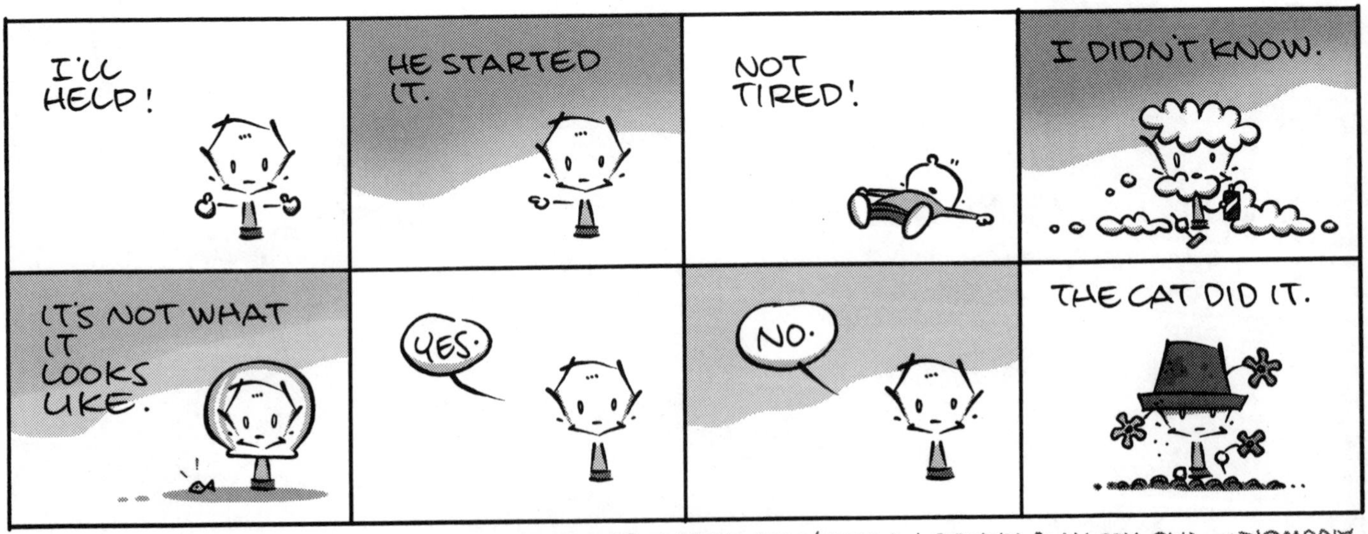
I'LL HELP!
HE STARTED IT.
NOT TIRED!
I DIDN'T KNOW.
IT'S NOT WHAT IT LOOKS LIKE.
YES.
NO.
THE CAT DID IT.

ANSWER: "THE TRUTH IS RARELY PURE, AND NEVER SIMPLE."

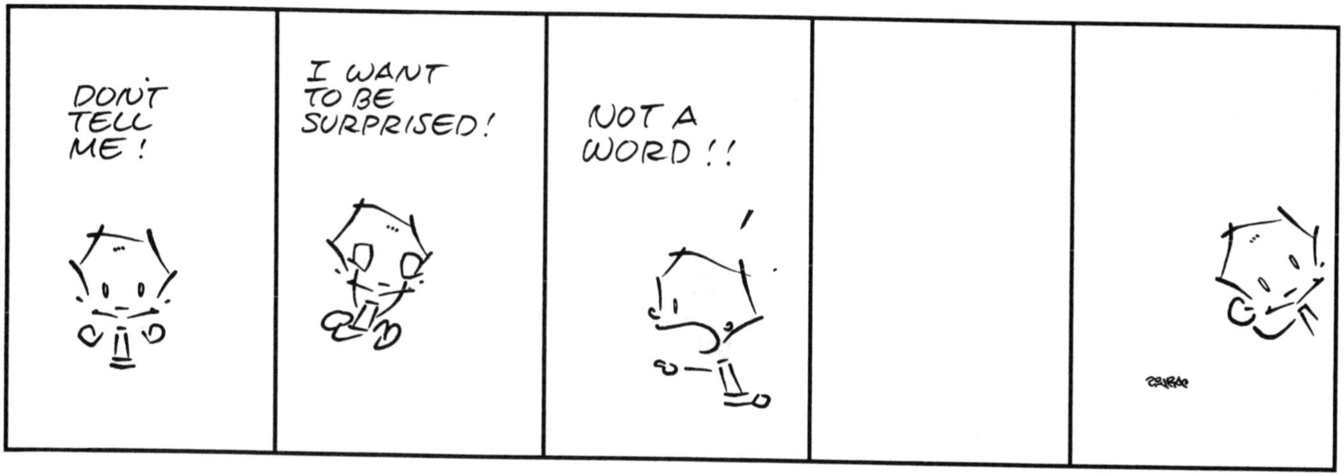
DON'T TELL ME!
I WANT TO BE SURPRISED!
NOT A WORD!!

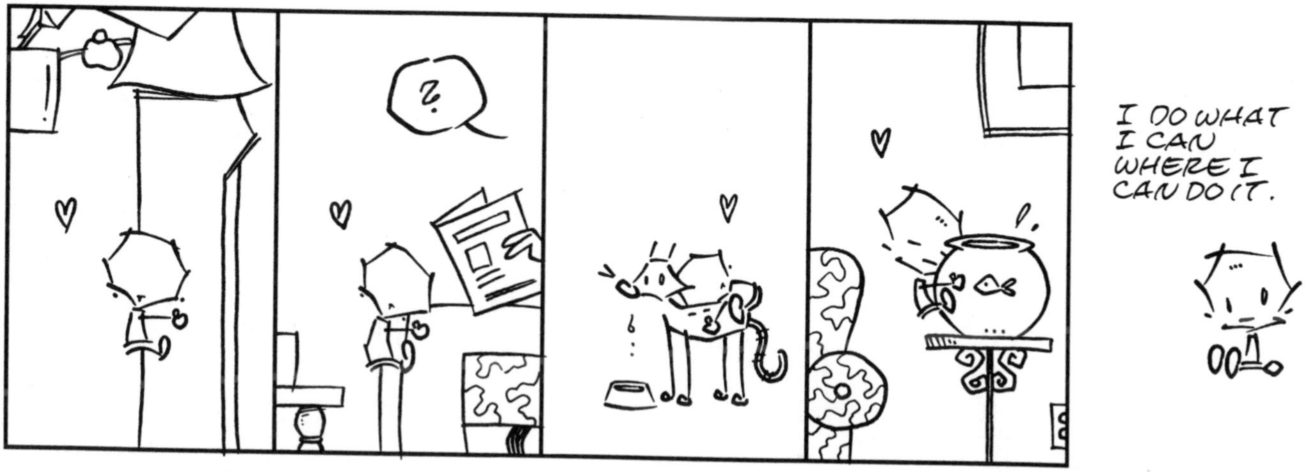
?
I DO WHAT I CAN WHERE I CAN DO IT.

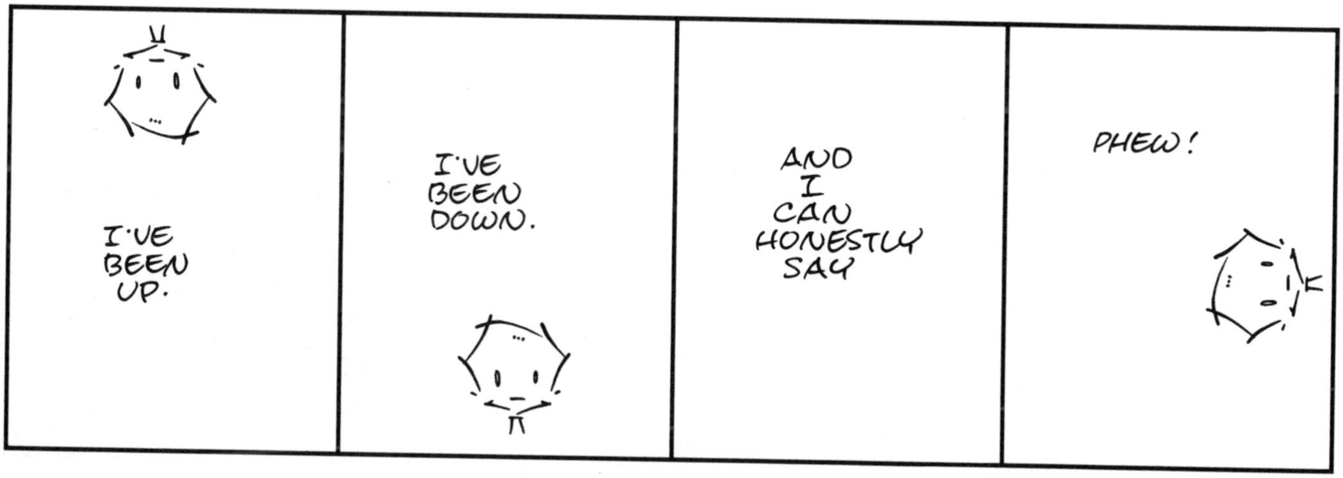
I'VE BEEN UP.
I'VE BEEN DOWN.
AND I CAN HONESTLY SAY
PHEW!

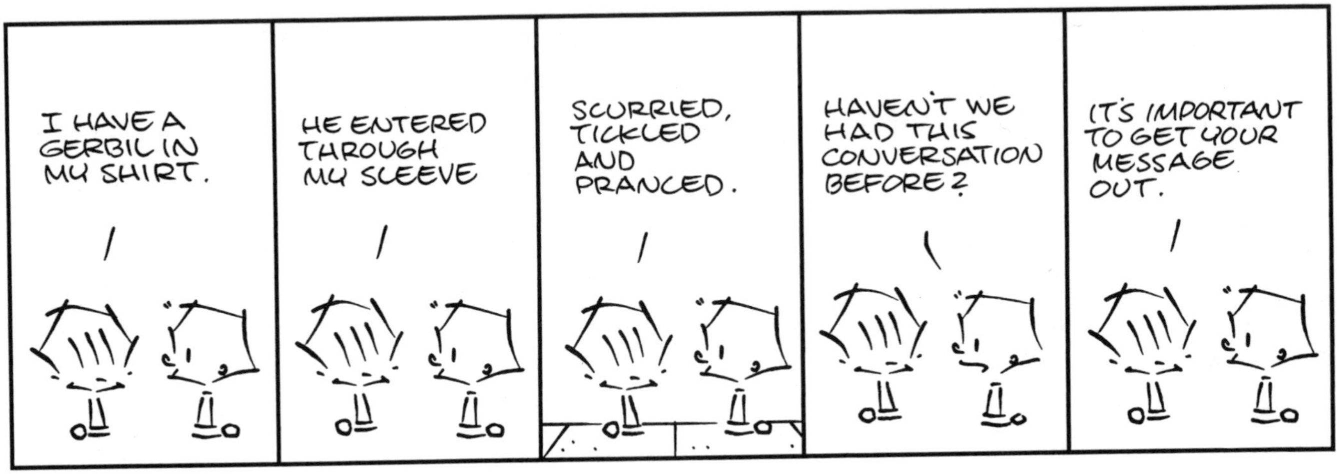
I HAVE A GERBIL IN MY SHIRT.
HE ENTERED THROUGH MY SLEEVE
SCURRIED, TICKLED AND PRANCED.
HAVEN'T WE HAD THIS CONVERSATION BEFORE?
IT'S IMPORTANT TO GET YOUR MESSAGE OUT.

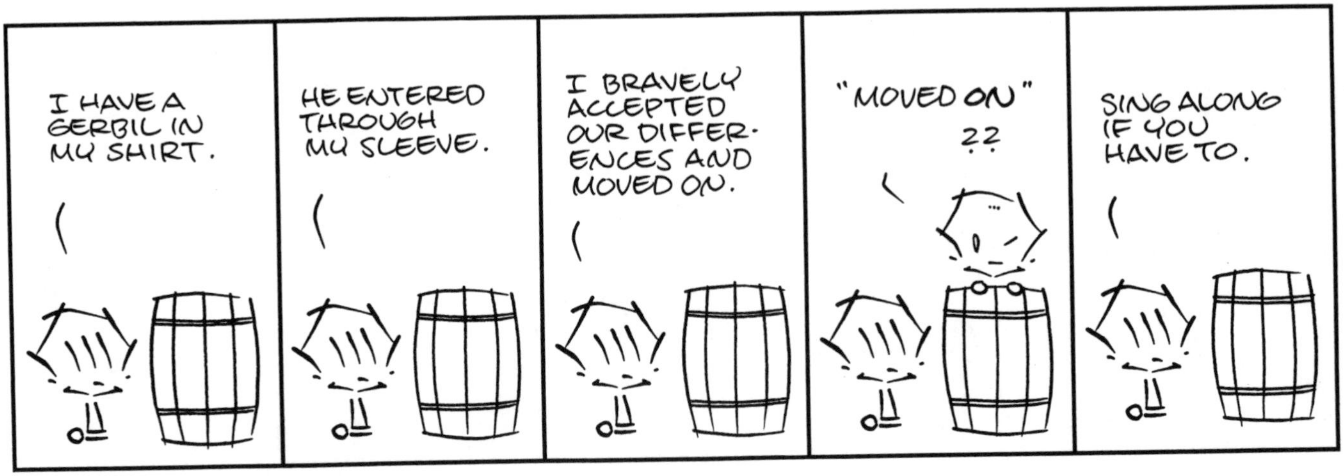
I HAVE A GERBIL IN MY SHIRT.
HE ENTERED THROUGH MY SLEEVE.
I BRAVELY ACCEPTED OUR DIFFER-ENCES AND MOVED ON.
"MOVED ON"
??
SING ALONG IF YOU HAVE TO.

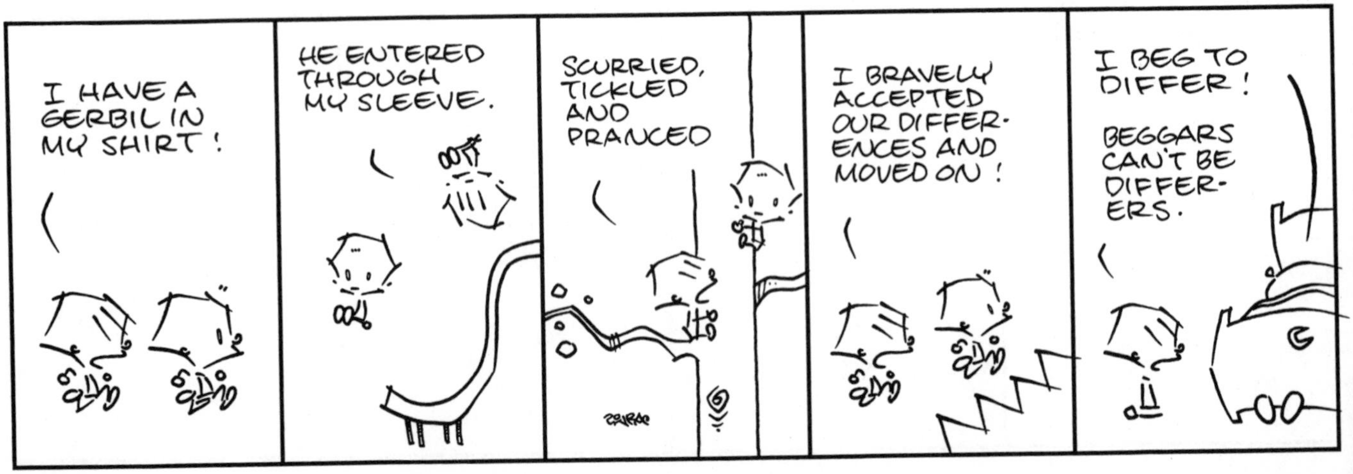
I HAVE A GERBIL IN MY SHIRT!
HE ENTERED THROUGH MY SLEEVE.
SCURRIED, TICKLED AND PRANCED
I BRAVELY ACCEPTED OUR DIFFER-ENCES AND MOVED ON!
I BEG TO DIFFER!
BEGGARS CAN'T BE DIFFER-ERS.

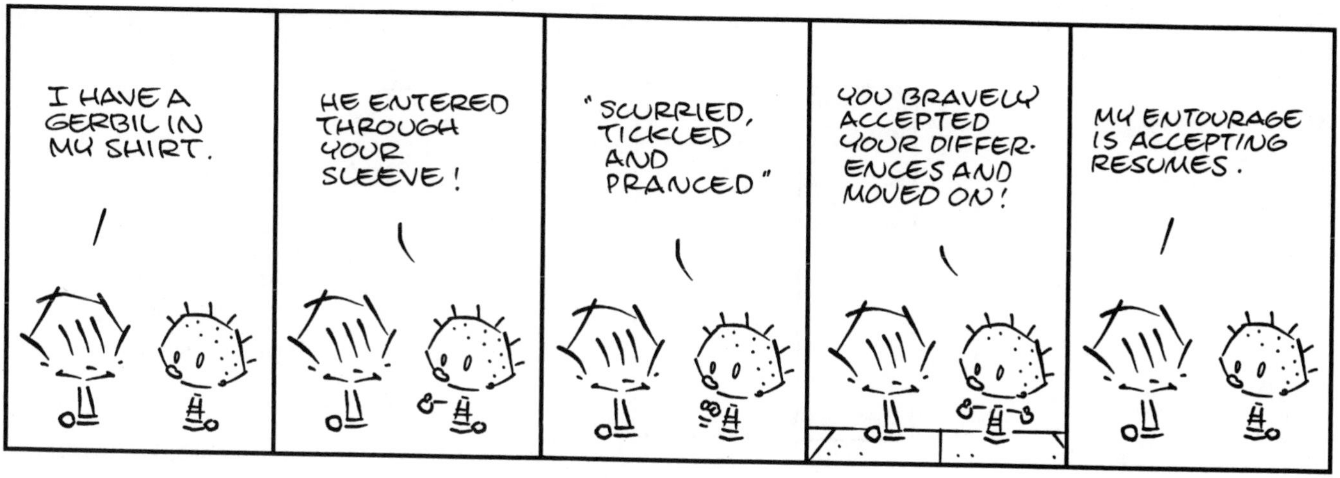
I HAVE A GERBIL IN MY SHIRT.
HE ENTERED THROUGH YOUR SLEEVE!
"SCURRIED, TICKLED AND PRANCED"
YOU BRAVELY ACCEPTED YOUR DIFFER-ENCES AND MOVED ON!
MY ENTOURAGE IS ACCEPTING RESUMES.

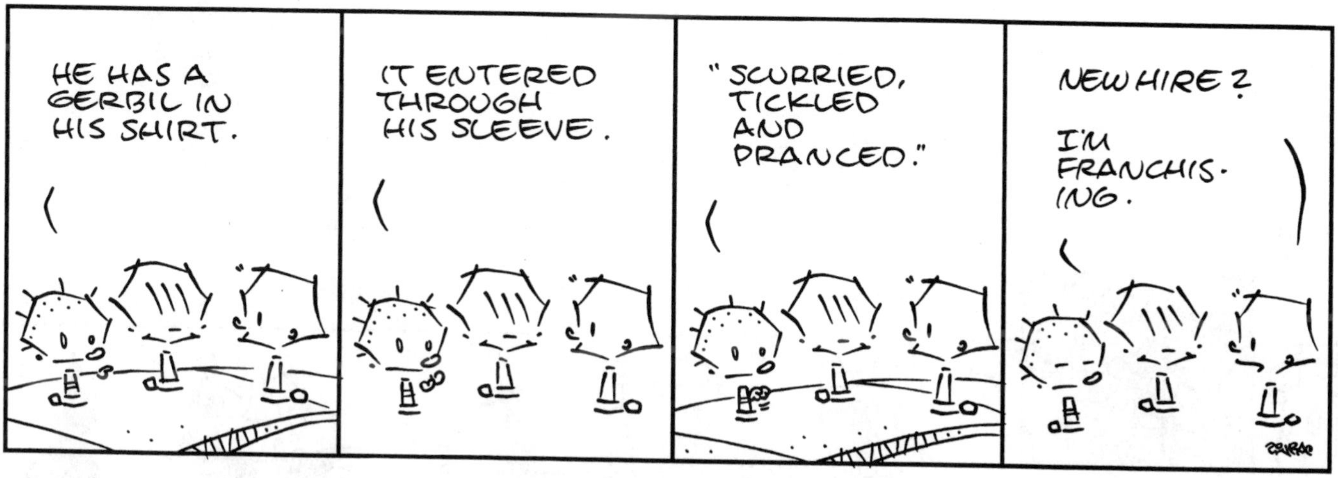
HE HAS A GERBIL IN HIS SHIRT.
IT ENTERED THROUGH HIS SLEEVE.
"SCURRIED, TICKLED AND PRANCED."
NEW HIRE?
I'M FRANCHIS-ING.

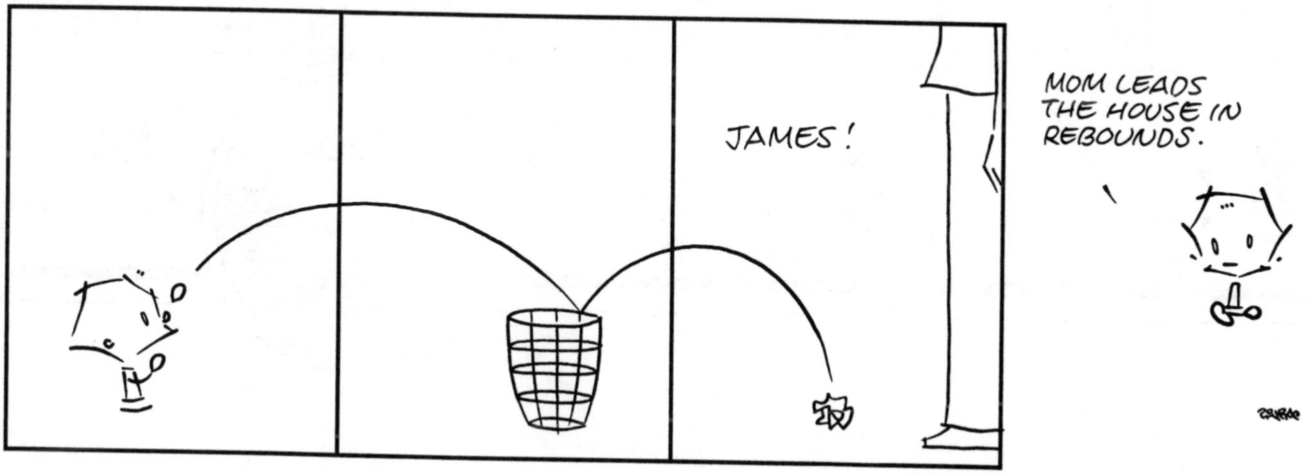
JAMES!
MOM LEADS THE HOUSE IN REBOUNDS.

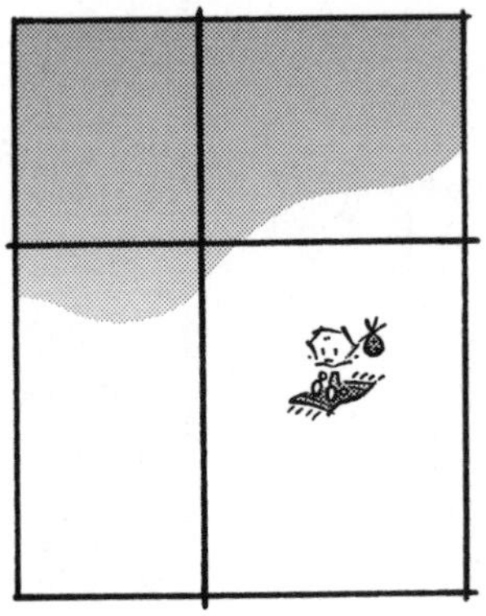

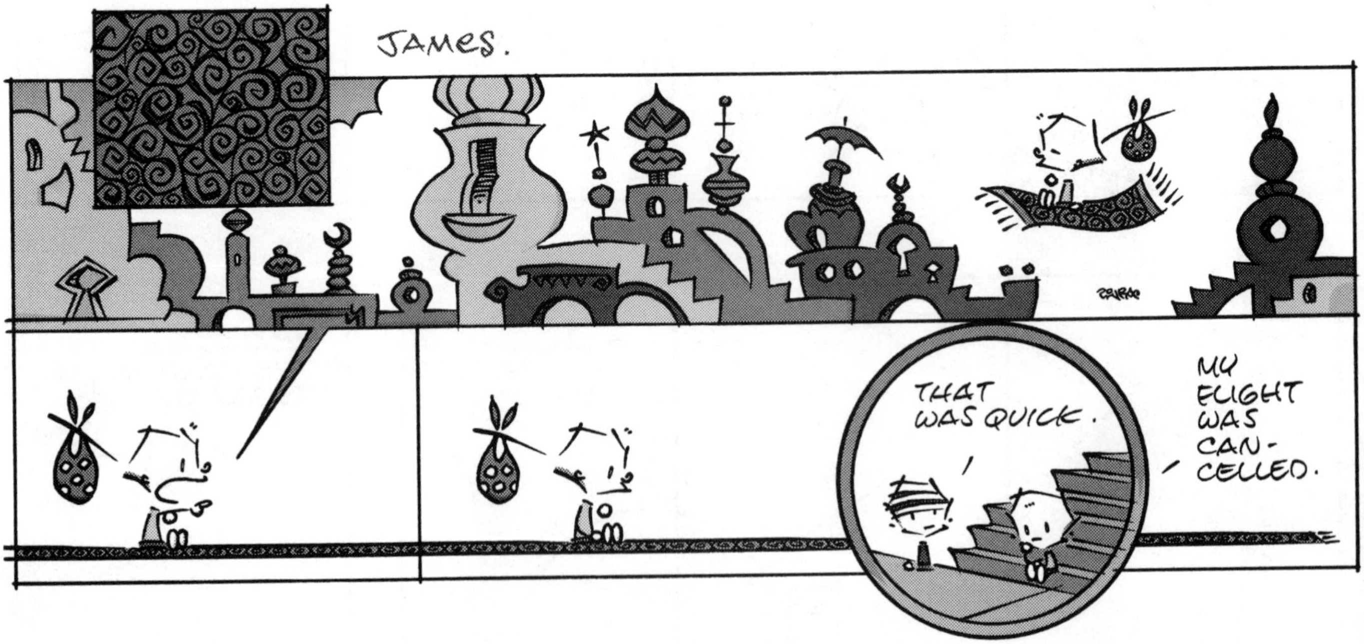
JAMES.
THAT WAS QUICK.
MY FLIGHT WAS CAN-CELLED.

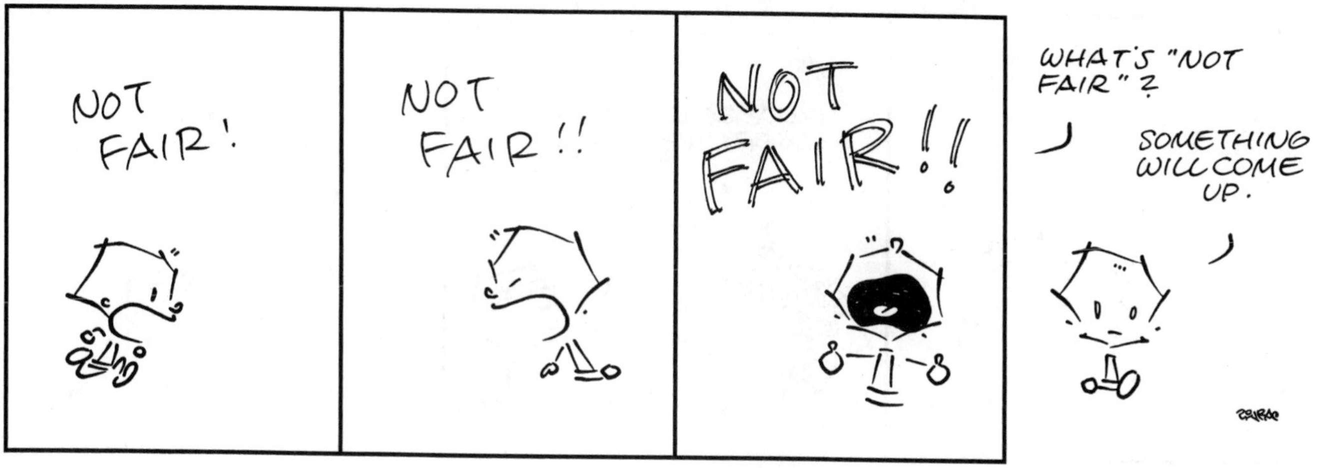
NOT FAIR!
NOT FAIR!!
NOT FAIR!!
WHAT'S "NOT FAIR"?
SOMETHING WILL COME UP.

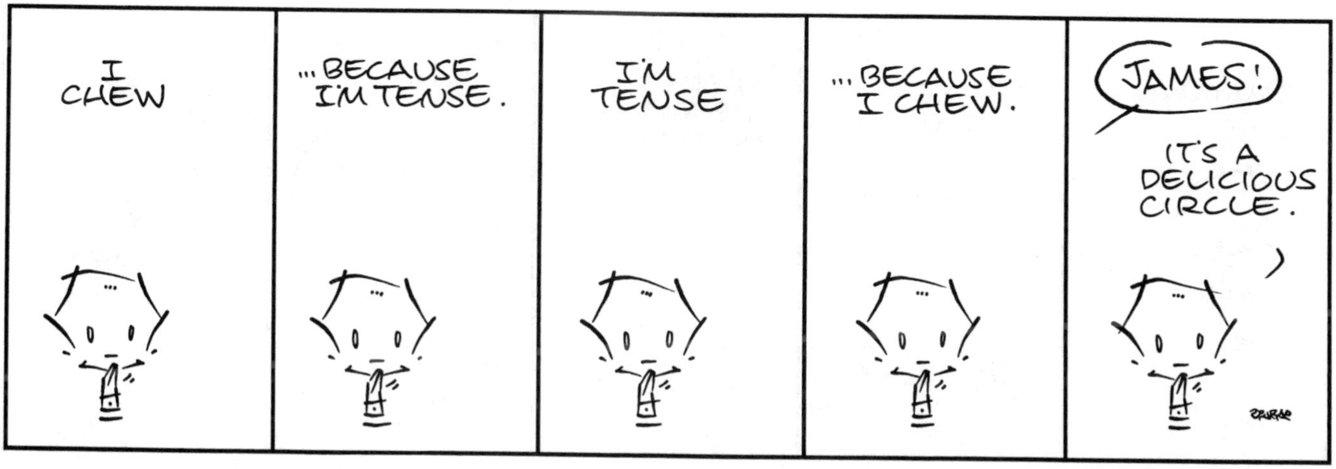
I CHEW
...BECAUSE I'M TENSE.
I'M TENSE
...BECAUSE I CHEW.
JAMES!
IT'S A DELICIOUS CIRCLE.

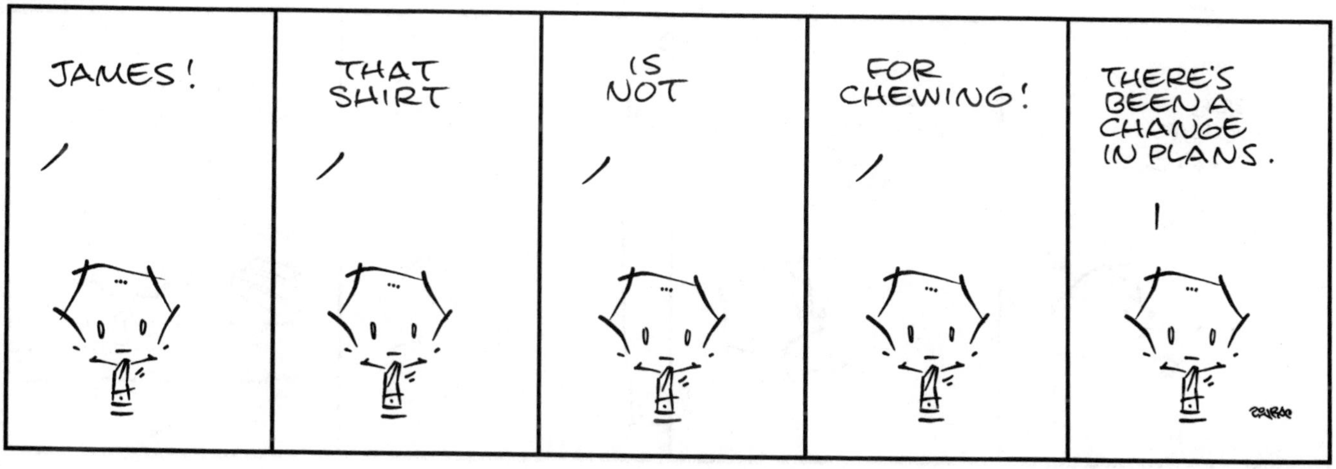
JAMES!
THAT SHIRT
IS NOT
FOR CHEWING!
THERE'S BEEN A CHANGE IN PLANS.

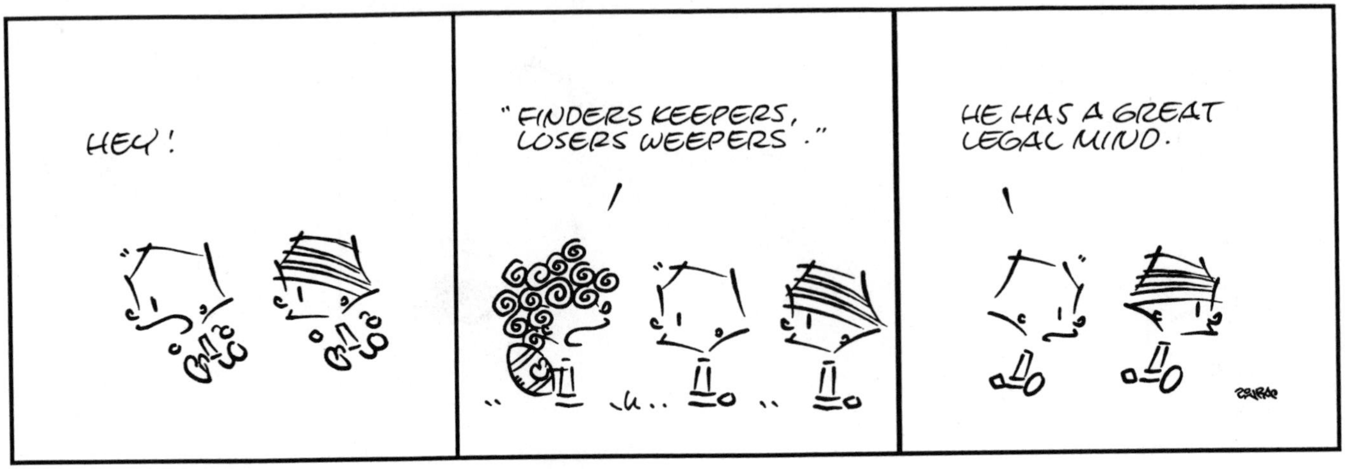
HEY!
"FINDERS KEEPERS, LOSERS WEEPERS."
HE HAS A GREAT LEGAL MIND.

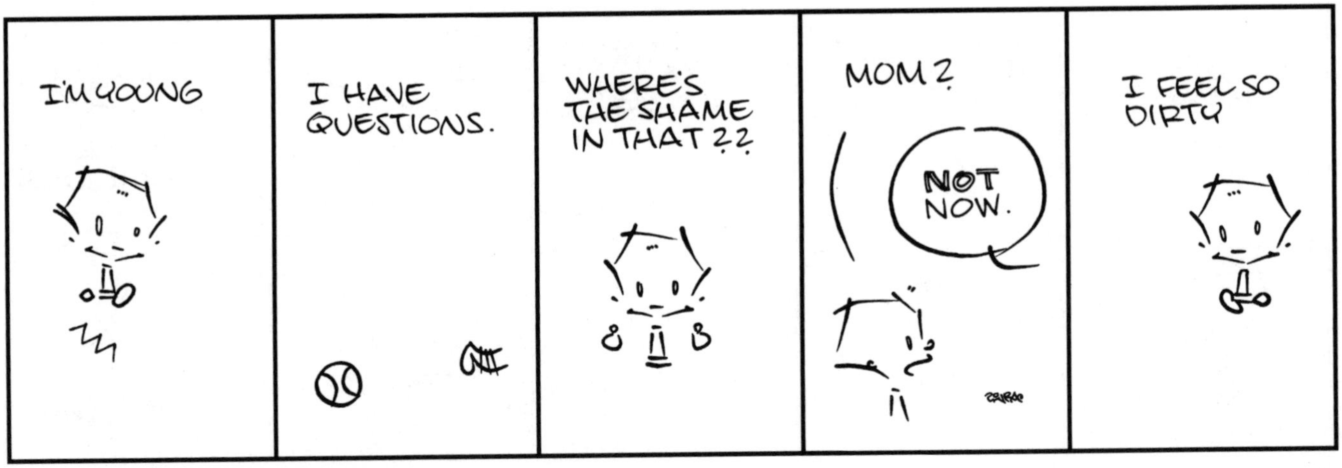
I'M YOUNG
I HAVE QUESTIONS.
WHERE'S THE SHAME IN THAT??
MOM?
NOT NOW.
I FEEL SO DIRTY

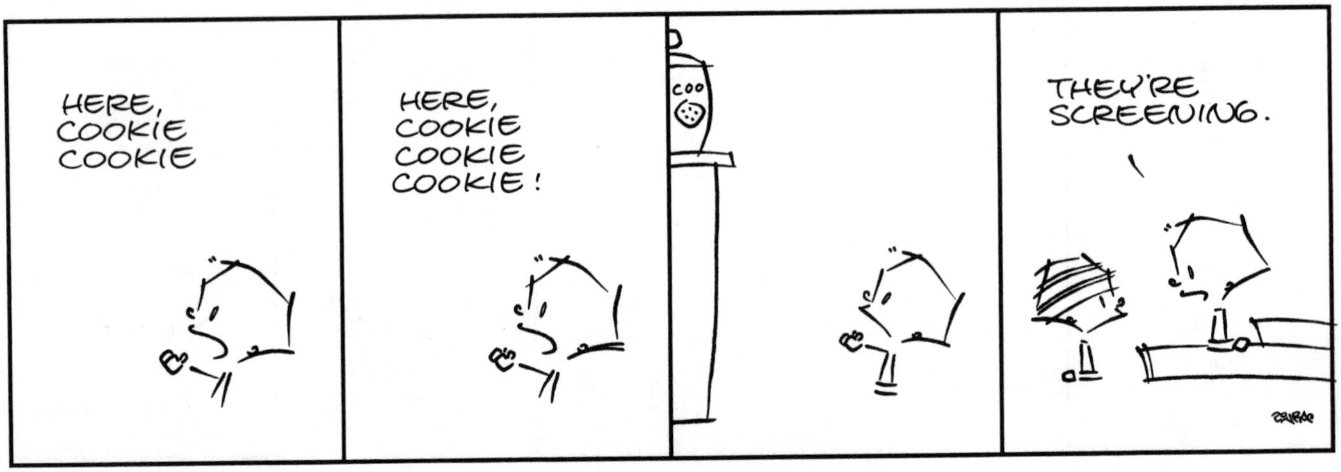
HERE, COOKIE COOKIE
HERE, COOKIE COOKIE COOKIE!
COO
THEY'RE SCREENING.

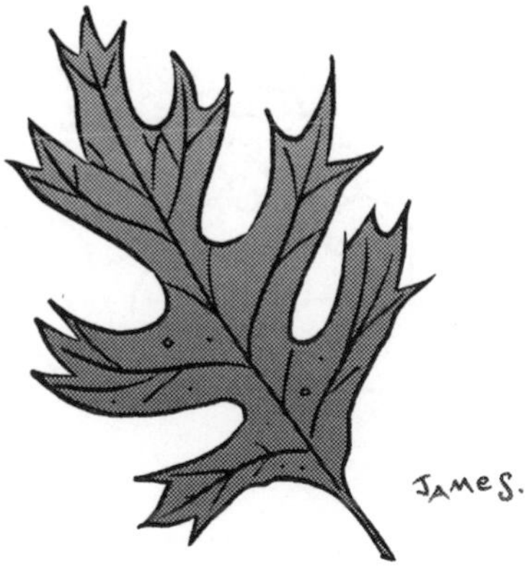
JAMES.

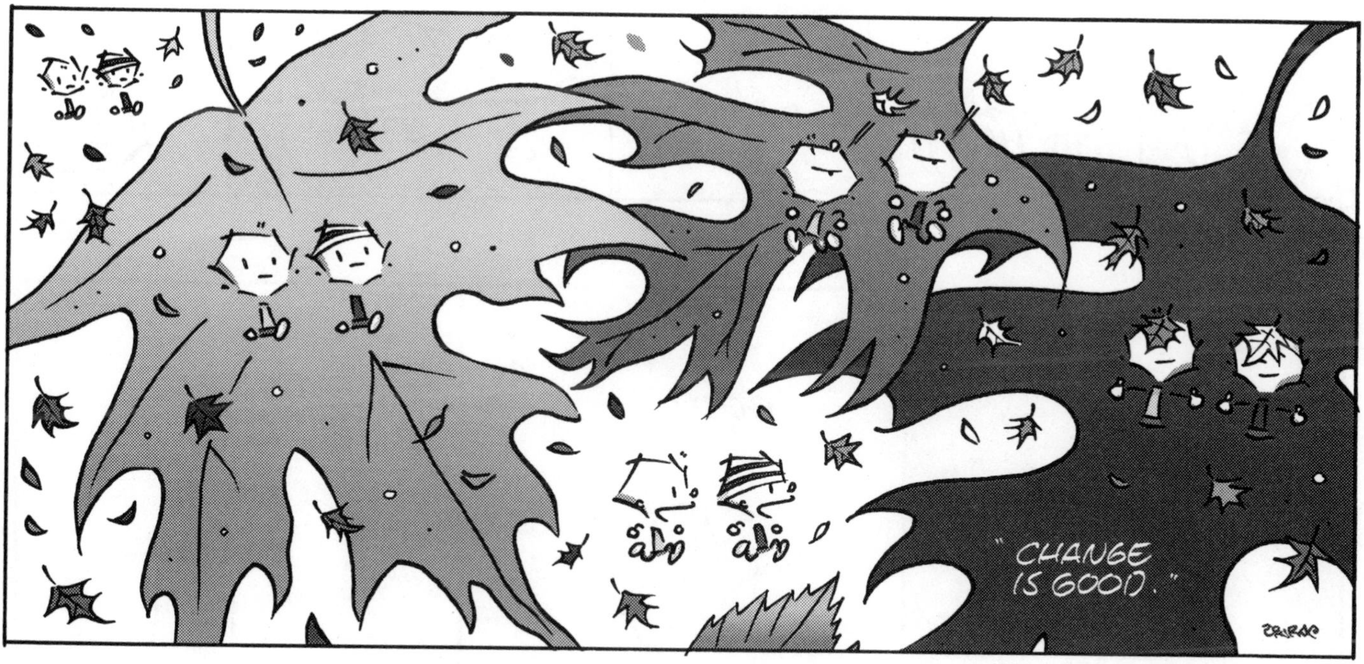
"CHANGE IS GOOD."

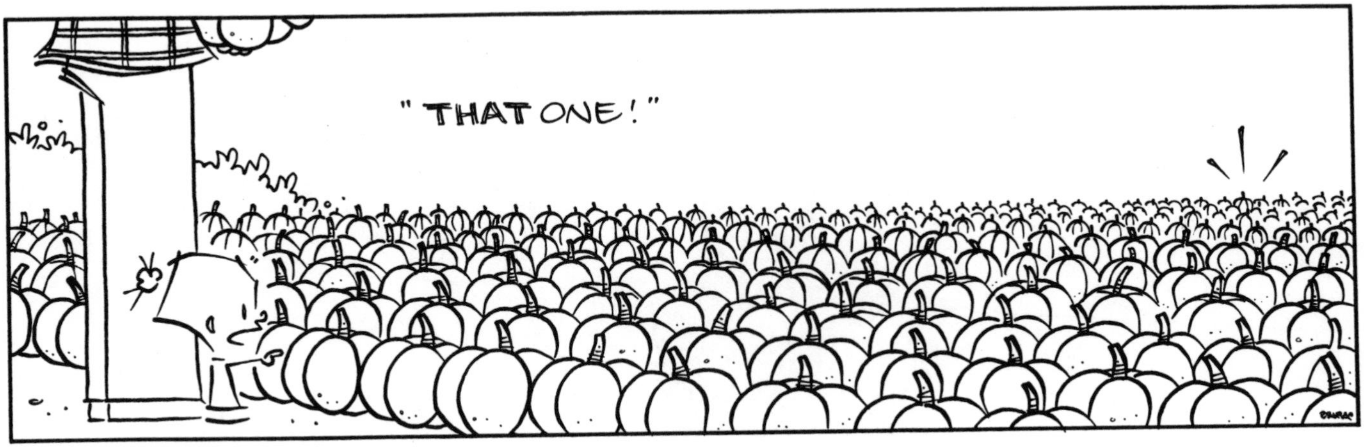
"THAT ONE!"

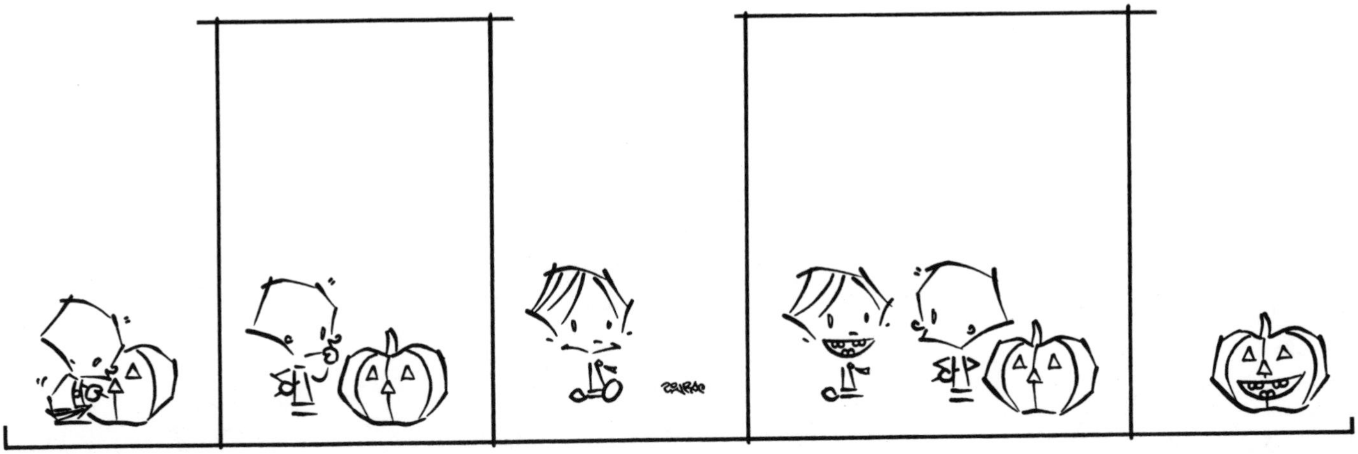

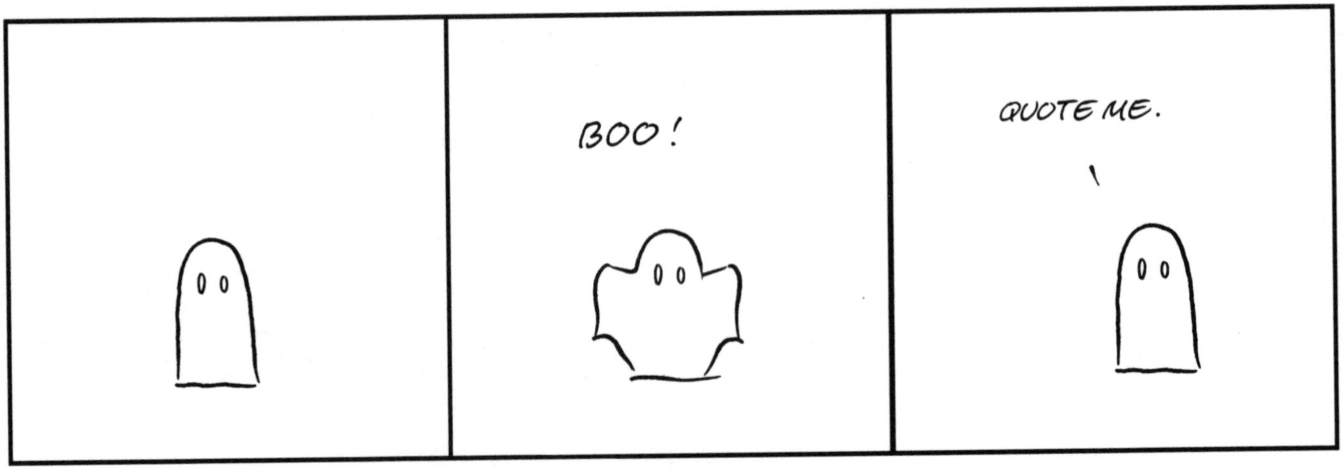
BOO!
QUOTE ME.

JAMES.

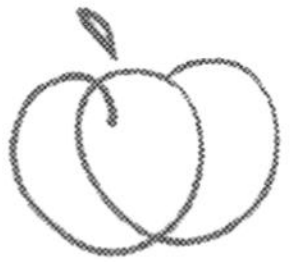

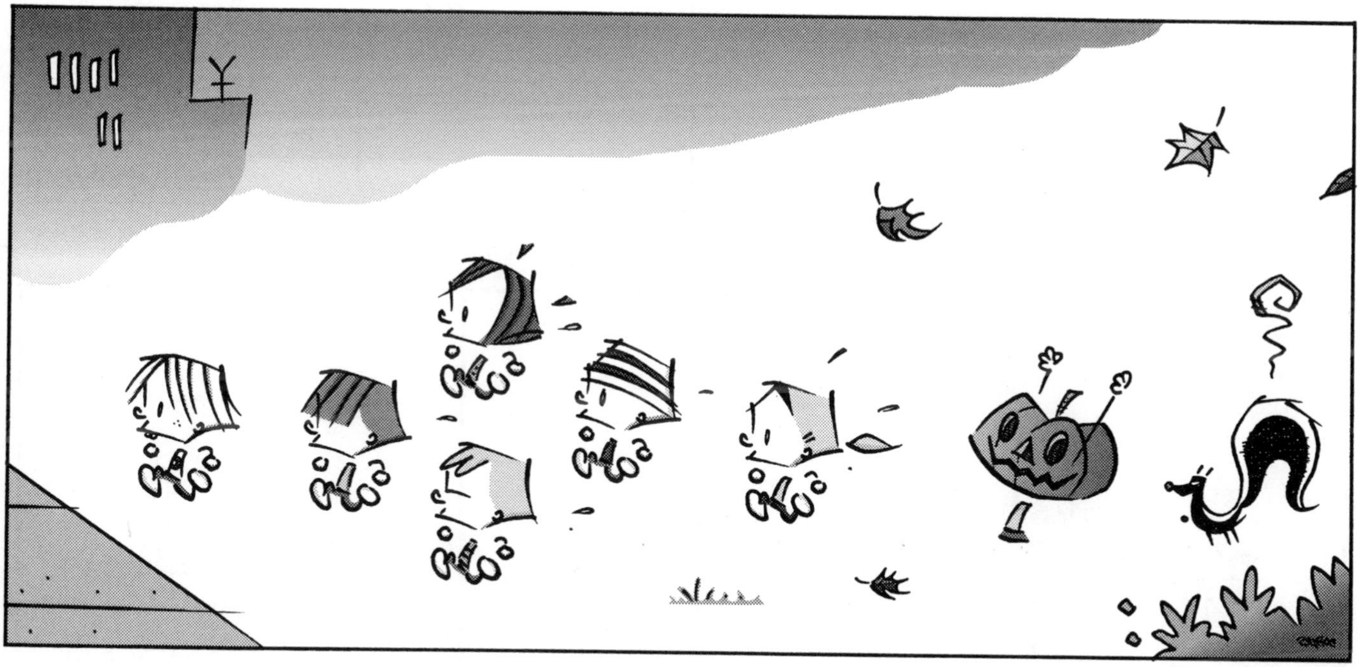

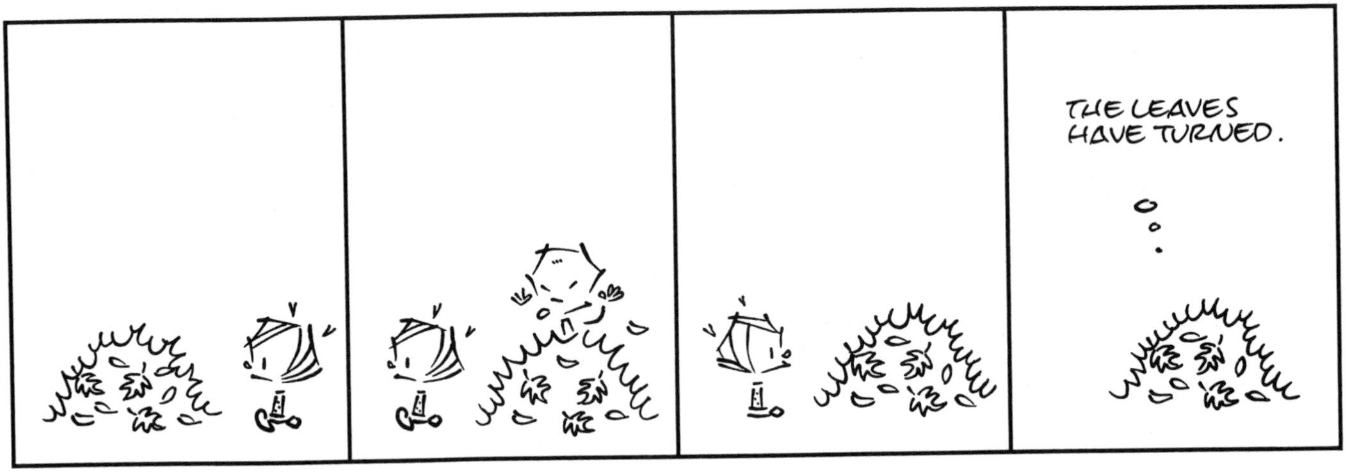
THE LEAVES
HAVE TURNED.

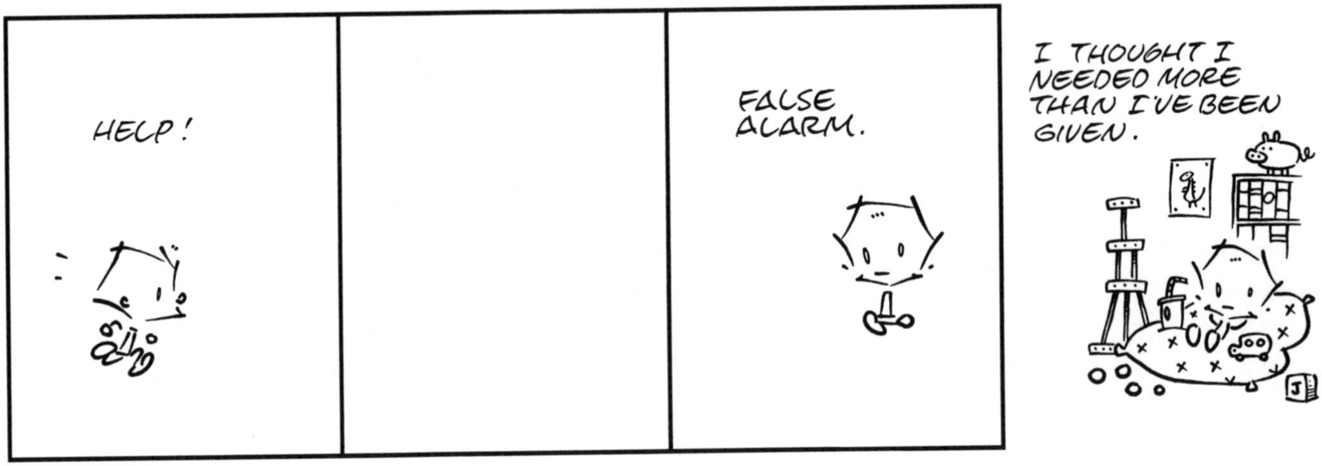
HELP!
FALSE
ALARM.
I THOUGHT I
NEEDED MORE
THAN I'VE BEEN
GIVEN.

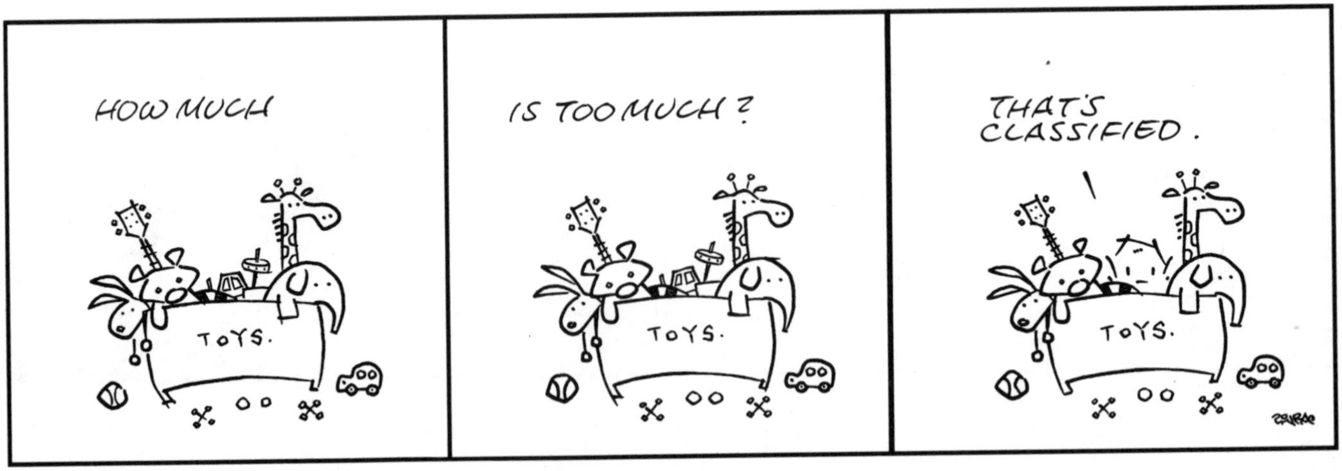
HOW MUCH
TOYS.
IS TOO MUCH?
TOYS.
THAT'S
CLASSIFIED.
TOYS.

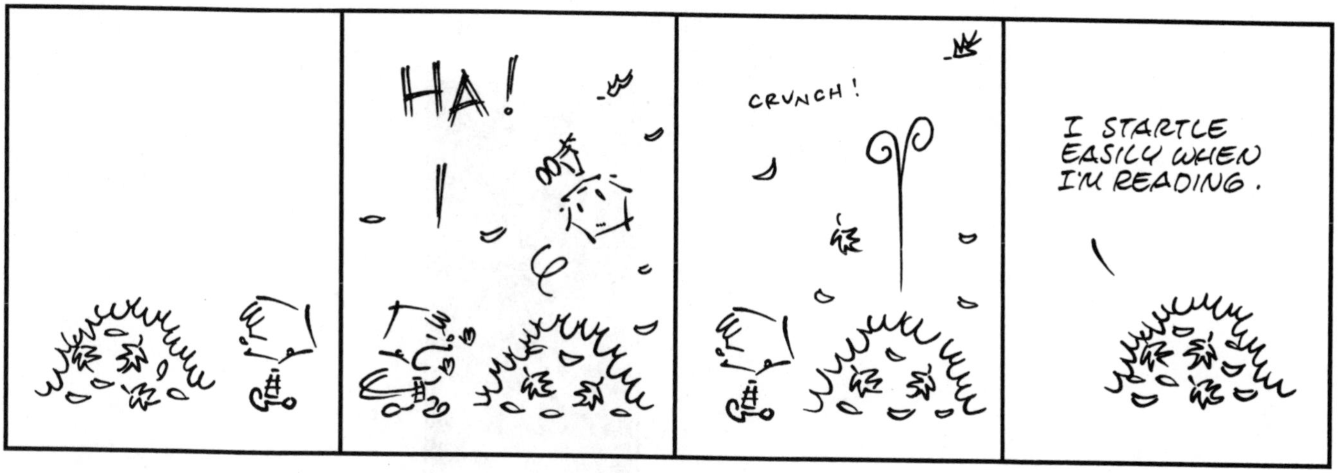
HA!
CRUNCH!
I STARTLE EASILY WHEN I'M READING.

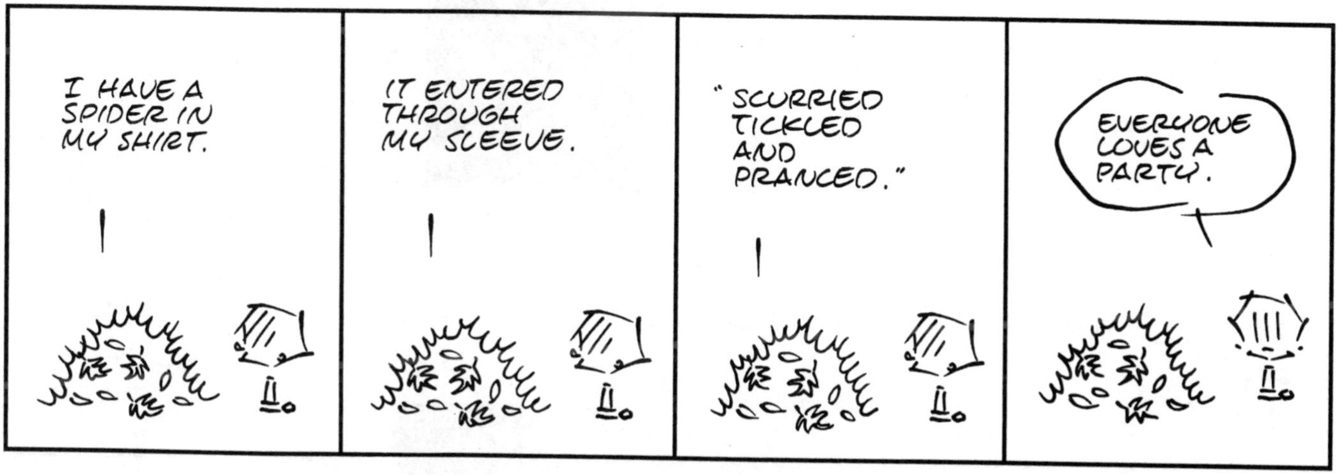
I HAVE A SPIDER IN MY SHIRT.
IT ENTERED THROUGH MY SLEEVE.
"SCURRIED TICKLED AND PRANCED."
EVERYONE LOVES A PARTY.

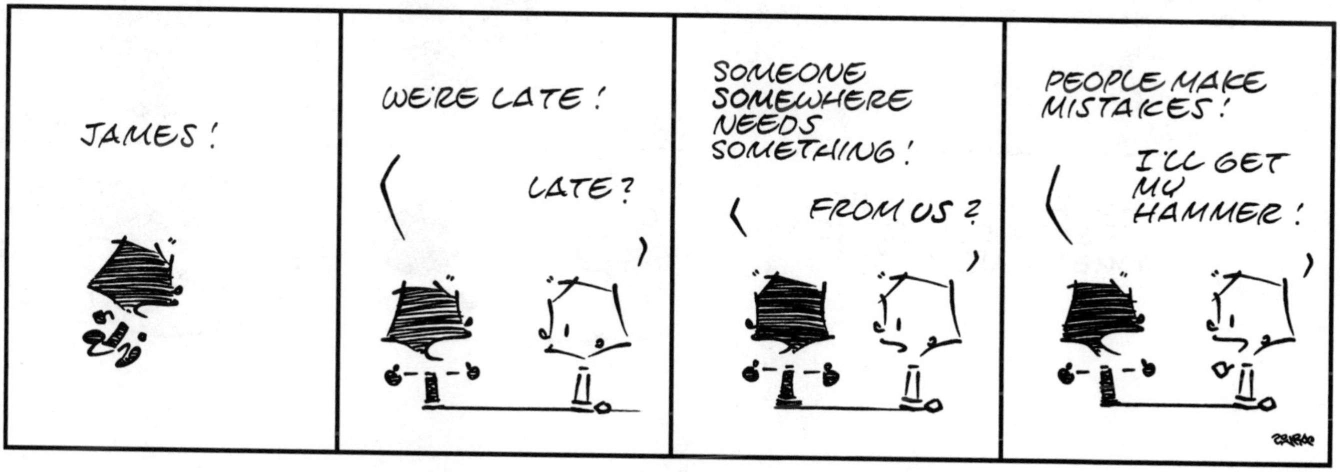
JAMES!
WE'RE LATE!
LATE?
SOMEONE SOMEWHERE NEEDS SOMETHING!
FROM US?
PEOPLE MAKE MISTAKES!
I'LL GET MY HAMMER!

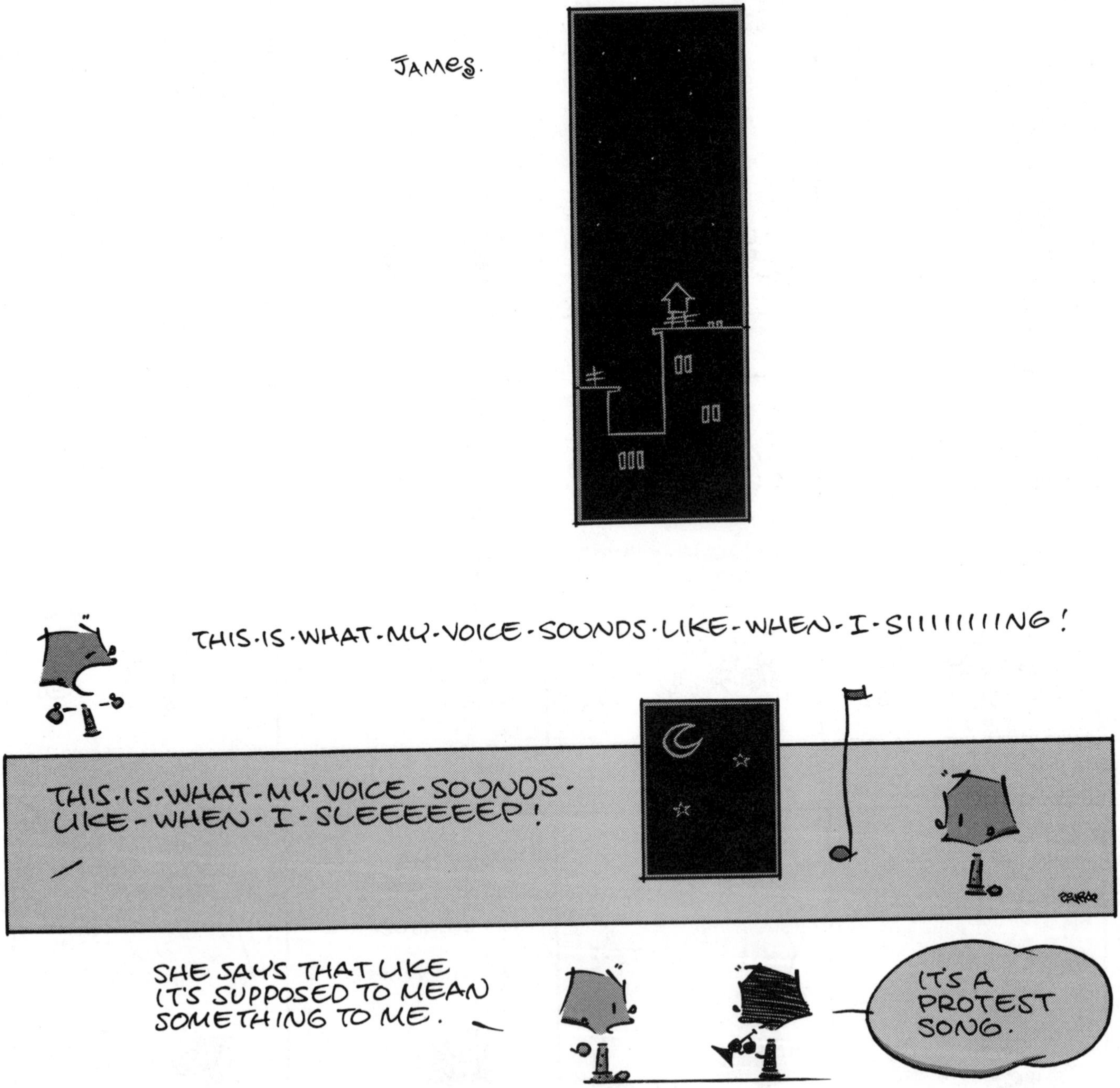
JAMES.
THIS·IS·WHAT·MY·VOICE·SOUNDS·LIKE·WHEN·I·SIIIIIIIING!
THIS·IS·WHAT·MY·VOICE·SOUNDS·LIKE·WHEN·I·SLEEEEEEEP!
SHE SAYS THAT LIKE IT'S SUPPOSED TO MEAN SOMETHING TO ME.
IT'S A PROTEST SONG.

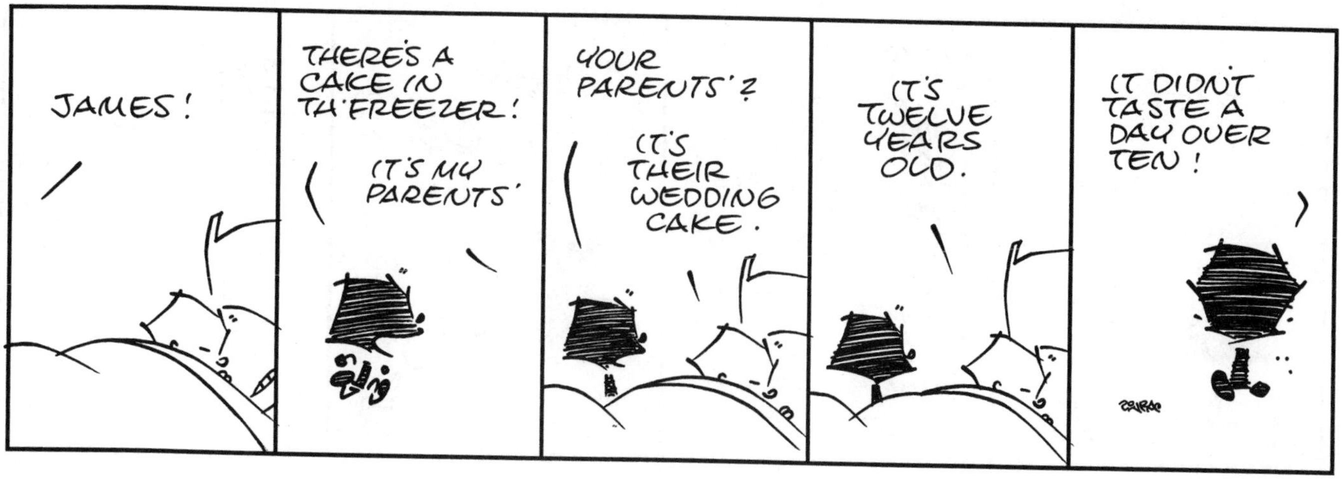
JAMES!
THERE'S A CAKE IN TH' FREEZER!
IT'S MY PARENTS'
YOUR PARENTS'?
IT'S THEIR WEDDING CAKE.
IT'S TWELVE YEARS OLD.
IT DIDN'T TASTE A DAY OVER TEN!

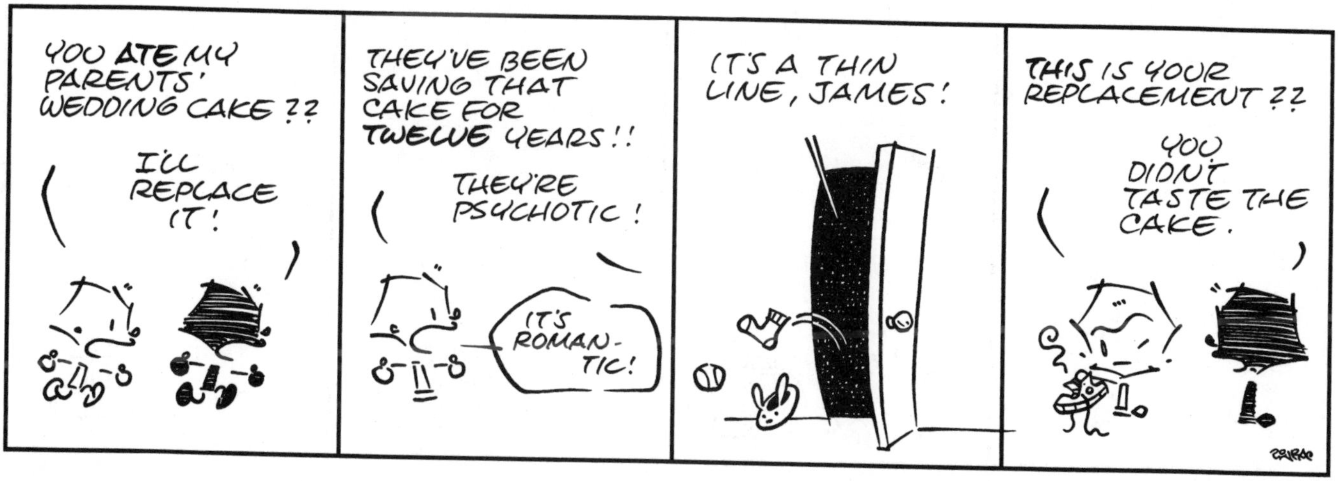
YOU ATE MY PARENTS' WEDDING CAKE??
I'LL REPLACE IT!
THEY'VE BEEN SAVING THAT CAKE FOR TWELVE YEARS!!
THEY'RE PSYCHOTIC!
IT'S ROMANTIC!
IT'S A THIN LINE, JAMES!
THIS IS YOUR REPLACEMENT??
YOU DIDN'T TASTE THE CAKE.

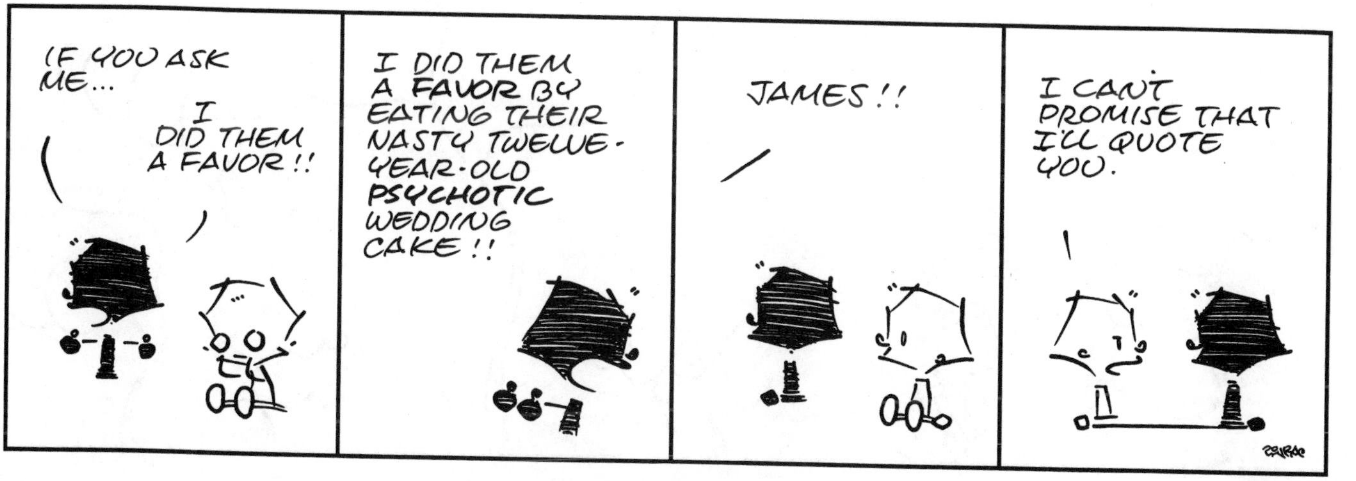
IF YOU ASK ME...
I DID THEM A FAVOR!!
I DID THEM A FAVOR BY EATING THEIR NASTY TWELVE-YEAR-OLD PSYCHOTIC WEDDING CAKE!!
JAMES!!
I CAN'T PROMISE THAT I'LL QUOTE YOU.

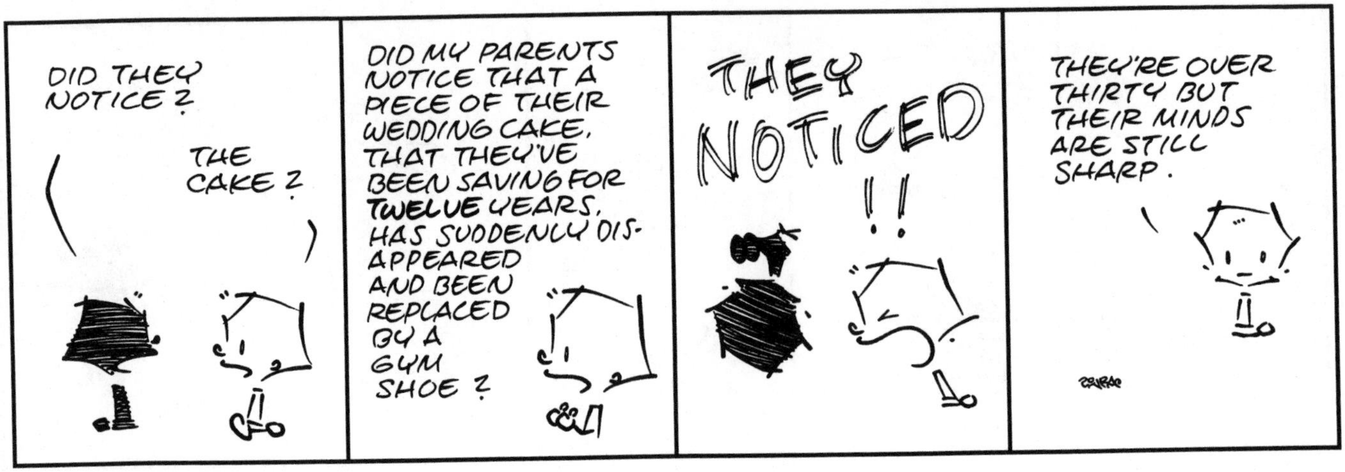
DID THEY NOTICE?
THE CAKE?
DID MY PARENTS NOTICE THAT A PIECE OF THEIR WEDDING CAKE, THAT THEY'VE BEEN SAVING FOR TWELVE YEARS, HAS SUDDENLY DISAPPEARED AND BEEN REPLACED BY A GYM SHOE?
THEY NOTICED
!!
THEY'RE OVER THIRTY BUT THEIR MINDS ARE STILL SHARP.

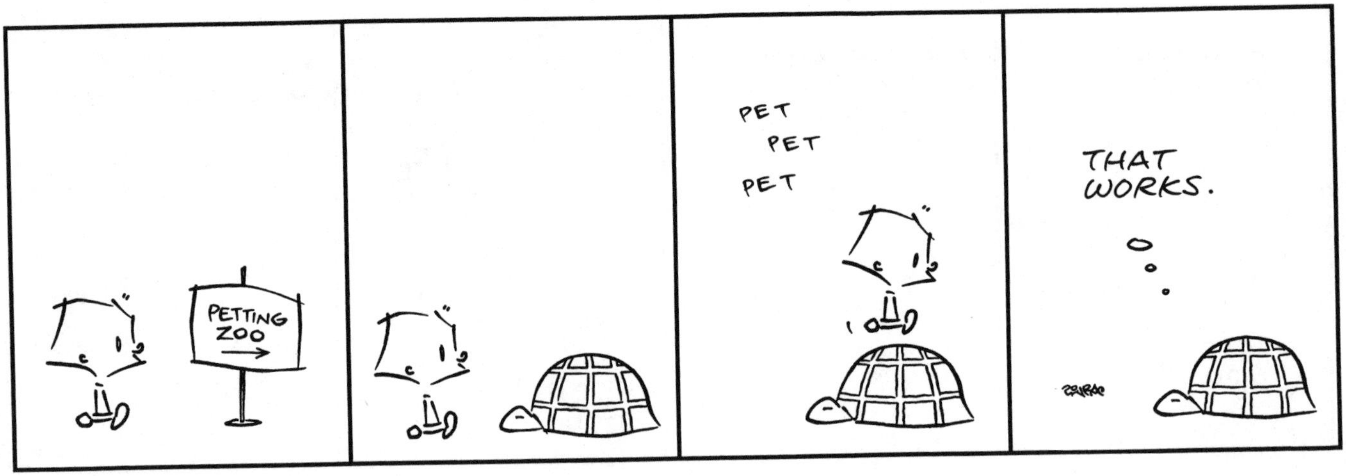
PETTING ZOO
PET PET PET
THAT WORKS.

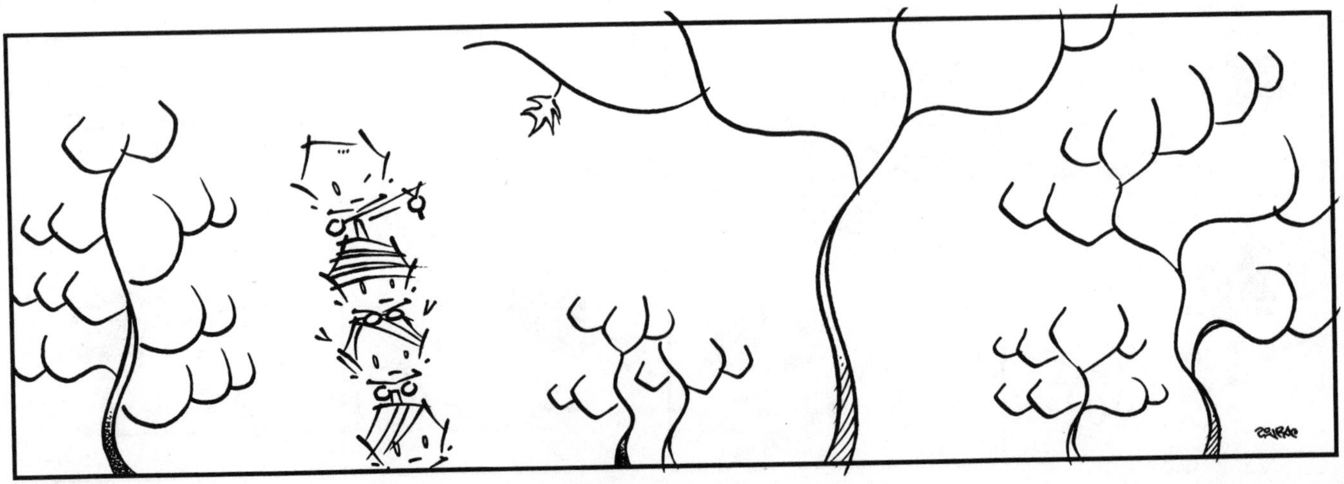

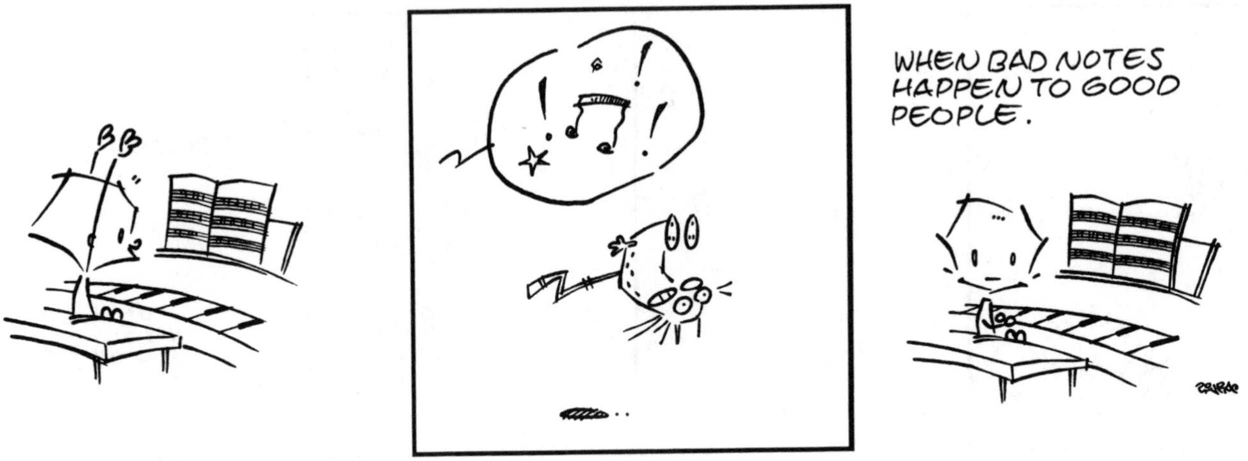
BB
WHEN BAD NOTES HAPPEN TO GOOD PEOPLE.

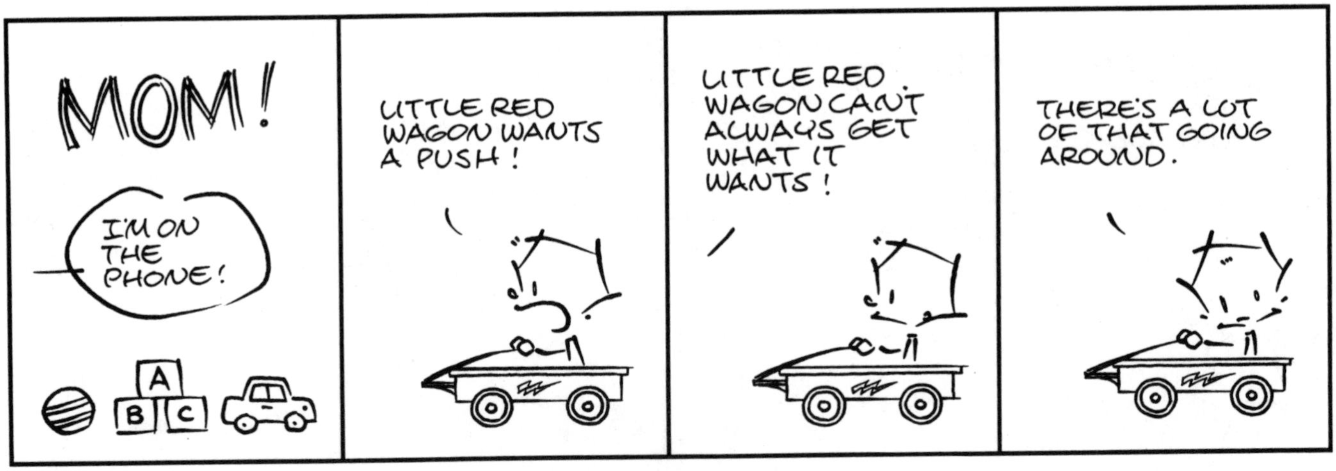
MOM!
I'M ON THE PHONE!
A
B C
LITTLE RED WAGON WANTS A PUSH!
LITTLE RED WAGON CAN'T ALWAYS GET WHAT IT WANTS!
THERE'S A LOT OF THAT GOING AROUND.

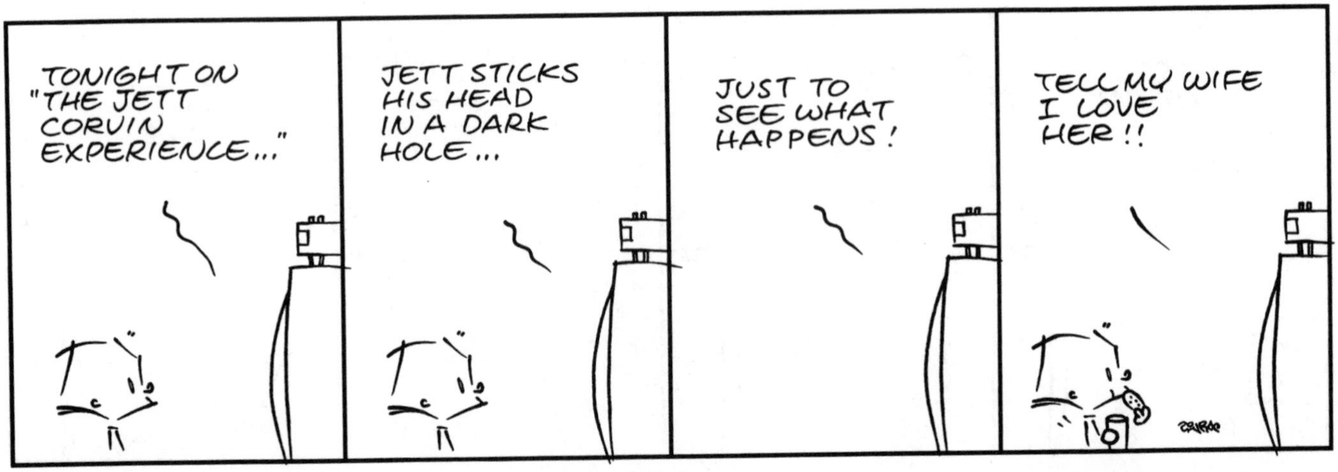
TONIGHT ON "THE JETT CORVIN EXPERIENCE..."
JETT STICKS HIS HEAD IN A DARK HOLE...
JUST TO SEE WHAT HAPPENS!
TELL MY WIFE I LOVE HER!!

JAMES

"THE CHARM OFFENSIVE."

WHO KNEW "CHARM" COULD BE SO OFFEN-SIVE?

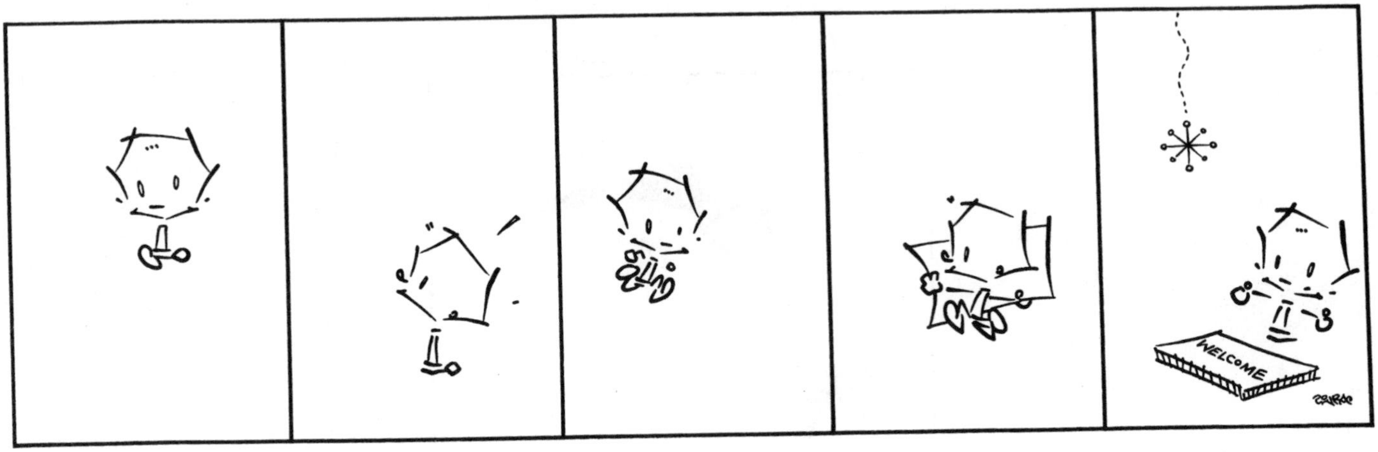
WELCOME

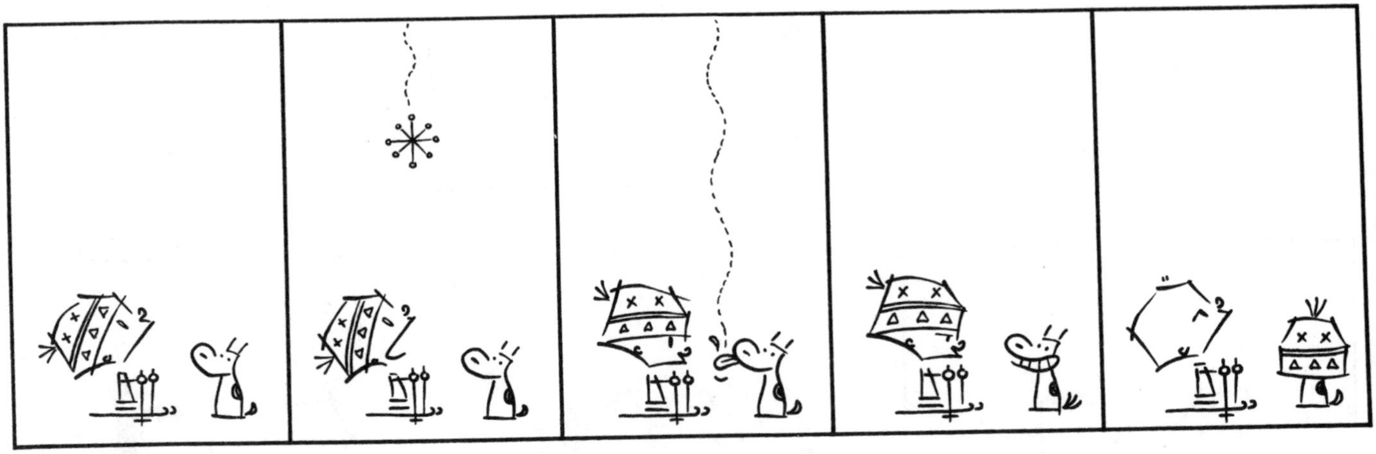

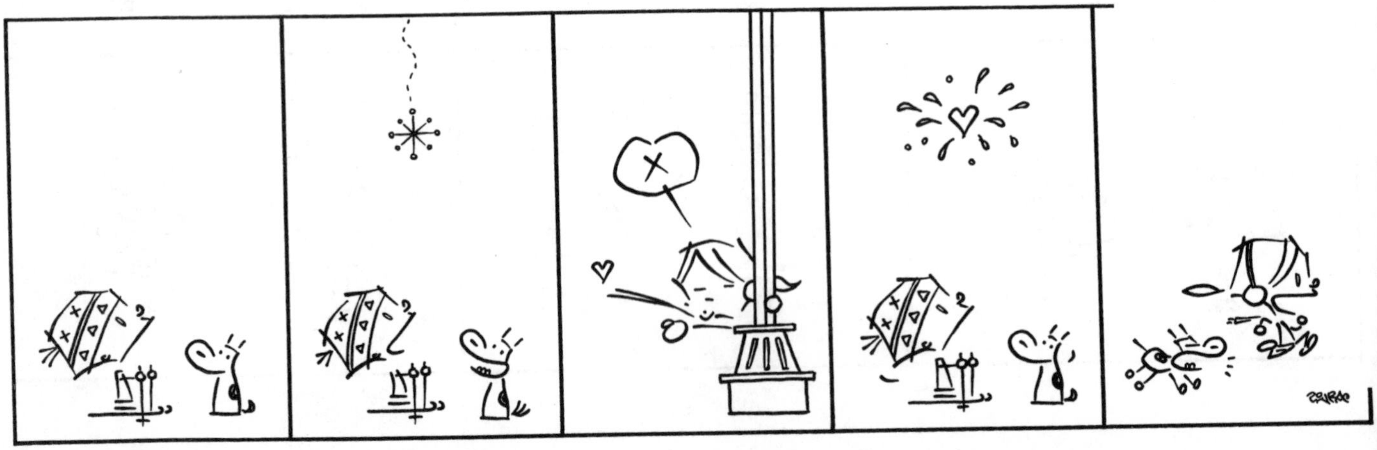

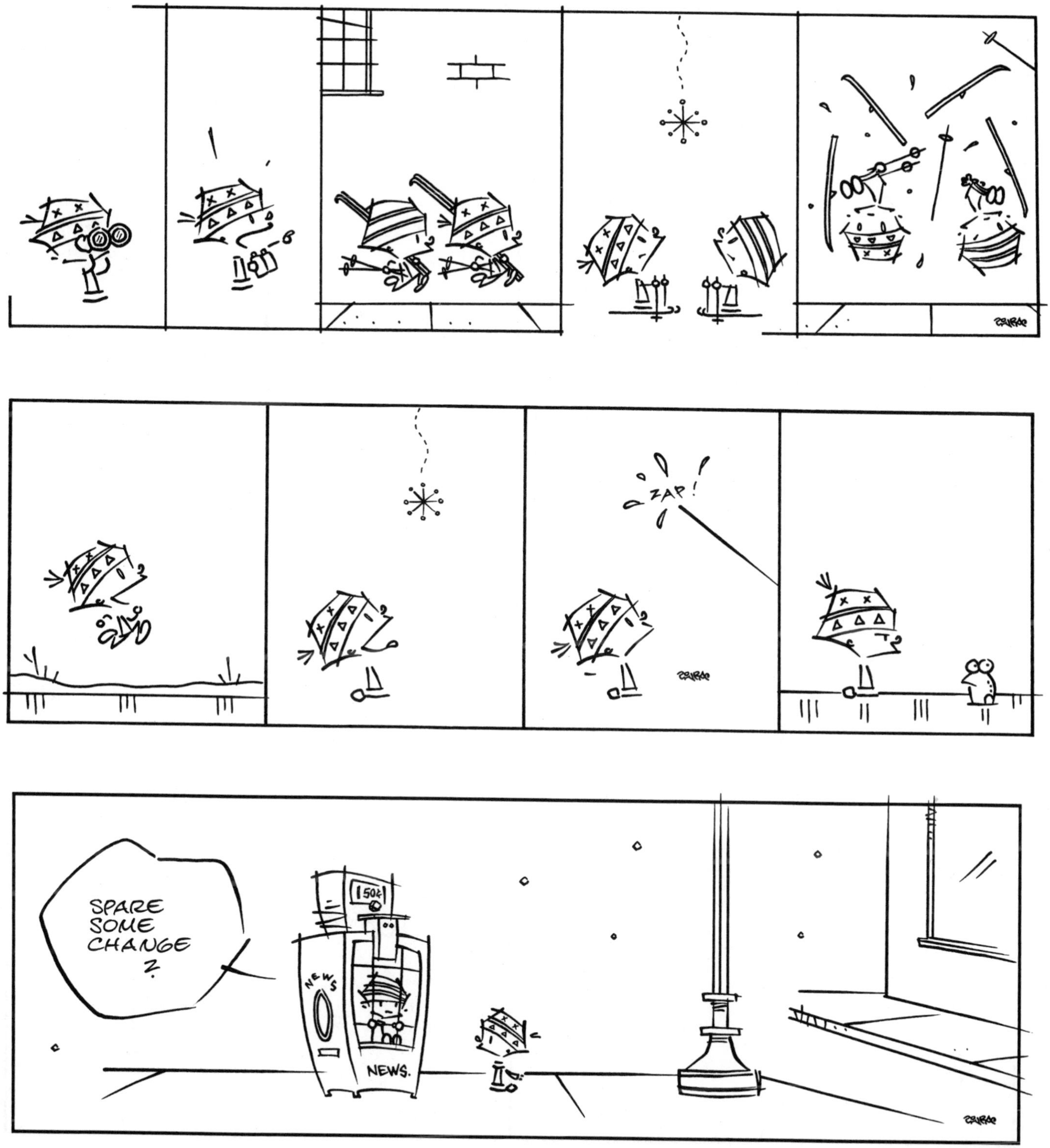
ZAP!
SPARE SOME CHANGE ?
50¢
NEWS
NEWS.

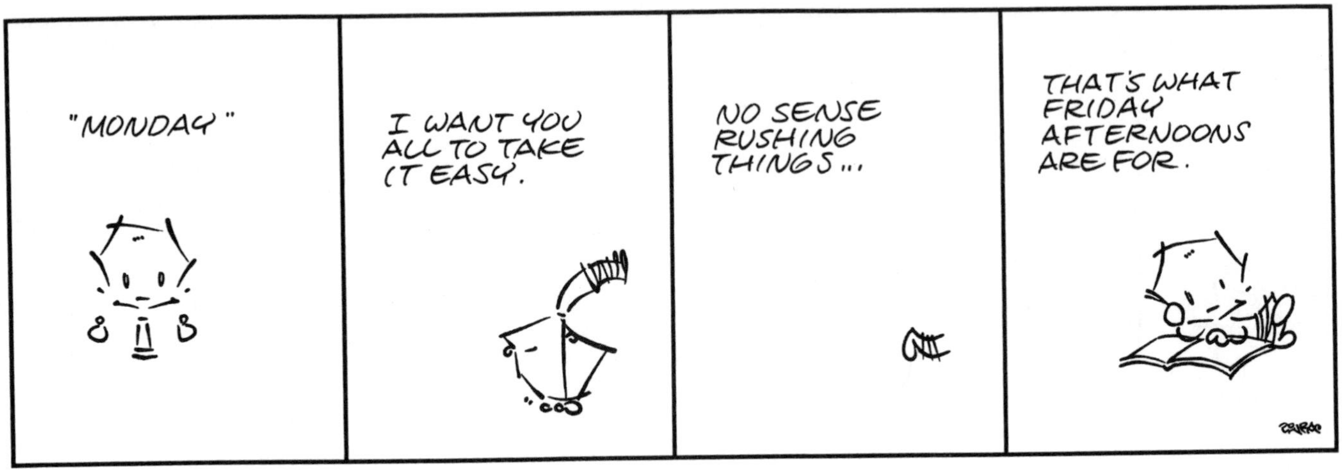
"MONDAY"
I WANT YOU ALL TO TAKE IT EASY.
NO SENSE RUSHING THINGS...
THAT'S WHAT FRIDAY AFTERNOONS ARE FOR.

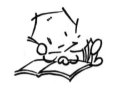

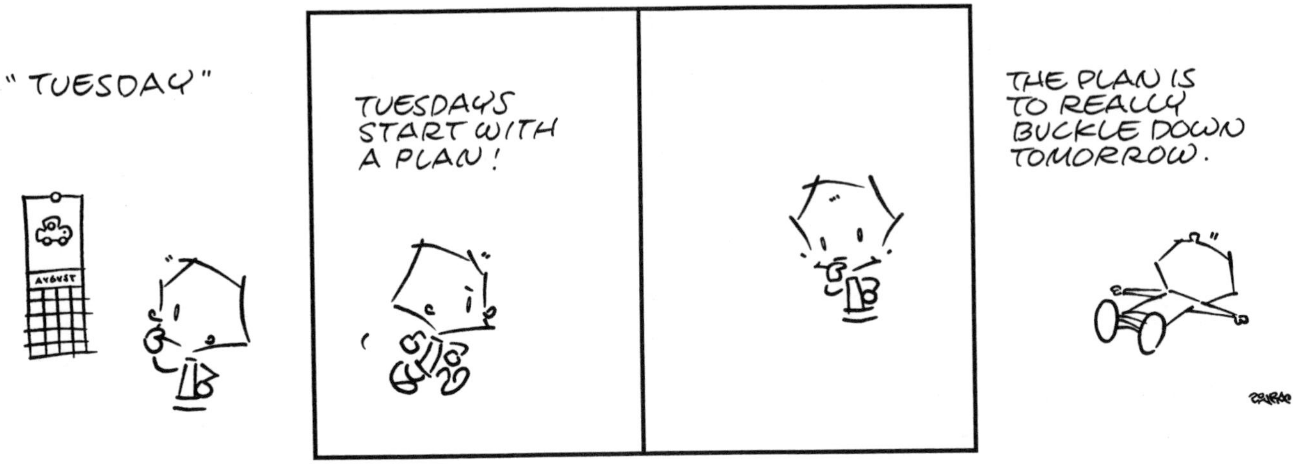
"TUESDAY"
AUGUST
TUESDAYS START WITH A PLAN!
THE PLAN IS TO REALLY BUCKLE DOWN TOMORROW.

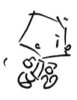

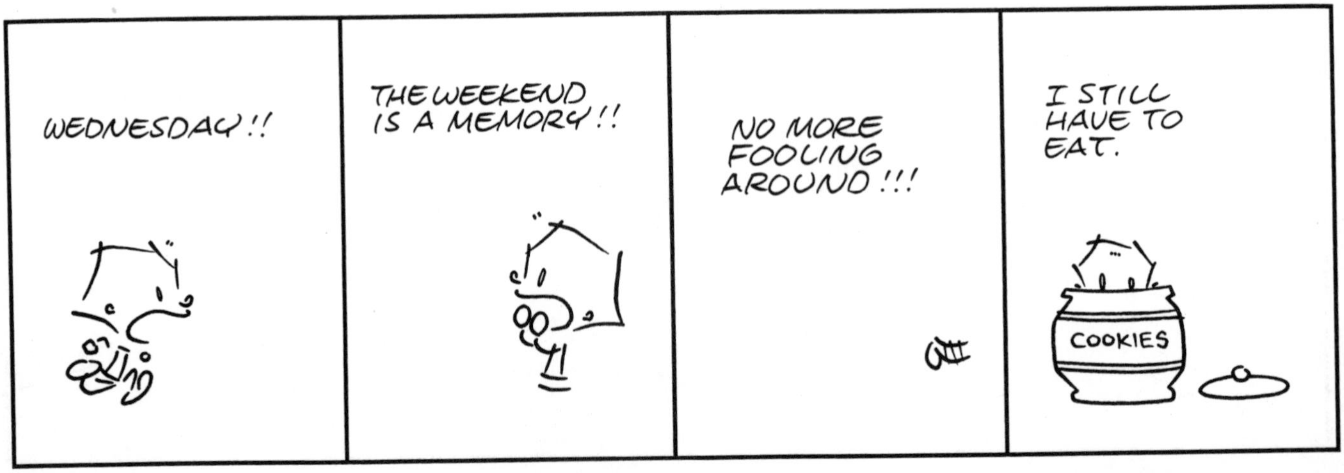
WEDNESDAY!!
THE WEEKEND IS A MEMORY!!
NO MORE FOOLING AROUND!!!
I STILL HAVE TO EAT.
COOKIES

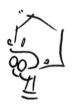

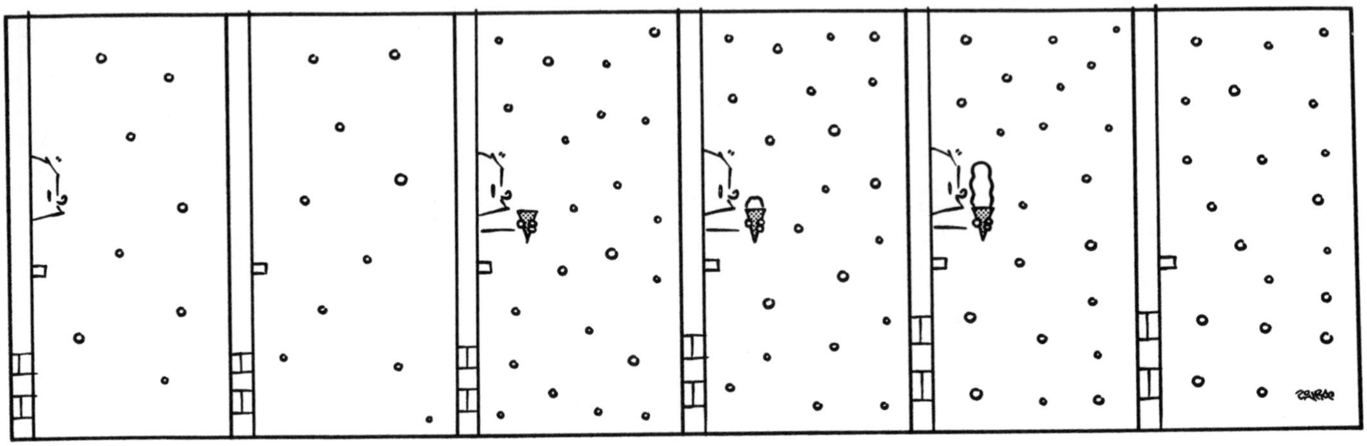

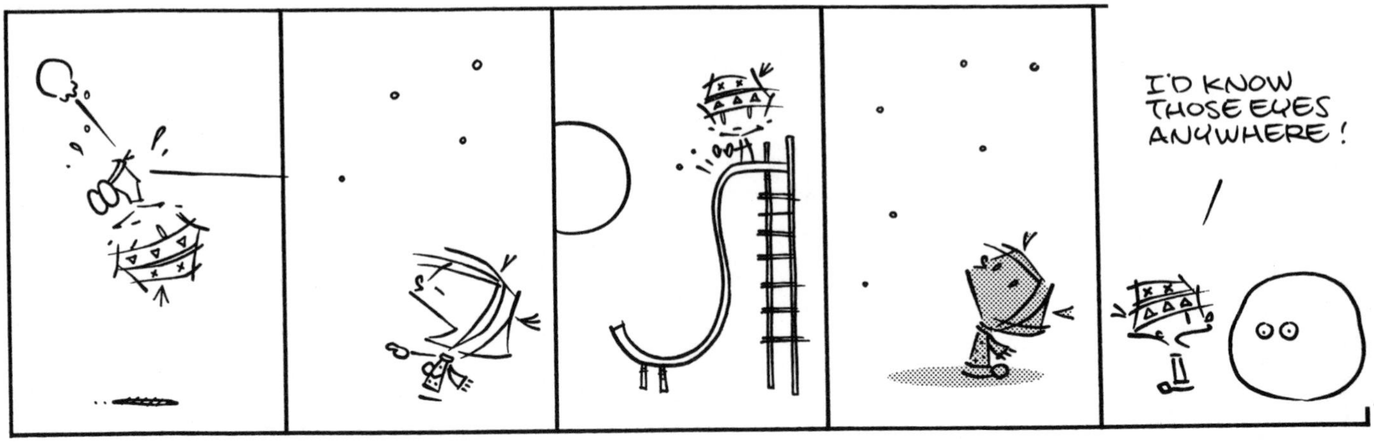
I'D KNOW THOSE EYES ANYWHERE!

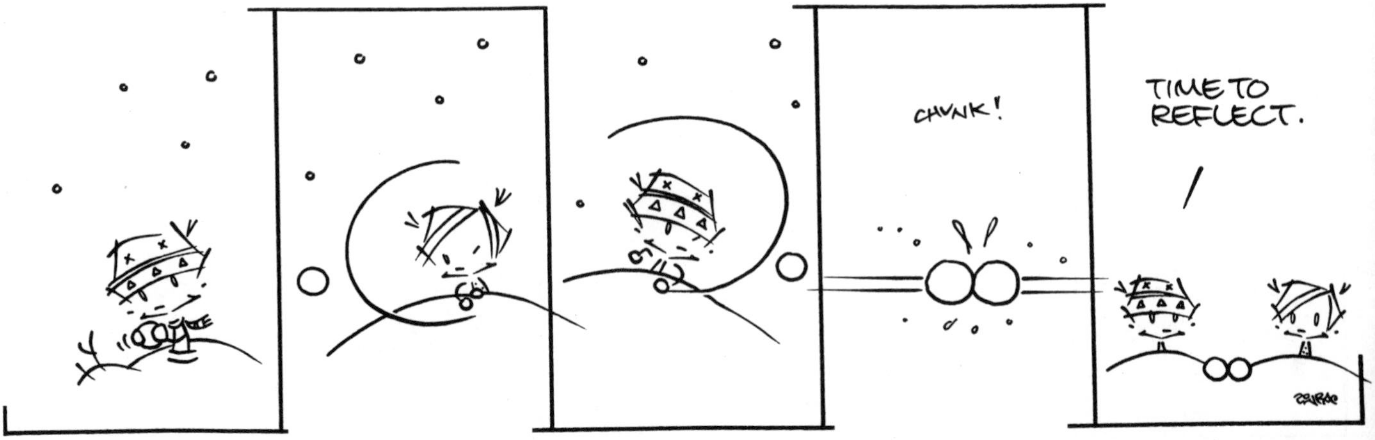
CHUNK!
TIME TO REFLECT.

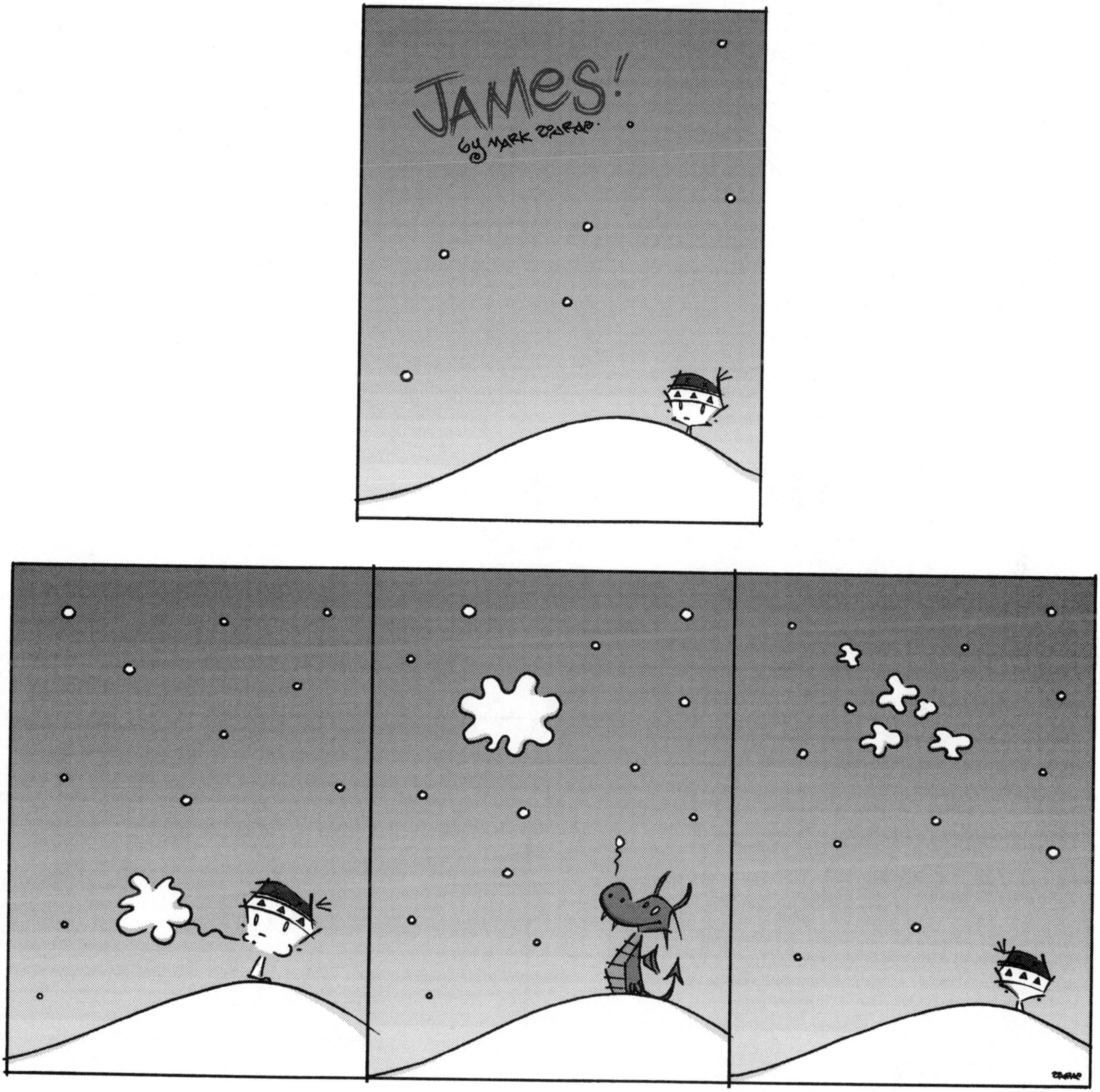
JAMES!

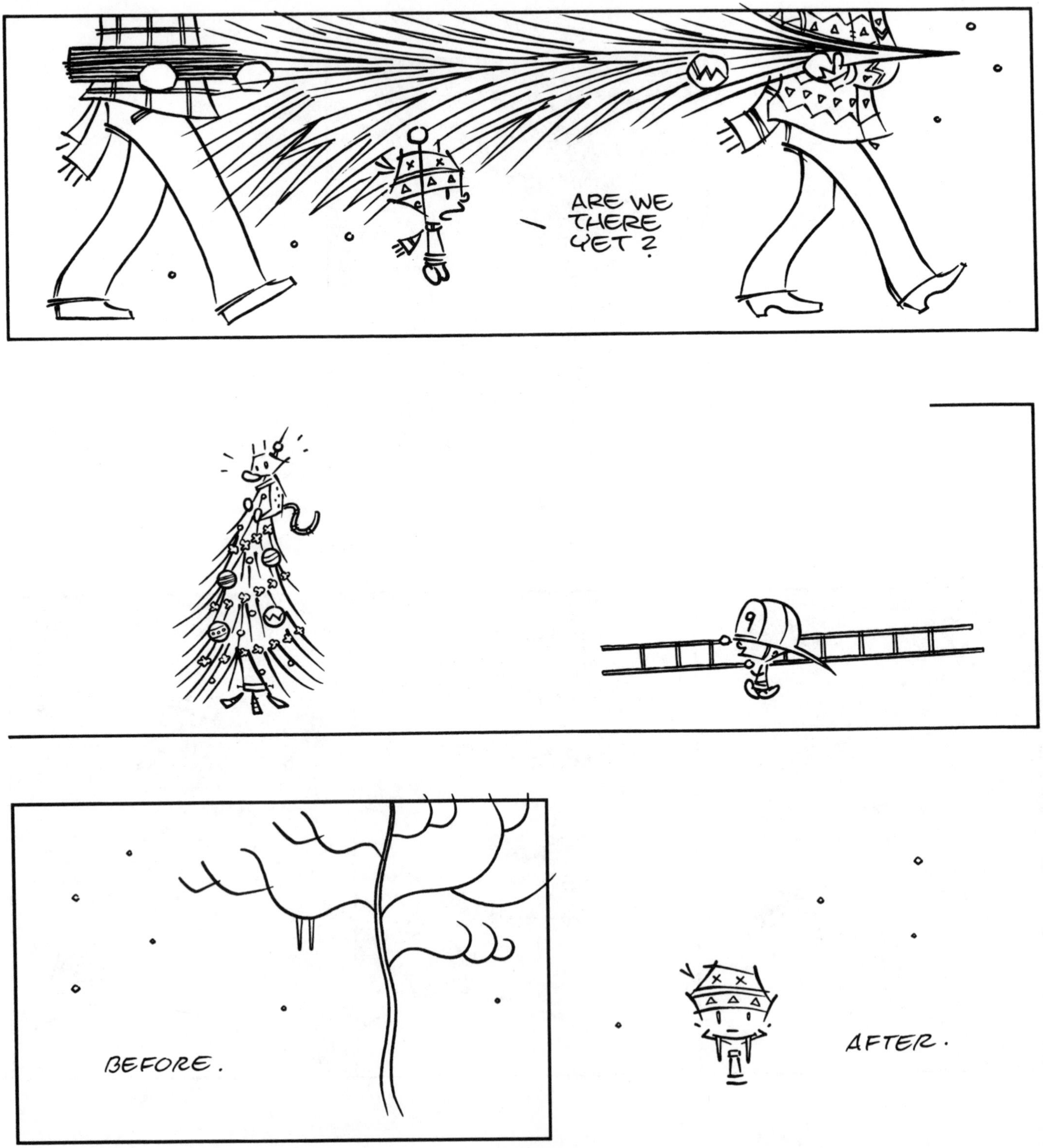
ARE WE THERE YET ?
BEFORE.
AFTER.

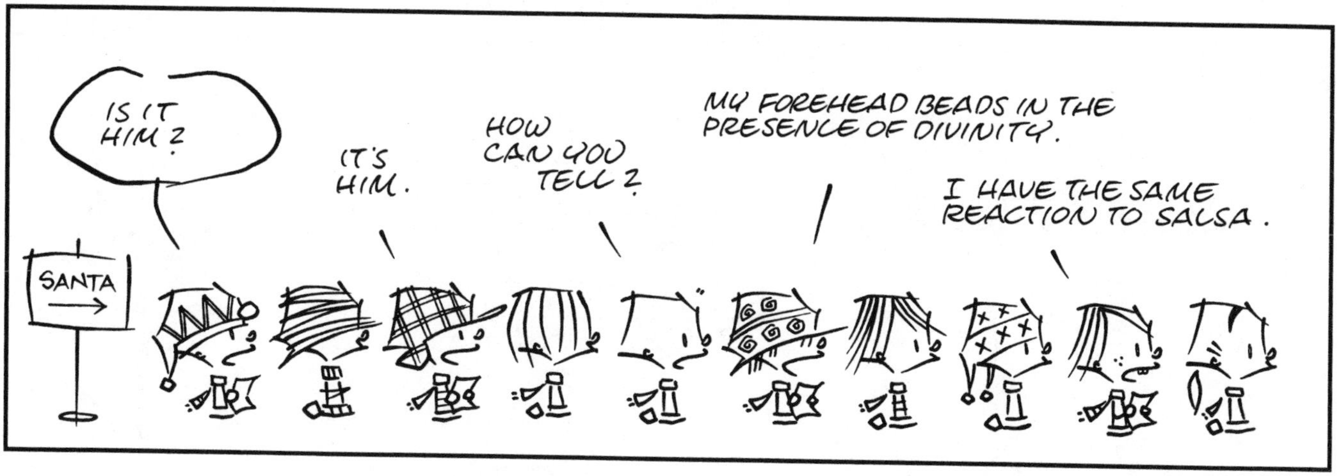
SANTA
IS IT HIM?
IT'S HIM.
HOW CAN YOU TELL?
MY FOREHEAD BEADS IN THE PRESENCE OF DIVINITY.
I HAVE THE SAME REACTION TO SALSA.

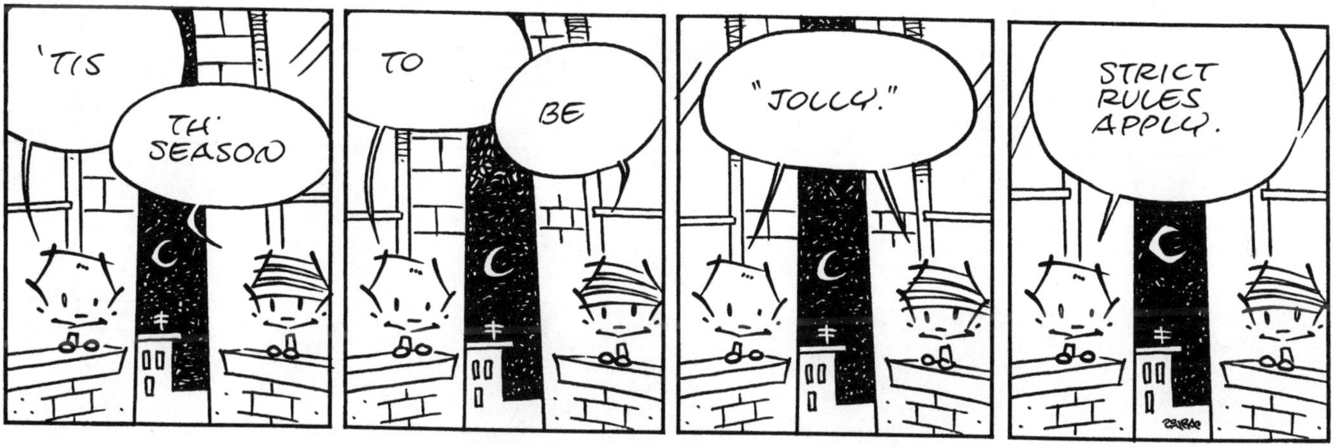
'TIS
TH' SEASON
TO
BE
"JOLLY."
STRICT RULES APPLY.

ATTACK OF THE XMAS SWEATERS!

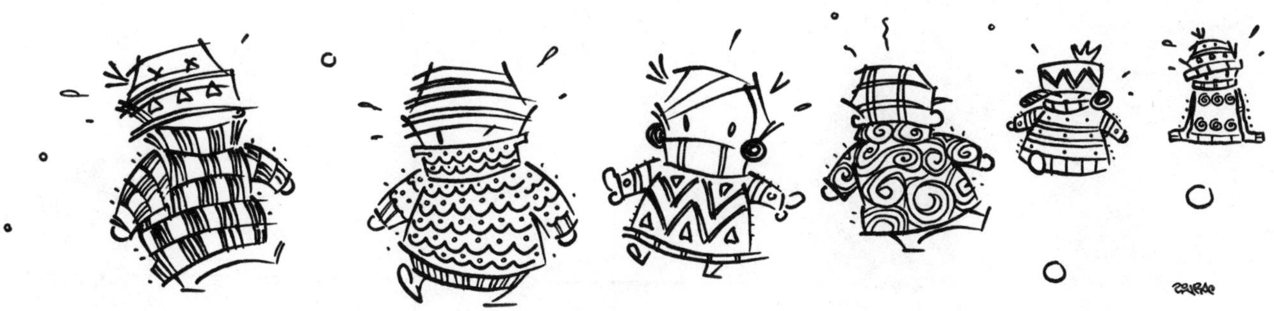

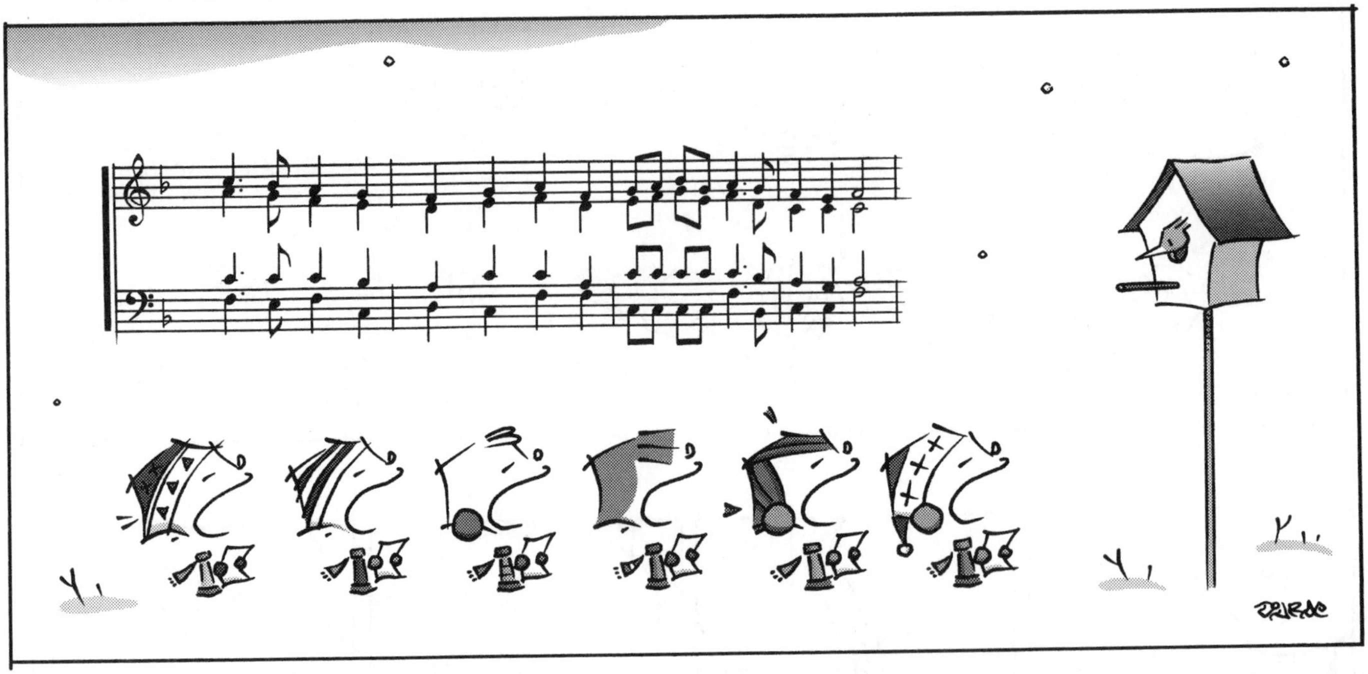

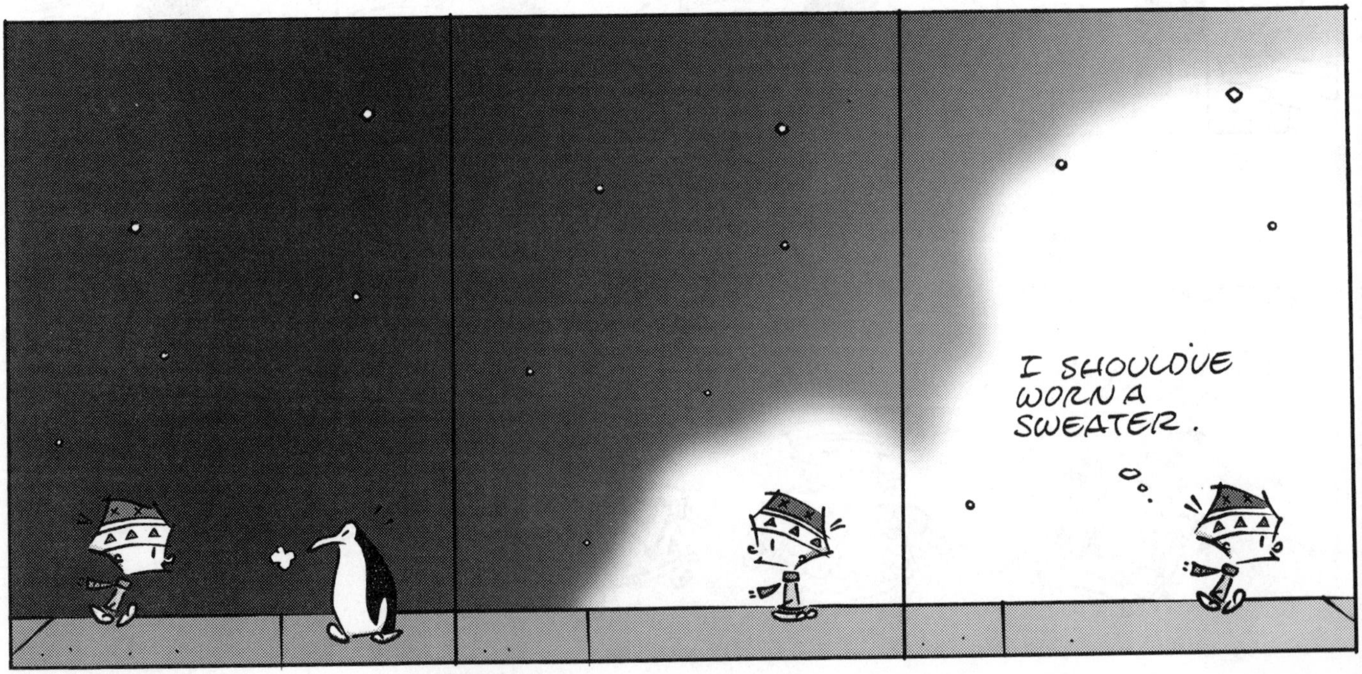
I SHOULD'VE WORN A SWEATER.

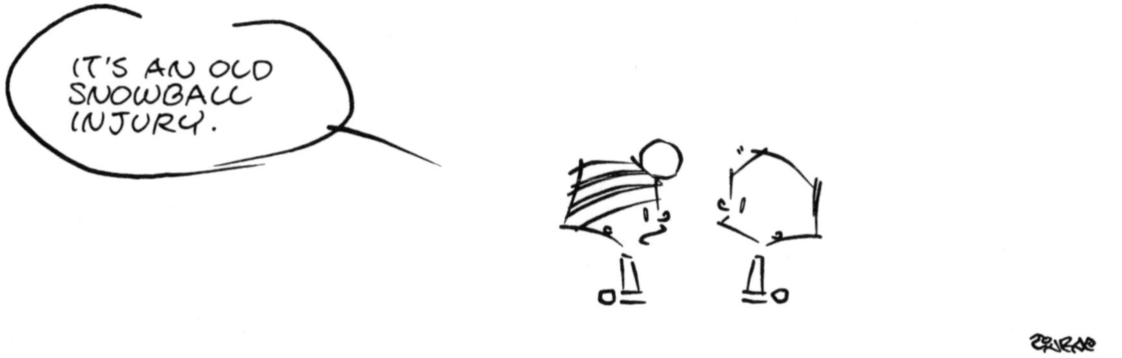
IT'S AN OLD SNOWBALL INJURY.

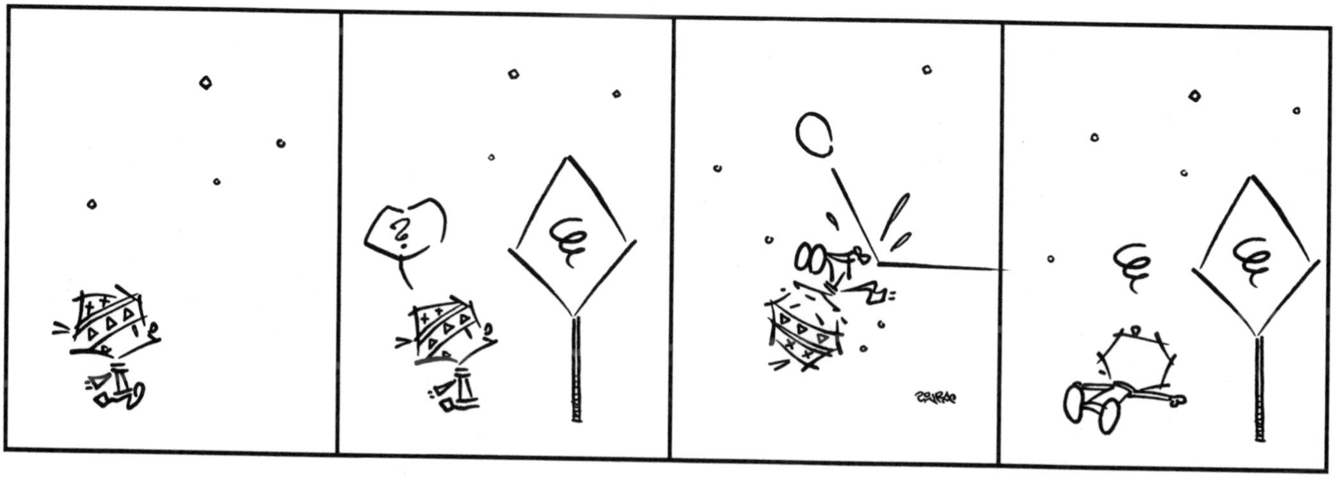

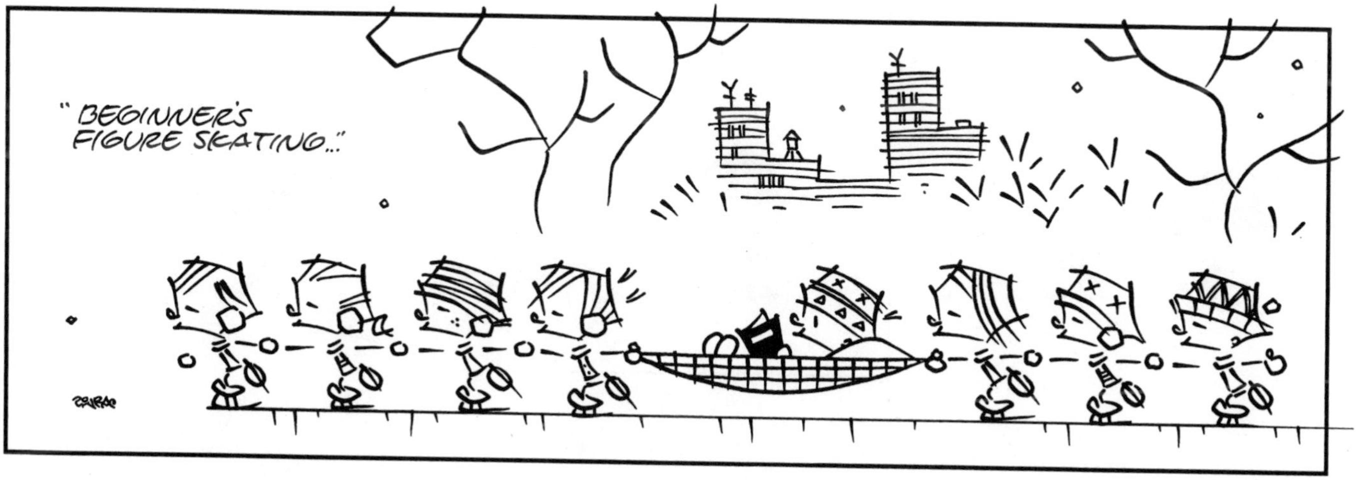
"BEGINNER'S FIGURE SKATING..."

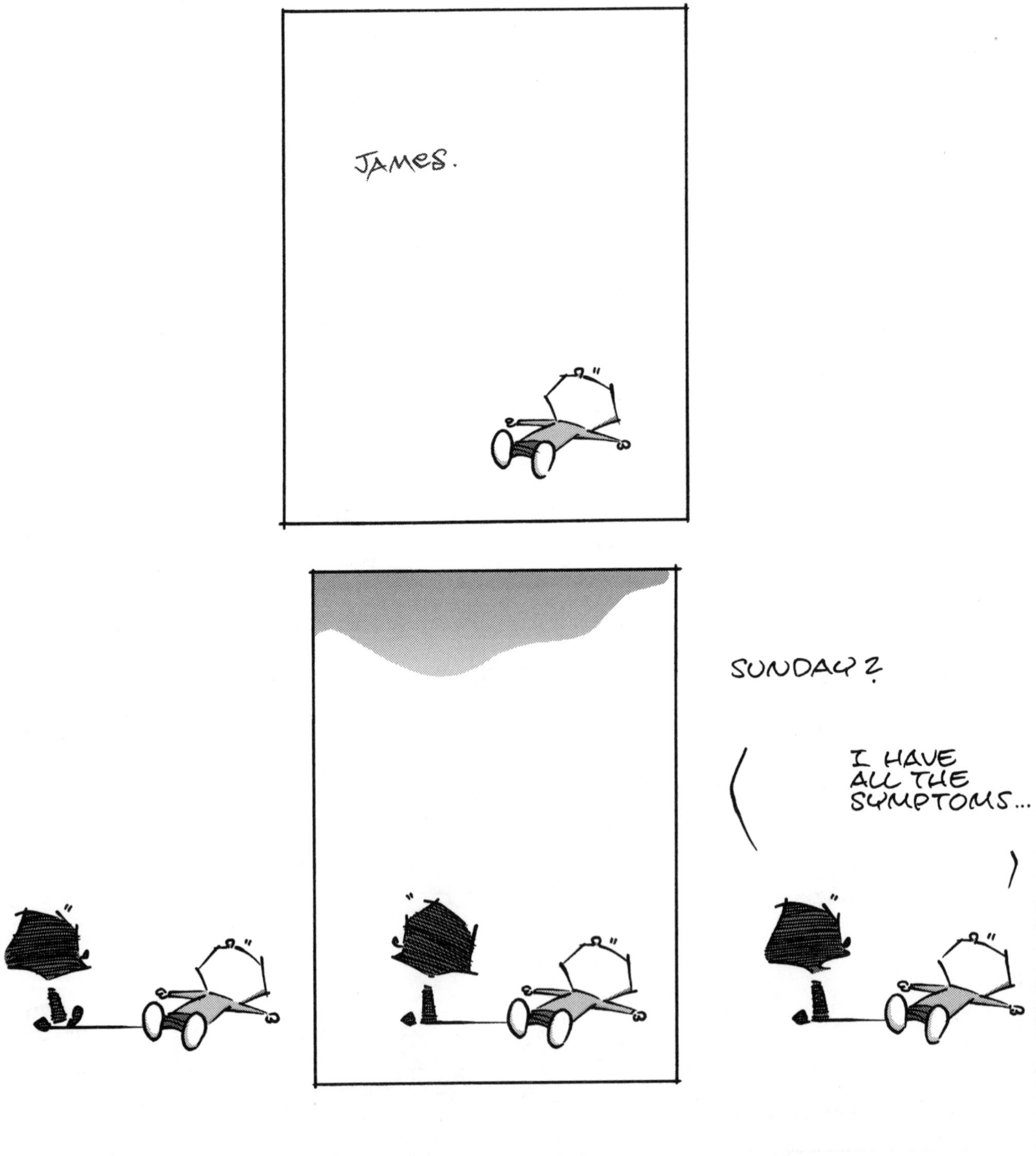

JAMES.
SUNDAY?
I HAVE ALL THE SYMPTOMS...

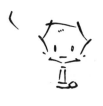

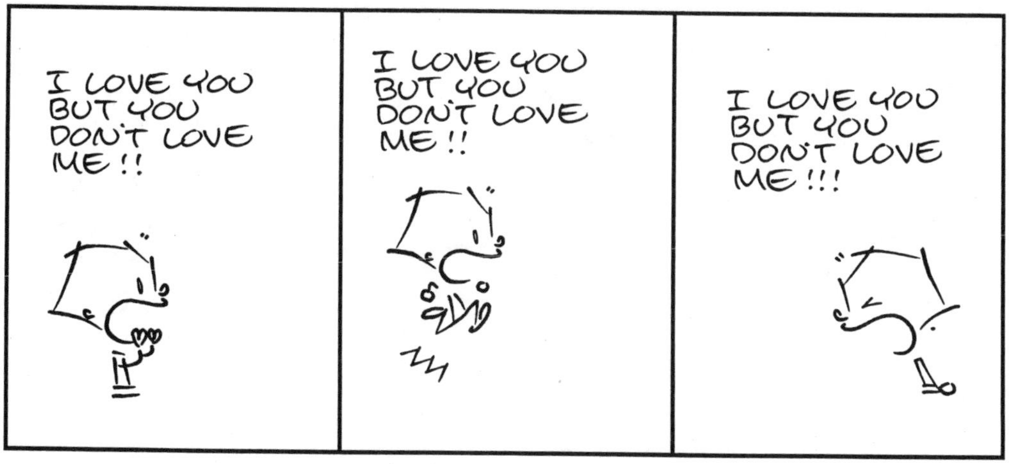
I LOVE YOU BUT YOU DON'T LOVE ME!!
I LOVE YOU BUT YOU DON'T LOVE ME!!
I LOVE YOU BUT YOU DON'T LOVE ME!!!
IT'S MAKING ME WACKY!

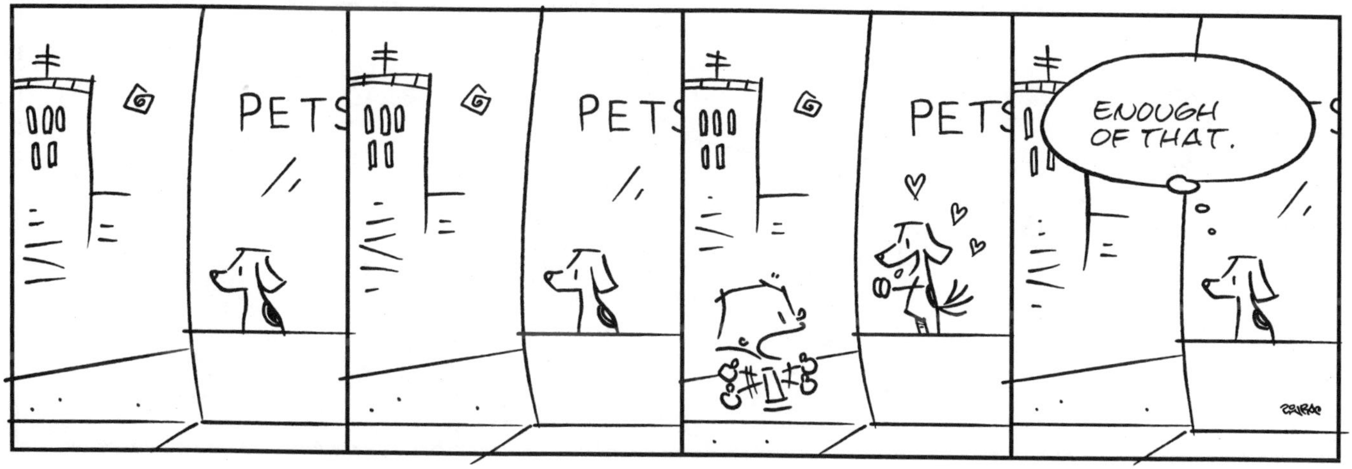
PETS
PETS
PETS
ENOUGH OF THAT.

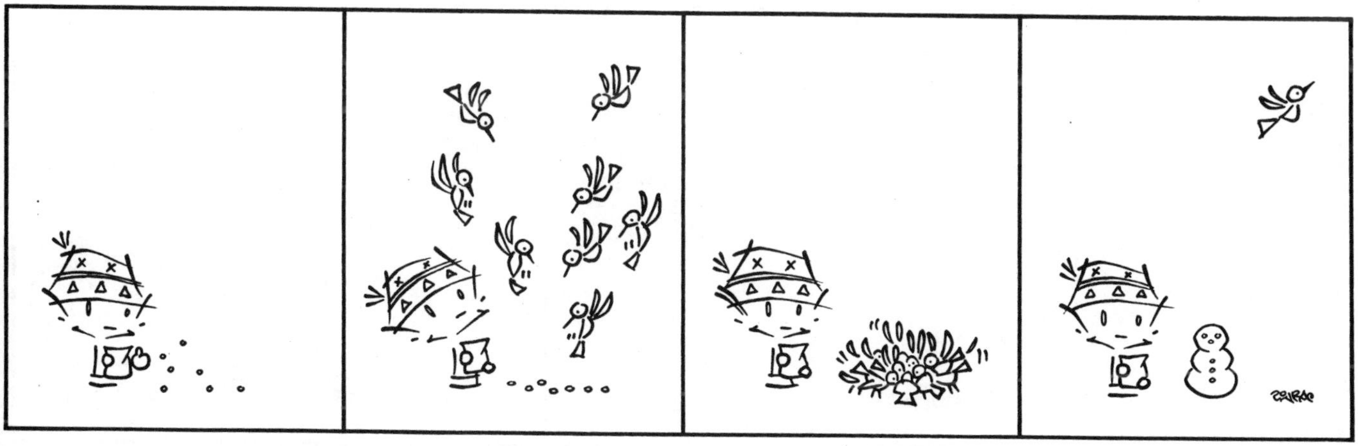

TODAY'S THE DAY!

I'M TAKING CHARGE!

YOU SAID THAT YESTERDAY!

IT SOUNDED GOOD THEN TOO.

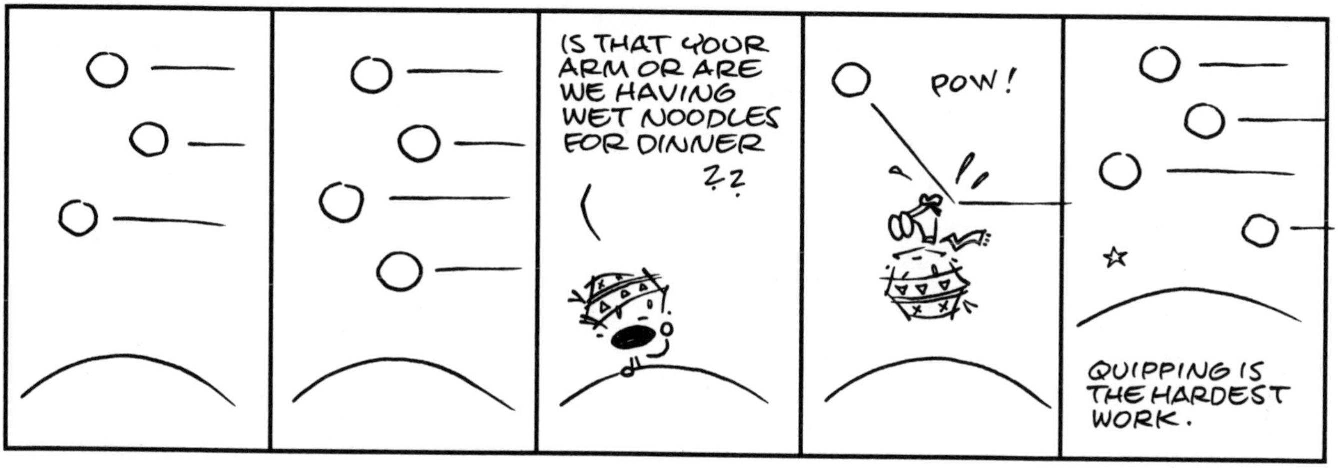
IS THAT YOUR ARM OR ARE WE HAVING WET NOODLES FOR DINNER
ZZ
POW!
QUIPPING IS THE HARDEST WORK.

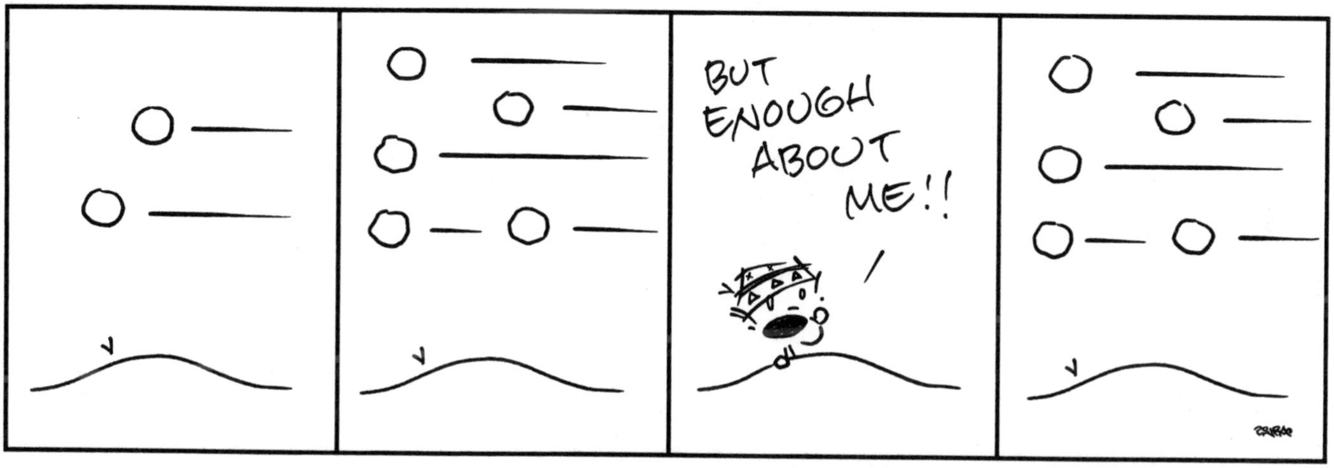
BUT ENOUGH ABOUT ME!!

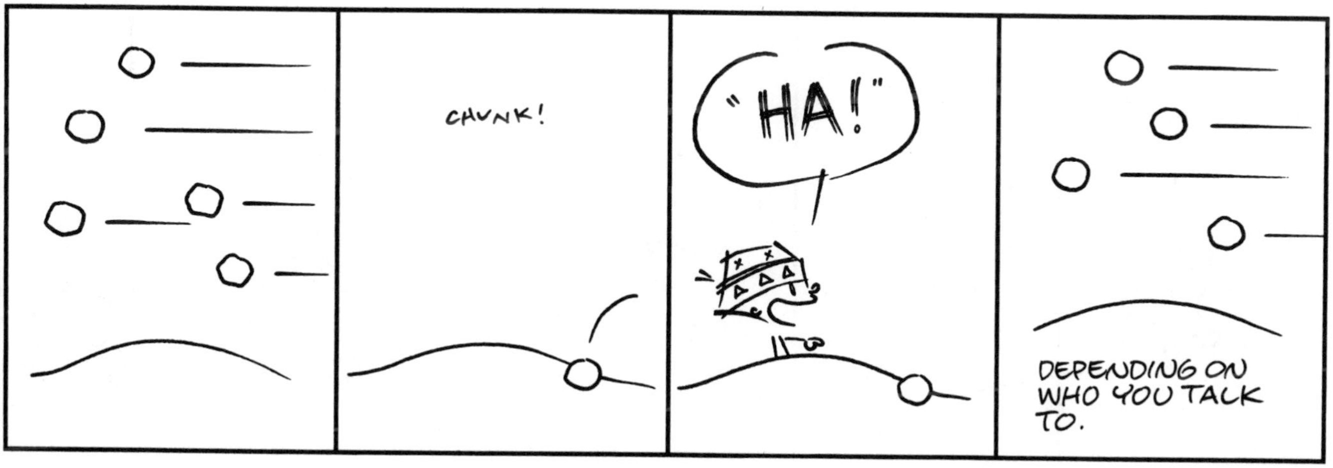
CHUNK!
"HA!"
DEPENDING ON WHO YOU TALK TO.

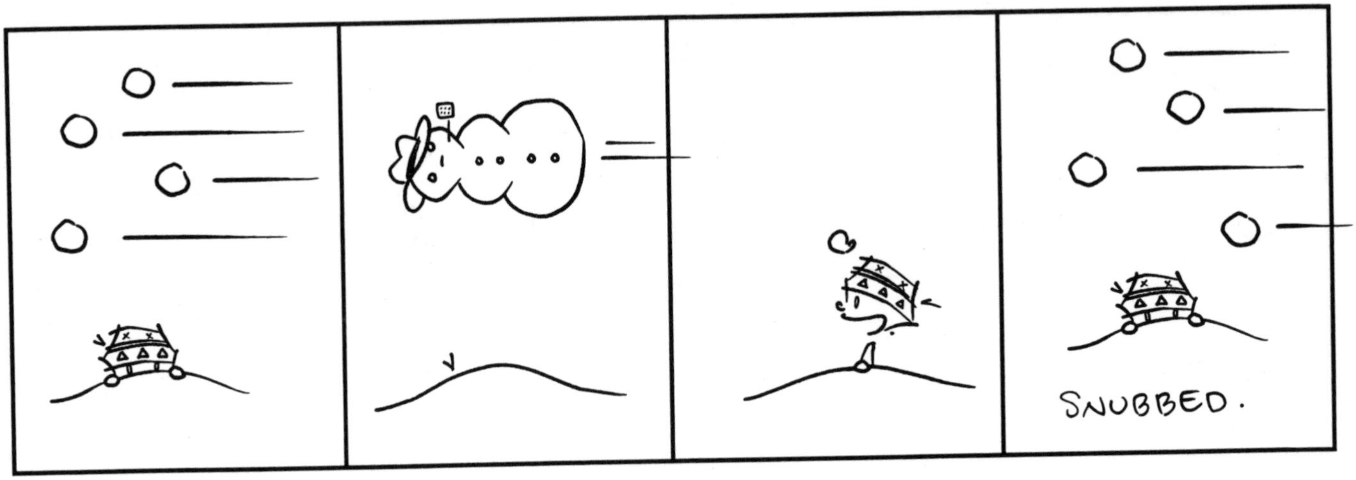
SNUBBED.

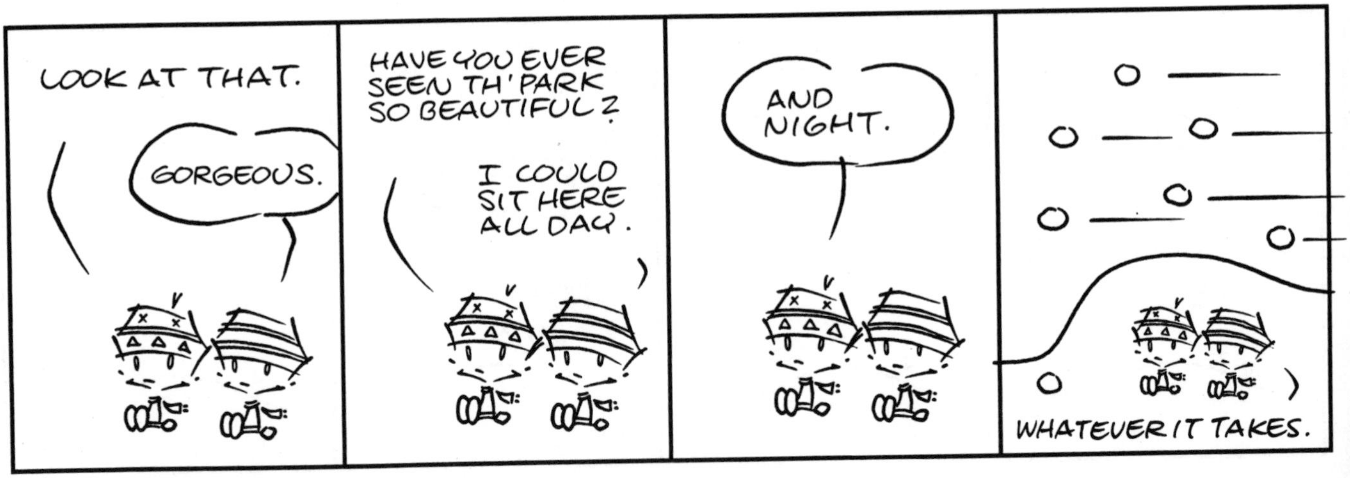
LOOK AT THAT.
GORGEOUS.
HAVE YOU EVER SEEN TH' PARK SO BEAUTIFUL?
I COULD SIT HERE ALL DAY.
AND NIGHT.
WHATEVER IT TAKES.

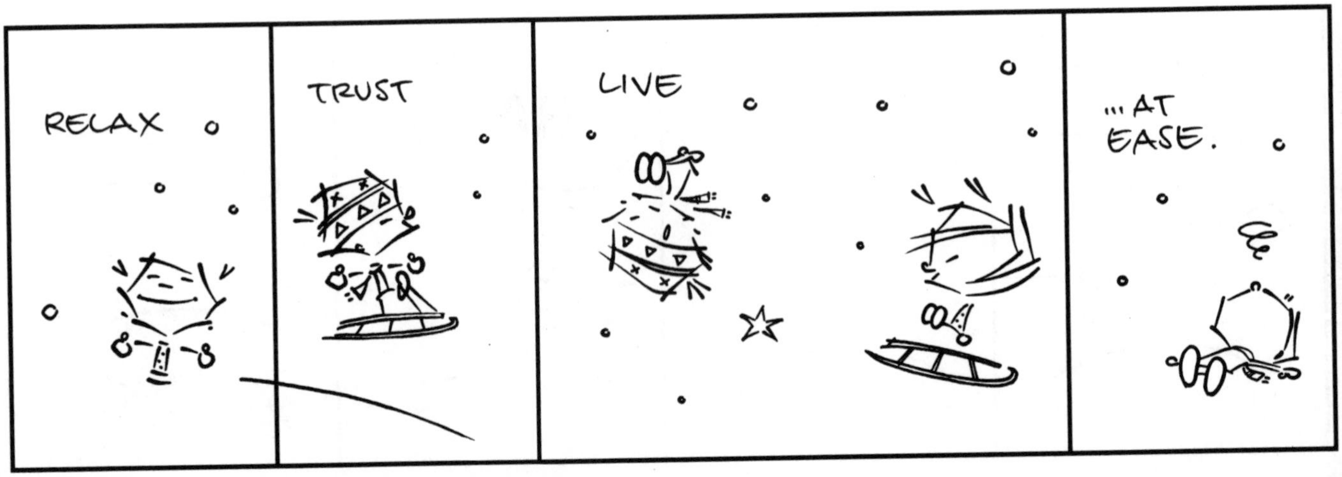
RELAX
TRUST
LIVE
...AT EASE.

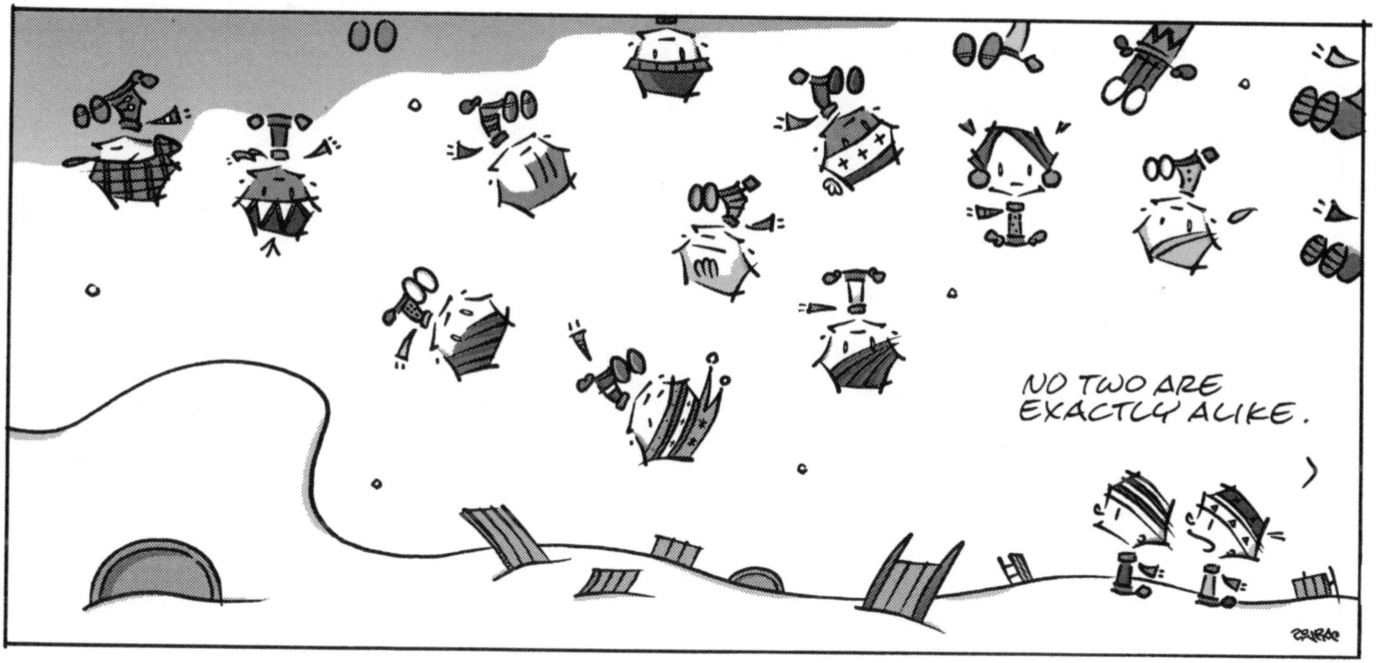
NO TWO ARE EXACTLY ALIKE.

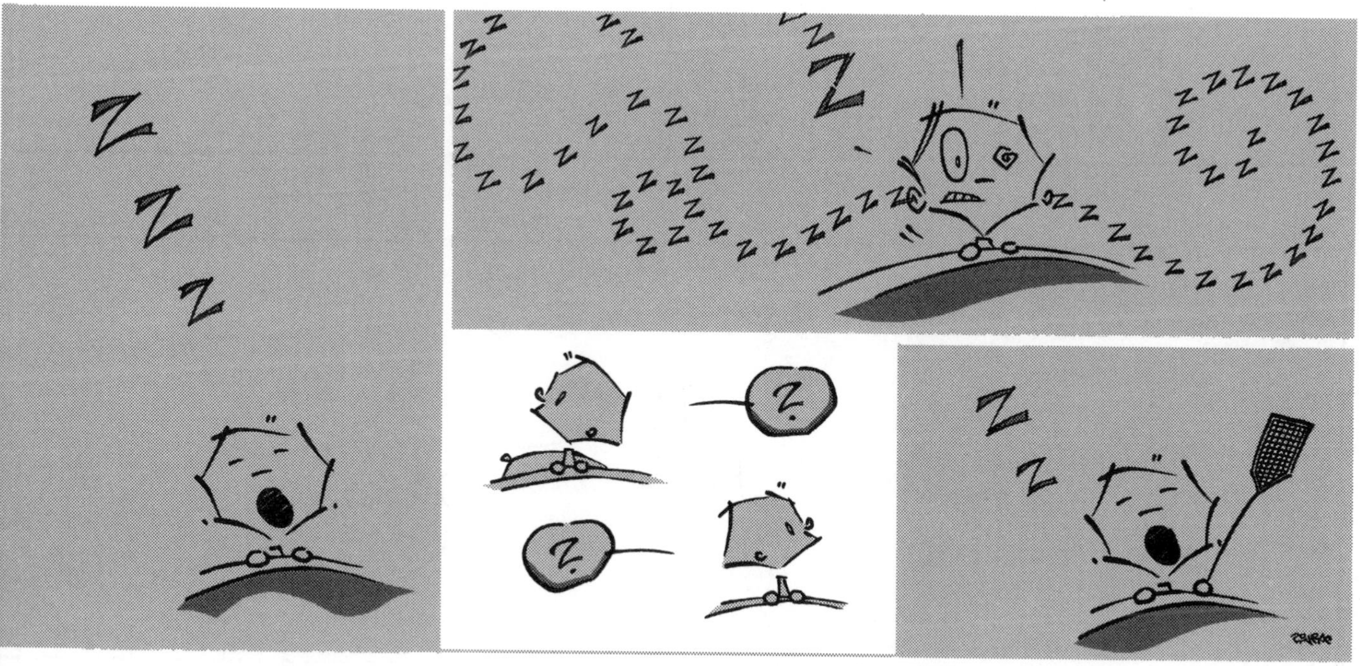

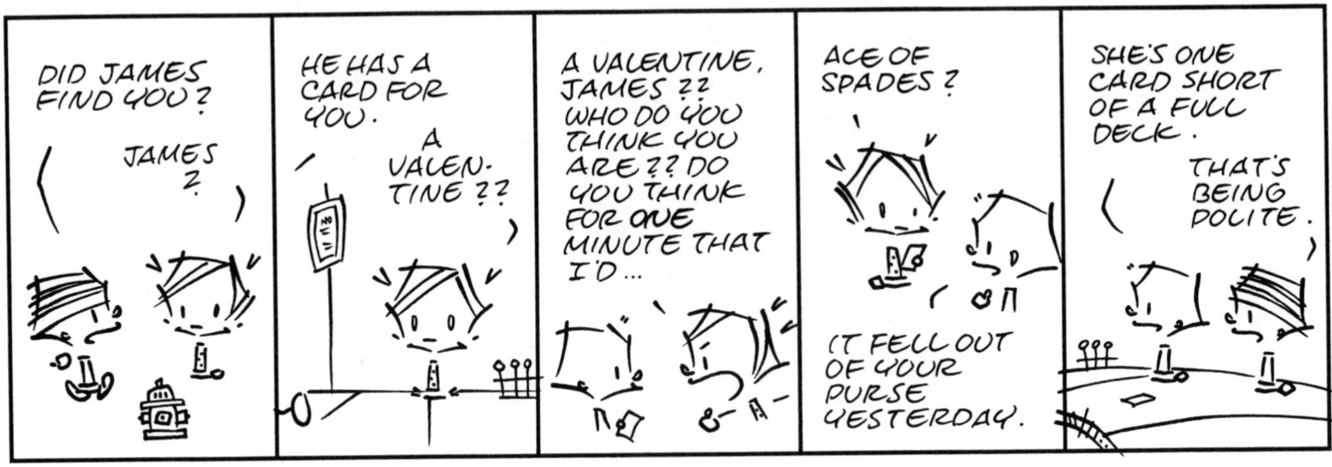
DID JAMES FIND YOU?
JAMES?
HE HAS A CARD FOR YOU.
A VALENTINE??
A VALENTINE, JAMES?? WHO DO YOU THINK YOU ARE?? DO YOU THINK FOR ONE MINUTE THAT I'D...
ACE OF SPADES?
IT FELL OUT OF YOUR PURSE YESTERDAY.
SHE'S ONE CARD SHORT OF A FULL DECK.
THAT'S BEING POLITE.

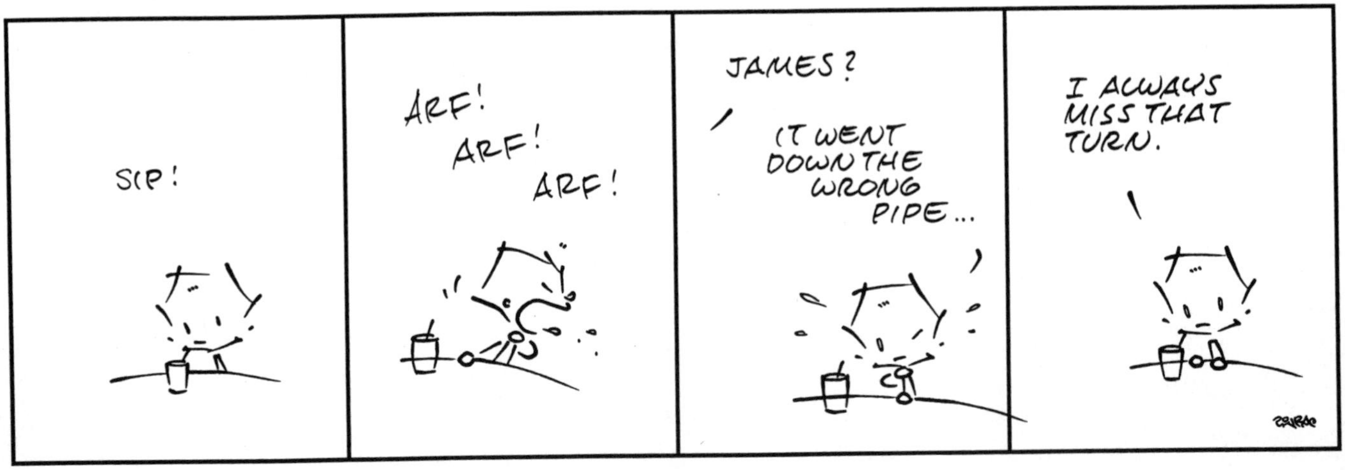
SIP!
ARF! ARF! ARF!
JAMES?
IT WENT DOWN THE WRONG PIPE...
I ALWAYS MISS THAT TURN.

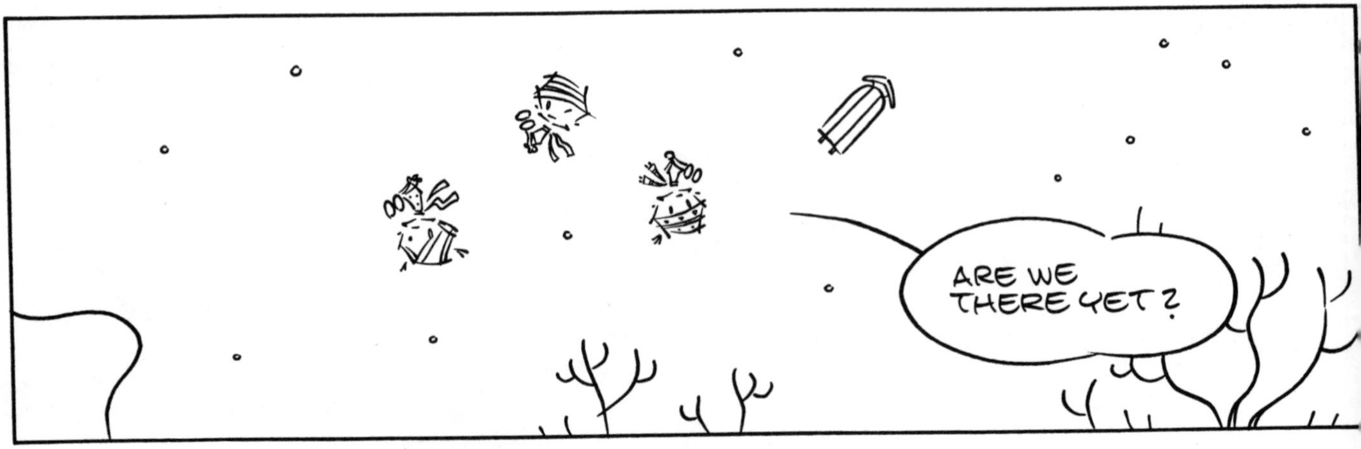
ARE WE THERE YET?

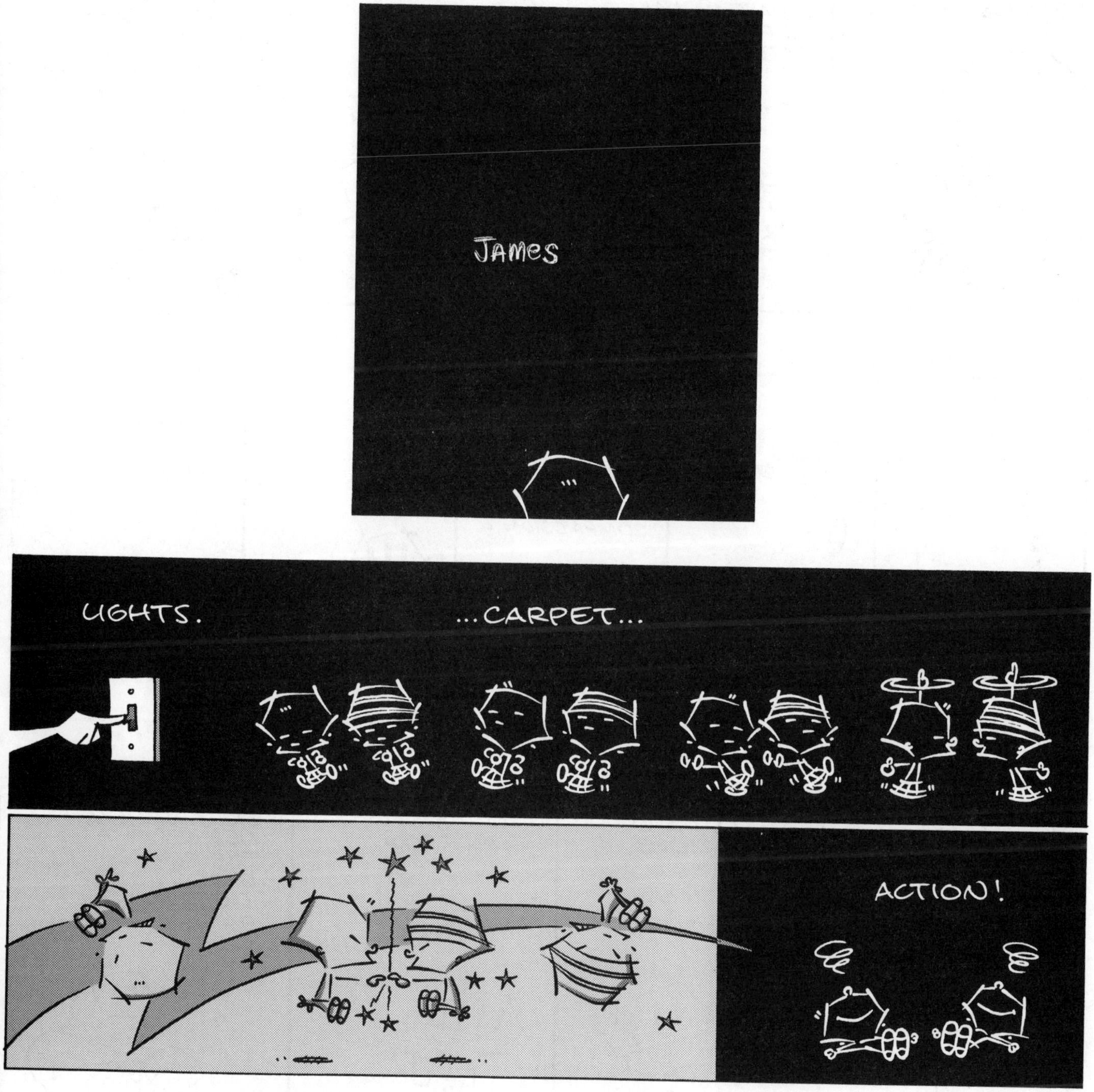
JAMES
LIGHTS.
...CARPET...
ACTION!

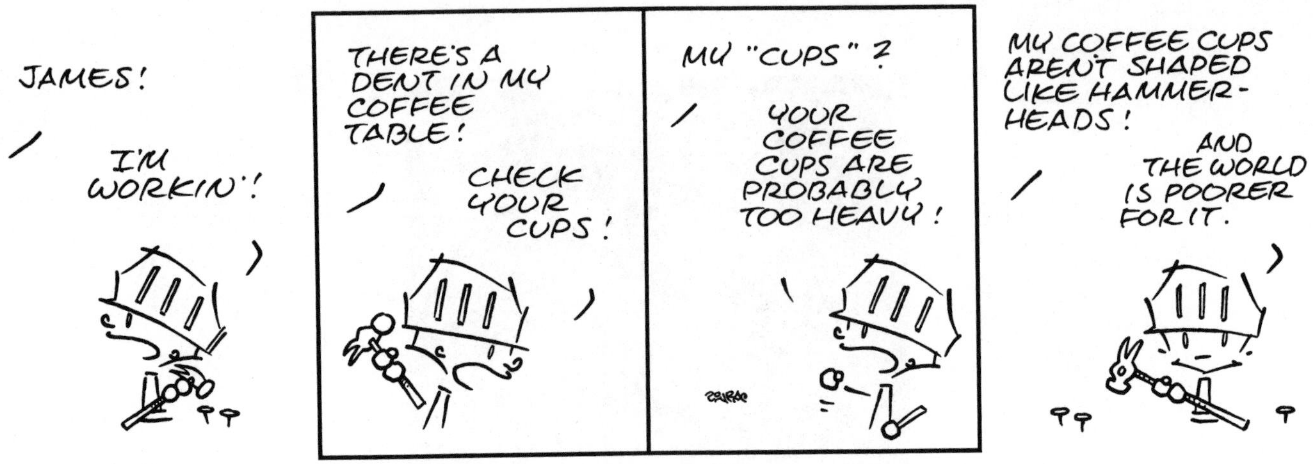
JAMES!
I'M WORKIN'!
THERE'S A DENT IN MY COFFEE TABLE!
CHECK YOUR CUPS!
MY "CUPS"?
YOUR COFFEE CUPS ARE PROBABLY TOO HEAVY!
MY COFFEE CUPS AREN'T SHAPED LIKE HAMMER-HEADS!
AND THE WORLD IS POORER FOR IT.

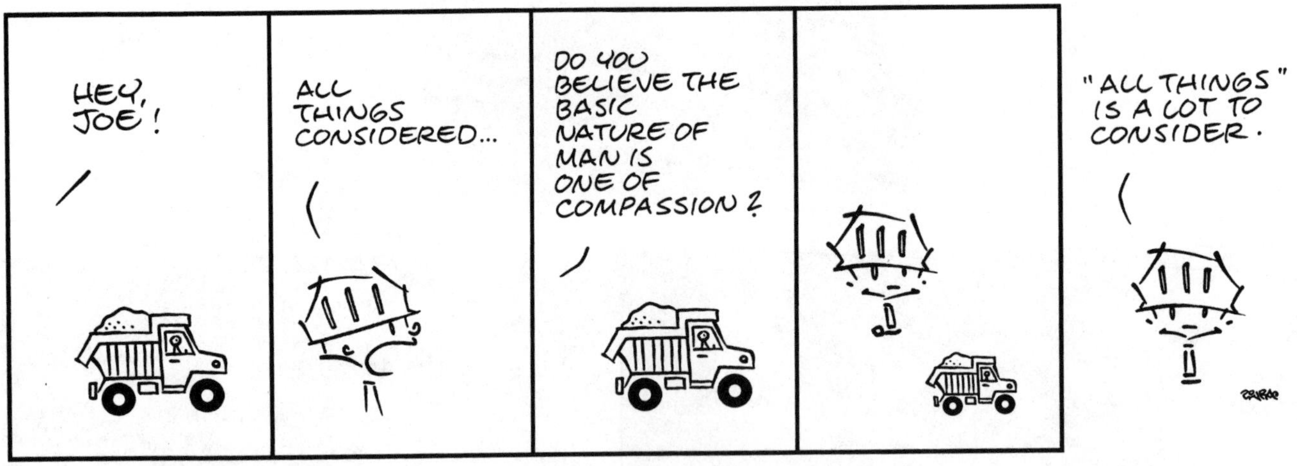
HEY, JOE!
ALL THINGS CONSIDERED...
DO YOU BELIEVE THE BASIC NATURE OF MAN IS ONE OF COMPASSION?
"ALL THINGS" IS A LOT TO CONSIDER.

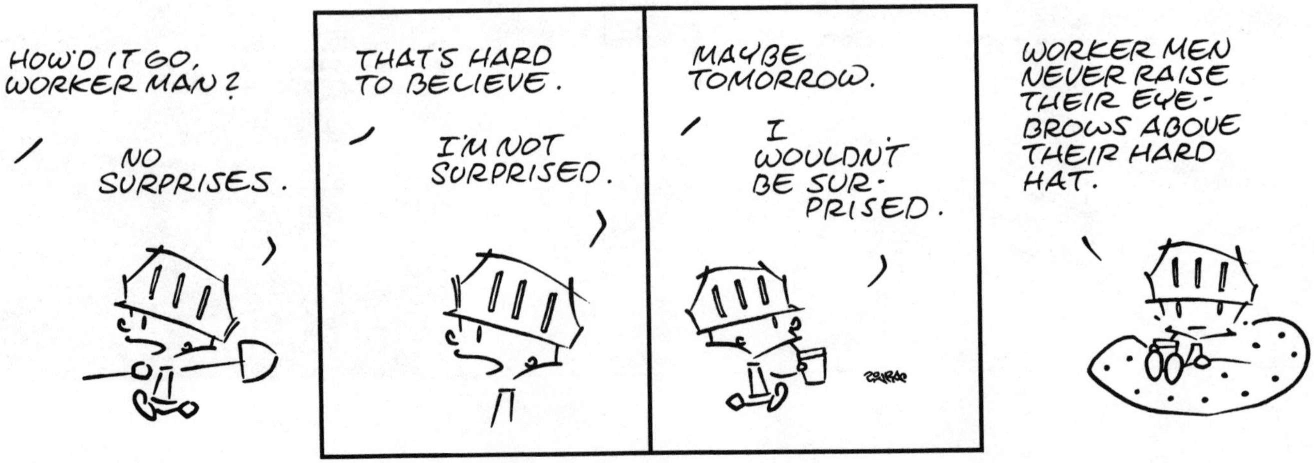
HOW'D IT GO, WORKER MAN?
NO SURPRISES.
THAT'S HARD TO BELIEVE.
I'M NOT SURPRISED.
MAYBE TOMORROW.
I WOULDN'T BE SUR-PRISED.
WORKER MEN NEVER RAISE THEIR EYE-BROWS ABOVE THEIR HARD HAT.

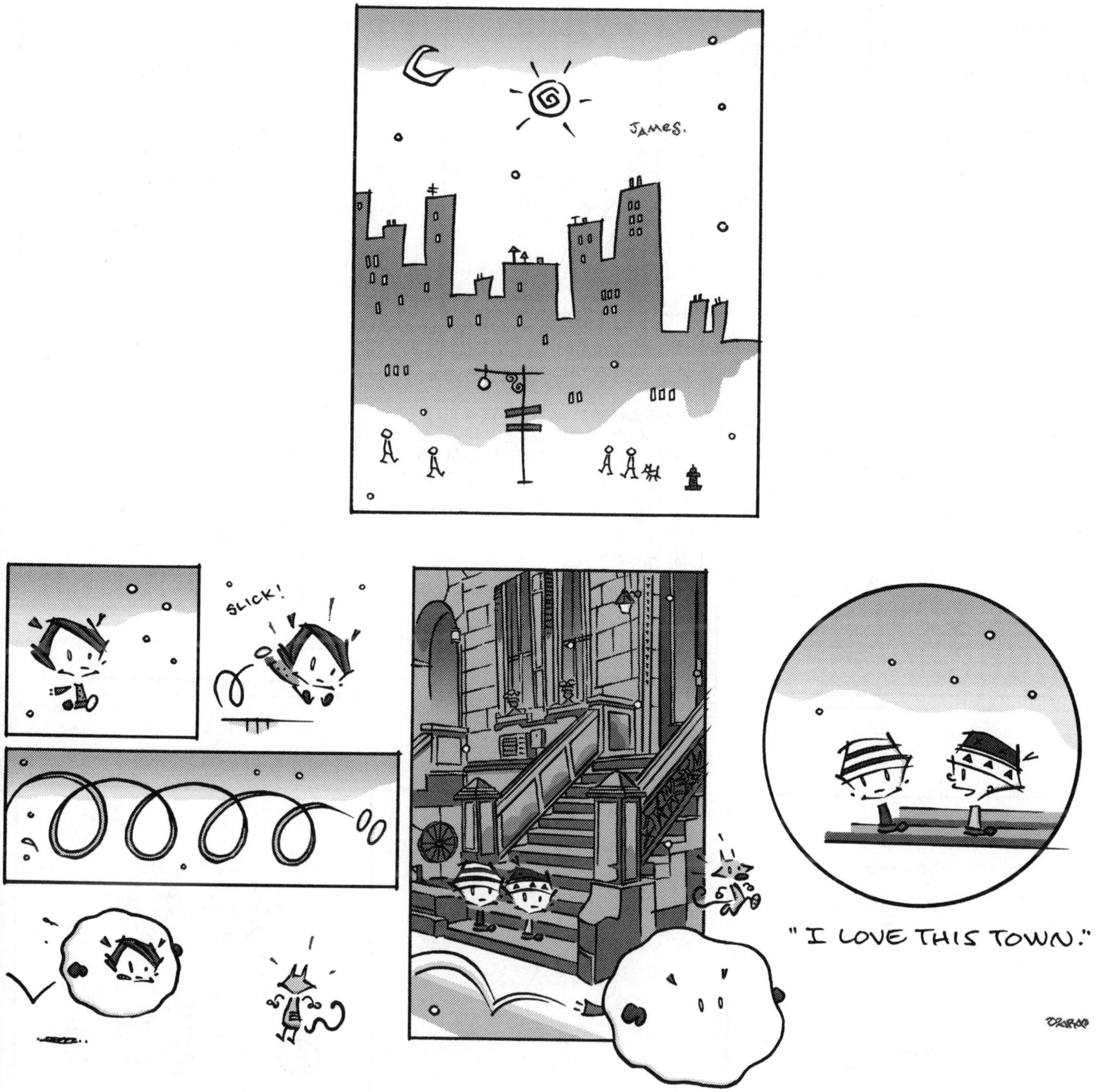
JAMES.
SLICK!
"I LOVE THIS TOWN."

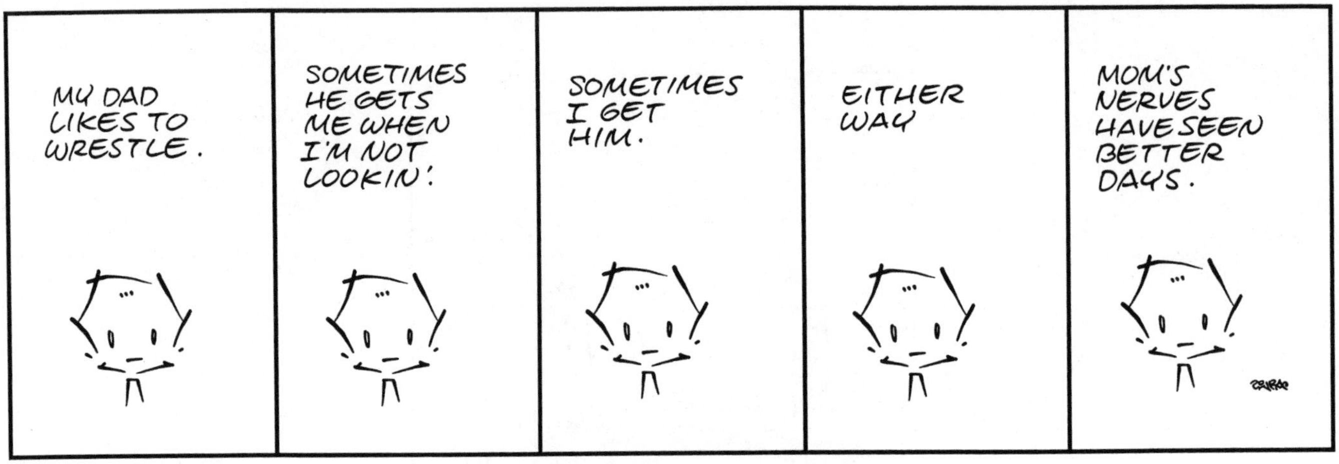
MY DAD LIKES TO WRESTLE.
SOMETIMES HE GETS ME WHEN I'M NOT LOOKIN'.
SOMETIMES I GET HIM.
EITHER WAY
MOM'S NERVES HAVE SEEN BETTER DAYS.

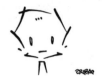

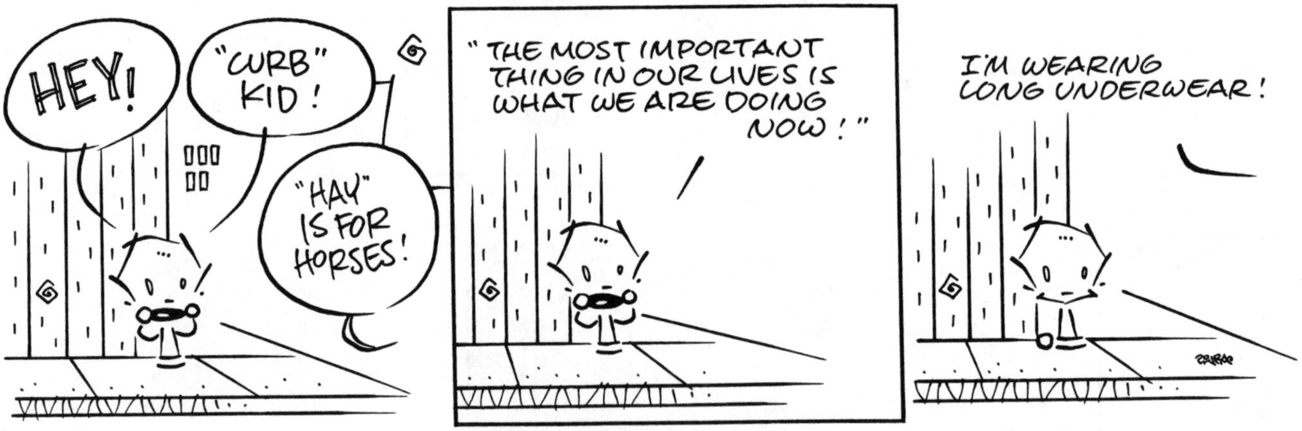
HEY!
"CURB" KID!
"HAY" IS FOR HORSES!
" THE MOST IMPORTANT THING IN OUR LIVES IS WHAT WE ARE DOING NOW ! "
I'M WEARING LONG UNDERWEAR!

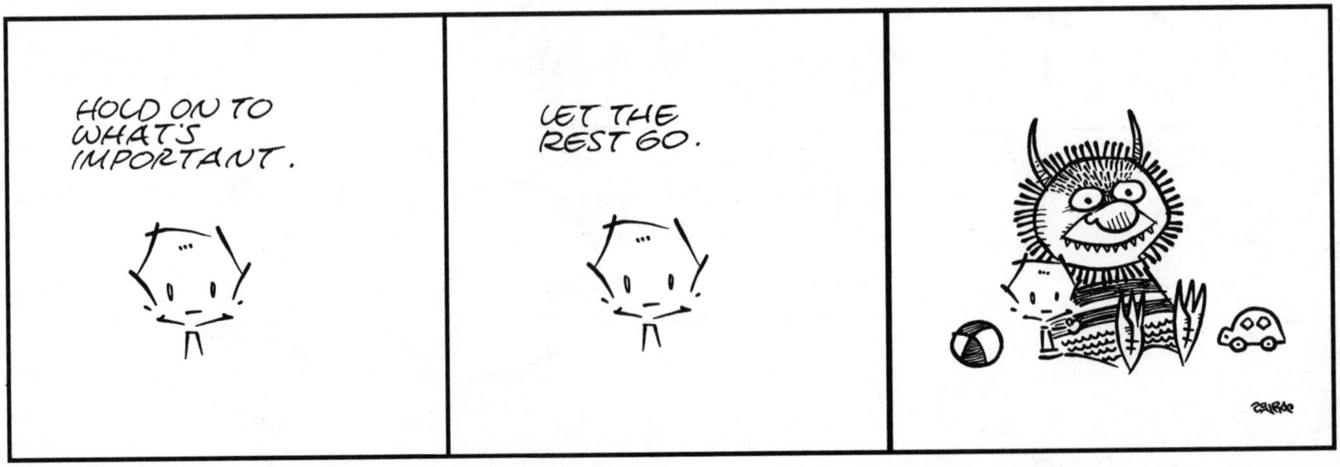
HOLD ON TO WHAT'S IMPORTANT.
LET THE REST GO.

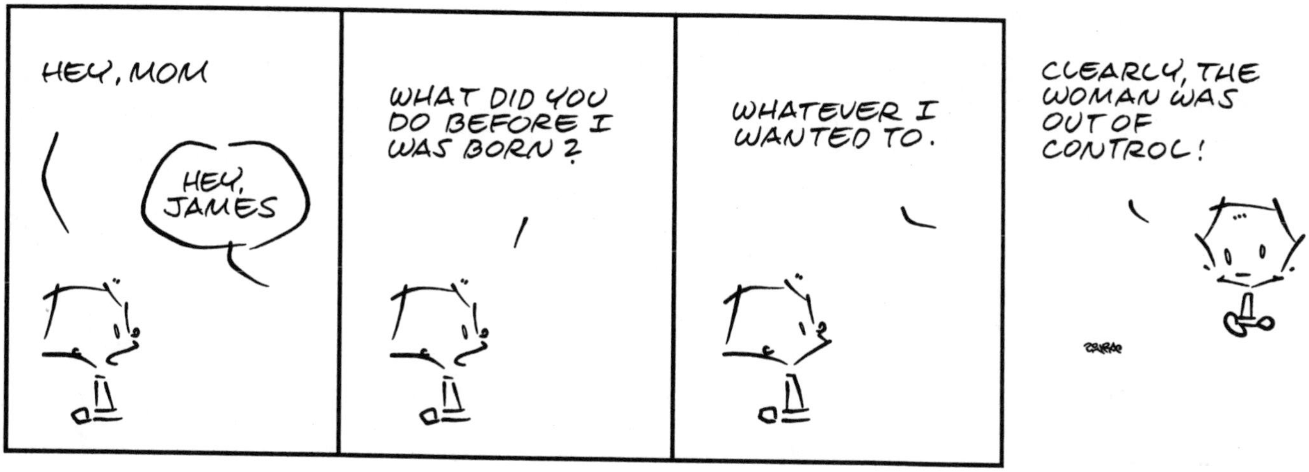
HEY, MOM
HEY, JAMES
WHAT DID YOU DO BEFORE I WAS BORN?
WHATEVER I WANTED TO.
CLEARLY, THE WOMAN WAS OUT OF CONTROL!

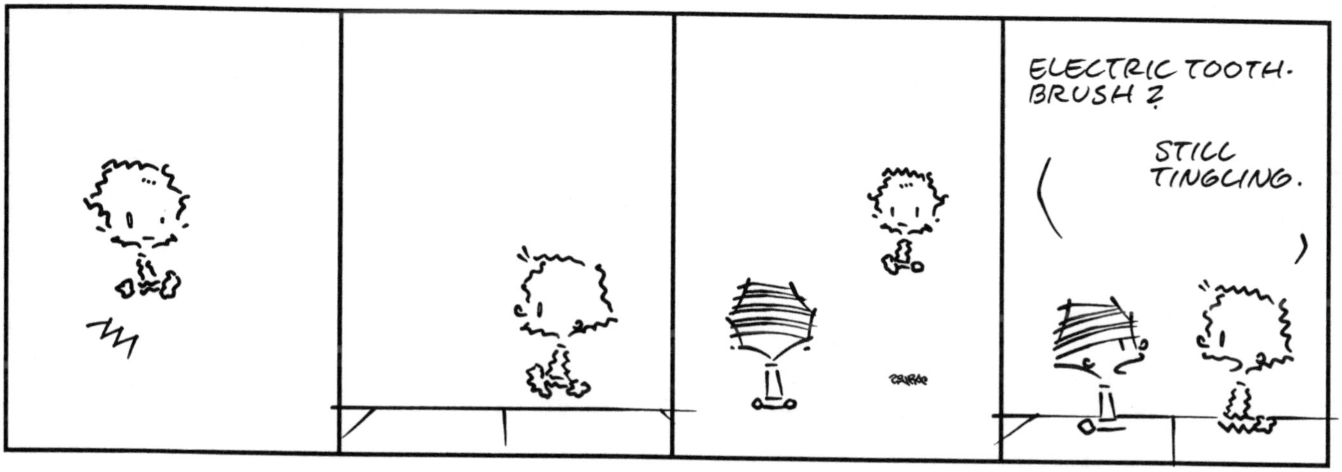
ELECTRIC TOOTH-BRUSH?
STILL TINGLING.

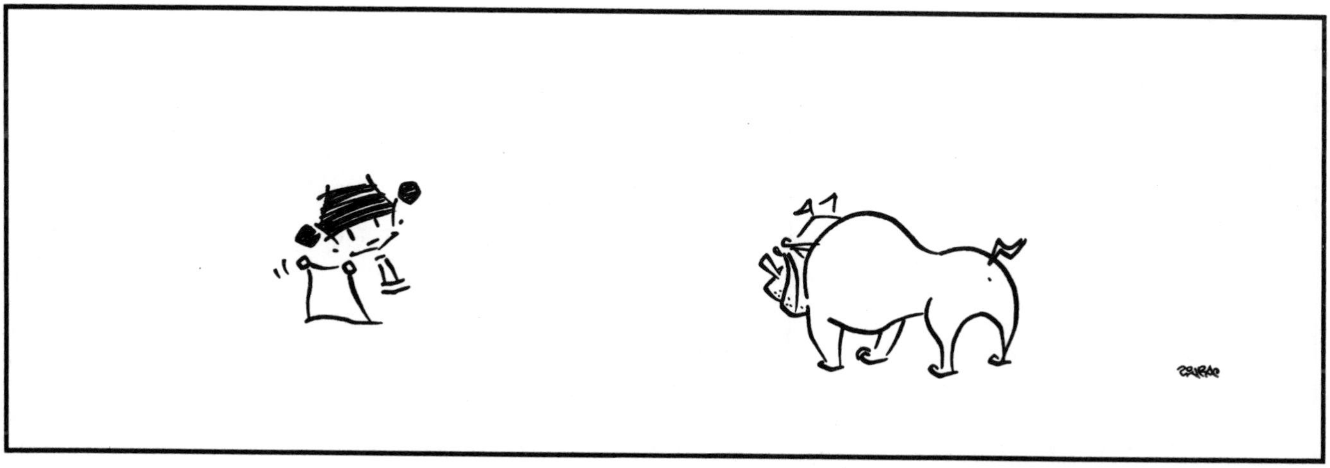

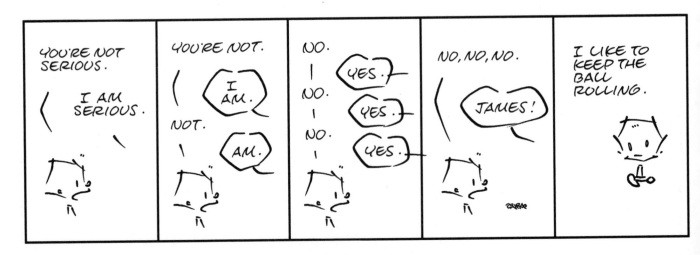

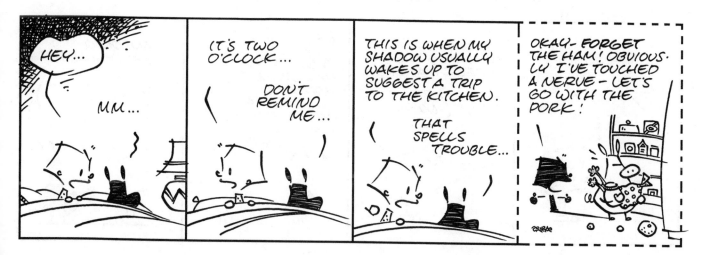

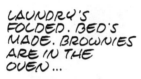

| OKAY,
JAMES. | JAMES... | DO IT FOR
DADDY. | WAVE FOR
DADDY! |
| JAMESY... | JAMES! | I GIVE UP. | WHAT I'D
REALLY LIKE
TO DO IS
DIRECT. |

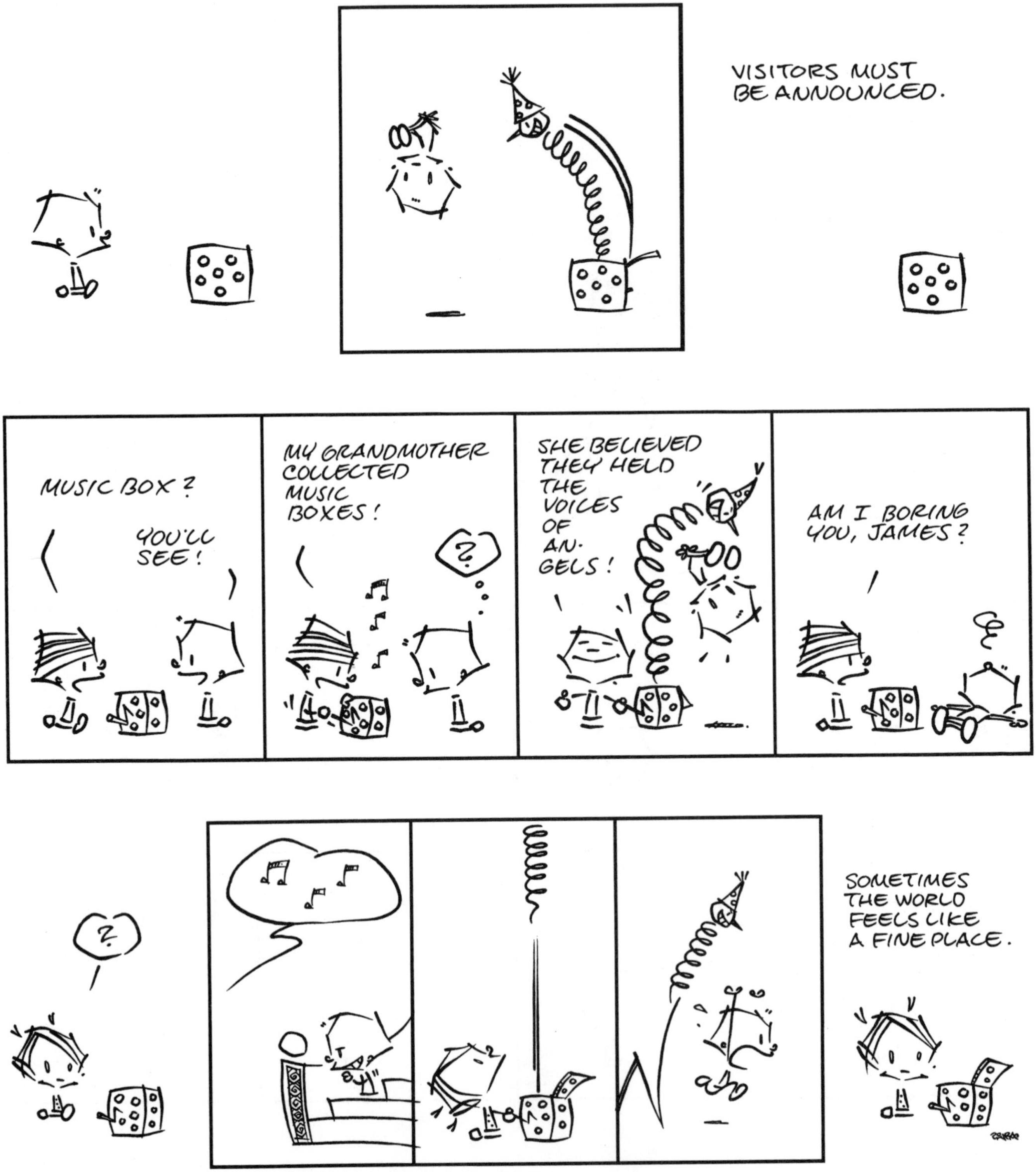
VISITORS MUST BE ANNOUNCED.
MUSIC BOX ?
YOU'LL SEE !
MY GRANDMOTHER COLLECTED MUSIC BOXES !
SHE BELIEVED THEY HELD THE VOICES OF AN-GELS !
AM I BORING YOU, JAMES ?
SOMETIMES THE WORLD FEELS LIKE A FINE PLACE.

JAMES.

"TOM TOM THE PIPER'S SON..."

STOLE A PIG

AND AWAY DID RUN."

I BLAME THE PIPER.

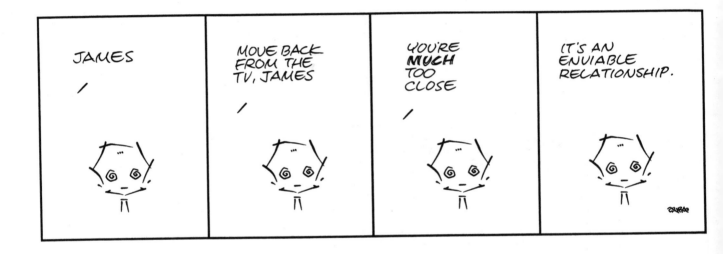

JAMES

MOVE BACK FROM THE TV, JAMES

YOU'RE **MUCH** TOO CLOSE

IT'S AN ENVIABLE RELATIONSHIP.

OKAY, JAMES...

DON'T YOU THINK THAT'S ENOUGH TV FOR ONE DAY?

MY HEAD SAYS "YES" BUT SCREWY THE PURPLE SQUIRREL SAYS "NO".

JAMES

TIMES OF CRISIS REVEAL TH' TRUTH ABOUT MEN.

PLOP!

NOOOOO!!

IT'S NOT ALWAYS ENCOURAGING.

THEY WERE
FRESH
YESTERDAY.

91

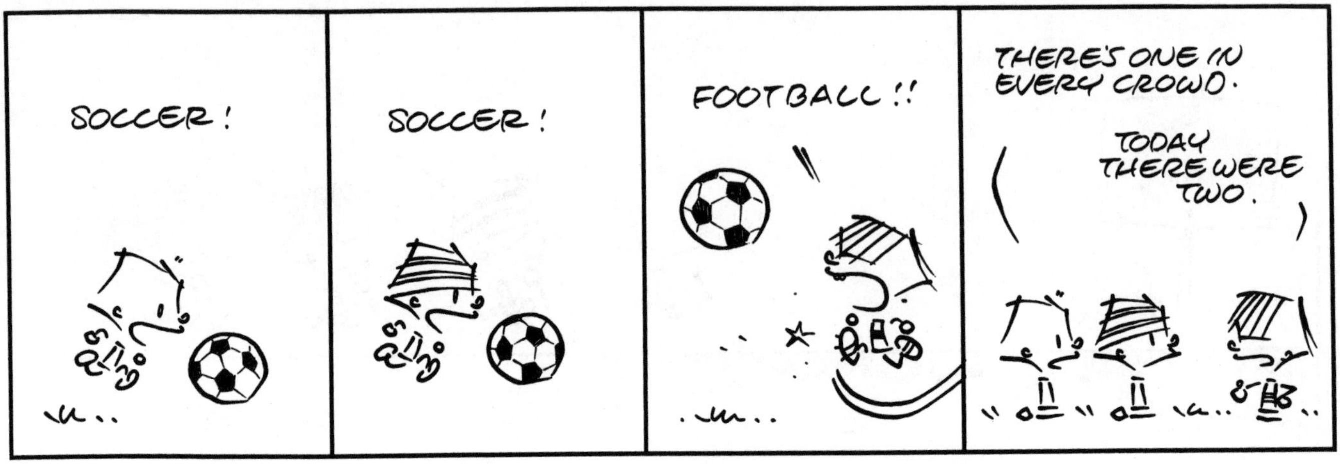
SOCCER!
SOCCER!
FOOTBALL!!
THERE'S ONE IN EVERY CROWD.
TODAY THERE WERE TWO.

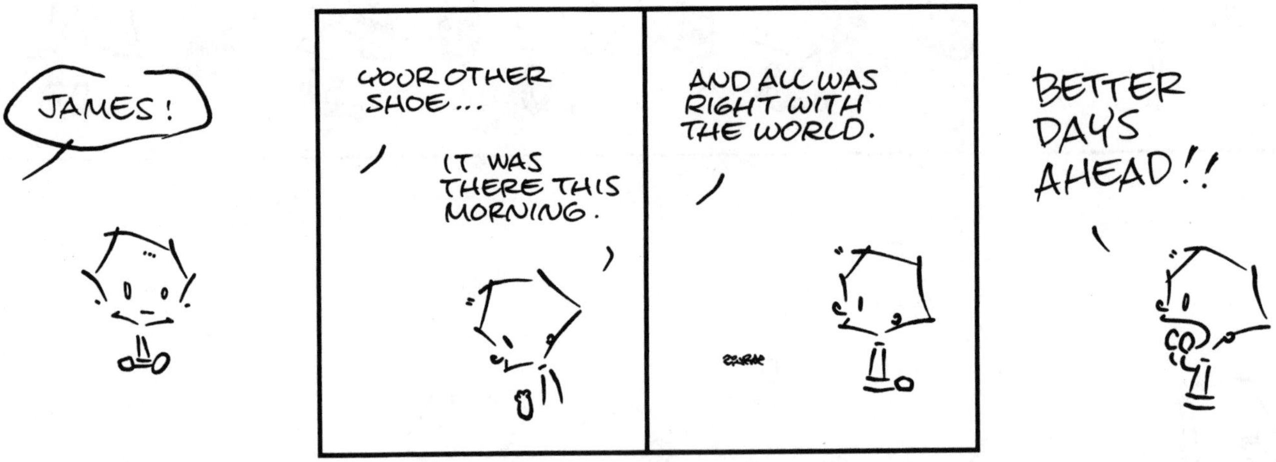
JAMES!
YOUR OTHER SHOE...
IT WAS THERE THIS MORNING.
AND ALL WAS RIGHT WITH THE WORLD.
BETTER DAYS AHEAD!!

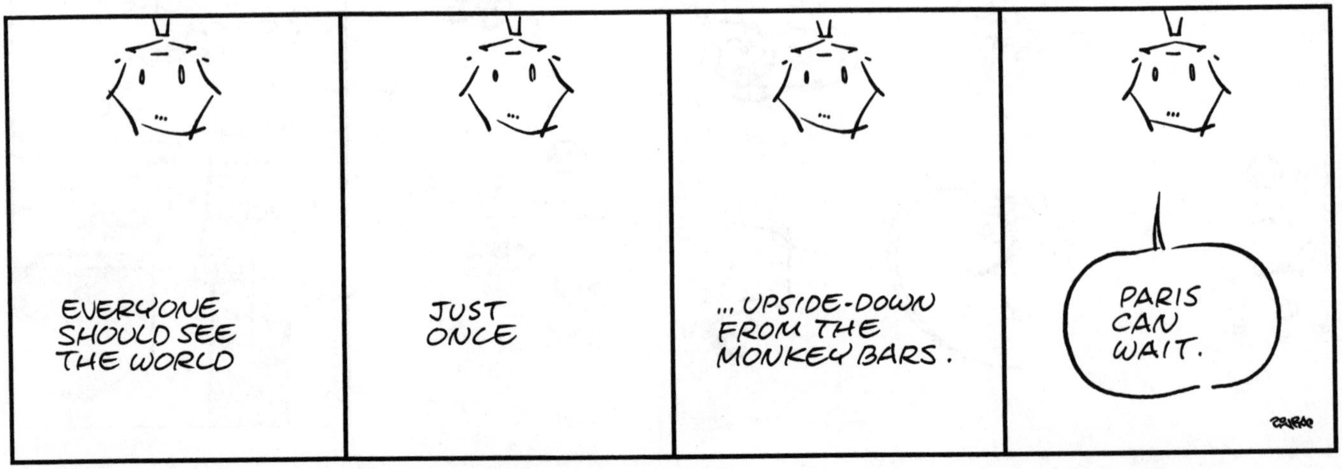
EVERYONE SHOULD SEE THE WORLD
JUST ONCE
... UPSIDE-DOWN FROM THE MONKEY BARS.
PARIS CAN WAIT.

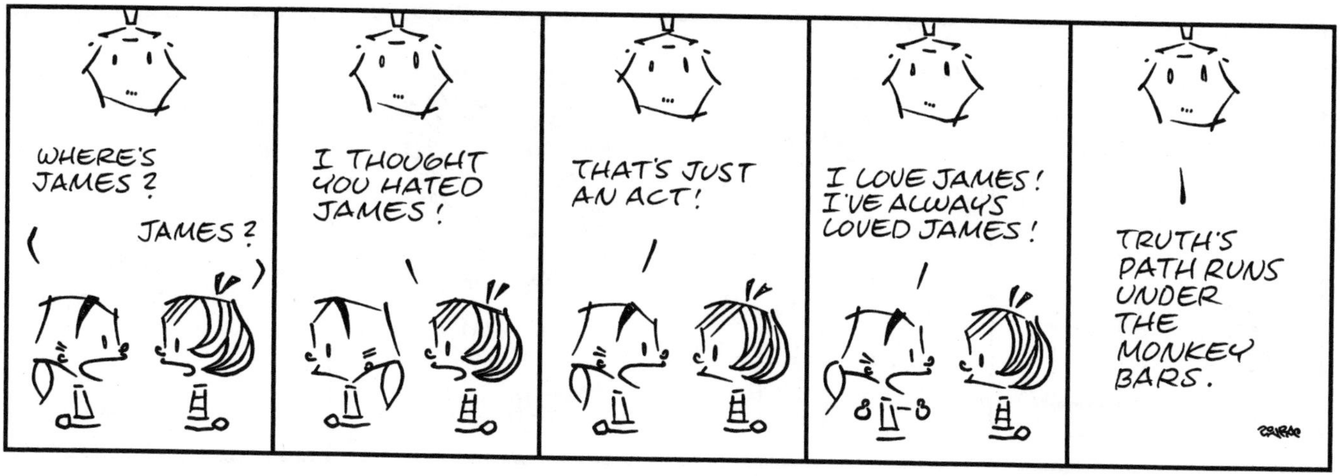
WHERE'S JAMES?
JAMES?
I THOUGHT YOU HATED JAMES!
THAT'S JUST AN ACT!
I LOVE JAMES! I'VE ALWAYS LOVED JAMES!
TRUTH'S PATH RUNS UNDER THE MONKEY BARS.

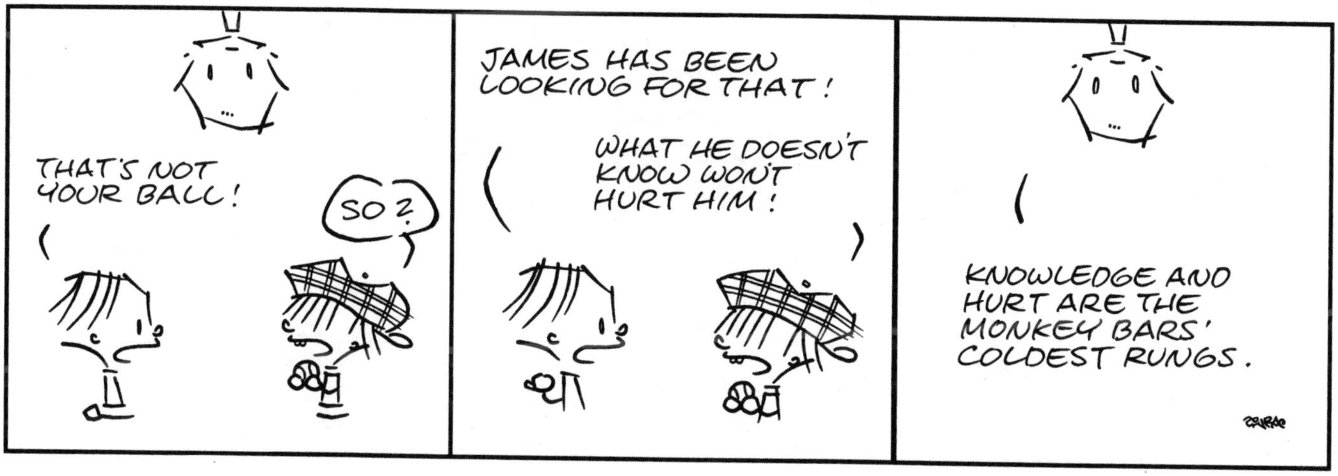
THAT'S NOT YOUR BALL!
SO?
JAMES HAS BEEN LOOKING FOR THAT!
WHAT HE DOESN'T KNOW WON'T HURT HIM!
KNOWLEDGE AND HURT ARE THE MONKEY BARS' COLDEST RUNGS.

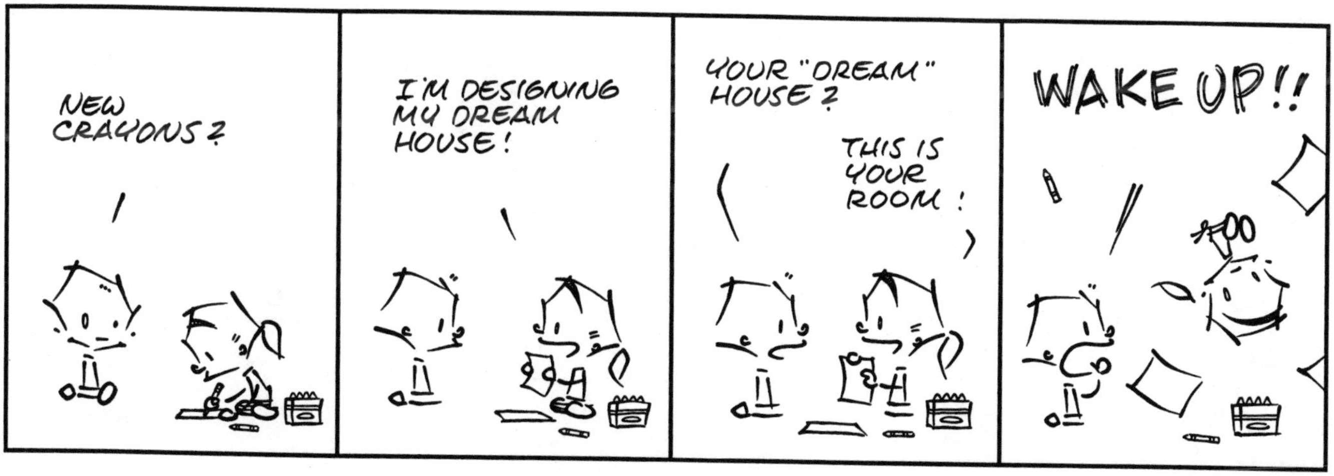
NEW CRAYONS?
I'M DESIGNING MY DREAM HOUSE!
YOUR "DREAM" HOUSE?
THIS IS YOUR ROOM!
WAKE UP!!

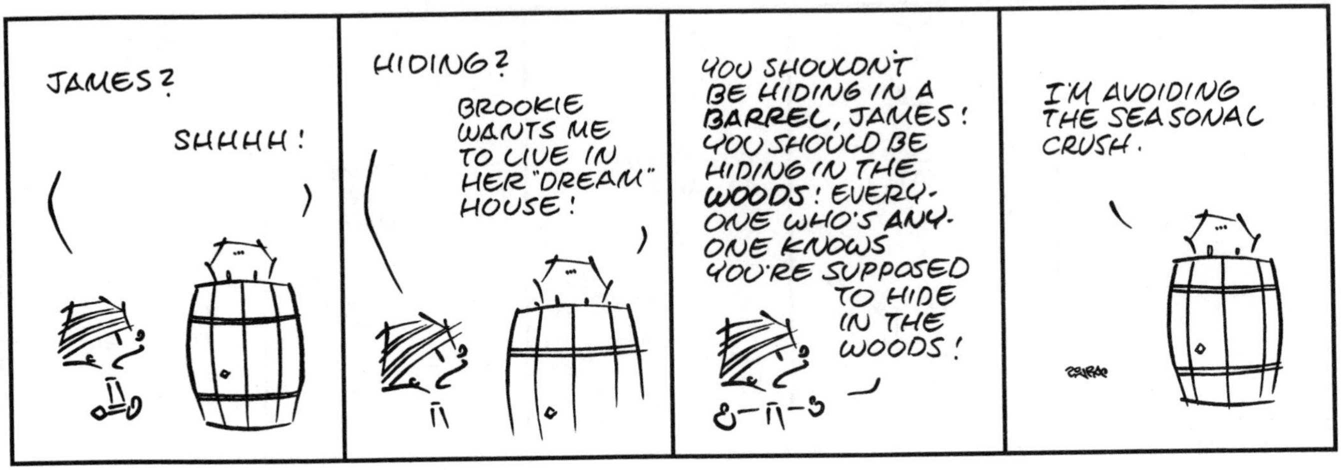
JAMES?
SHHHH!
HIDING?
BROOKIE WANTS ME TO LIVE IN HER "DREAM" HOUSE!
YOU SHOULDN'T BE HIDING IN A **BARREL**, JAMES! YOU SHOULD BE HIDING IN THE **WOODS**: EVERYONE WHO'S **ANY**ONE KNOWS YOU'RE SUPPOSED TO HIDE IN THE WOODS!
I'M AVOIDING THE SEASONAL CRUSH.

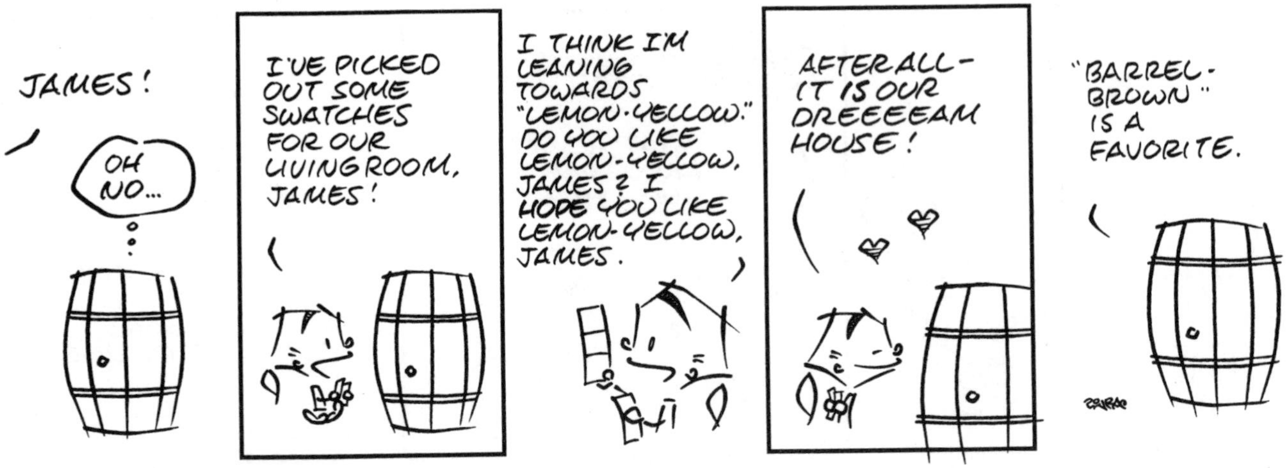
JAMES!
OH NO...
I'VE PICKED OUT SOME SWATCHES FOR OUR LIVING ROOM, JAMES!
I THINK I'M LEANING TOWARDS "LEMON-YELLOW." DO YOU LIKE LEMON-YELLOW, JAMES? I **HOPE** YOU LIKE LEMON-YELLOW, JAMES.
AFTER ALL - IT **IS** OUR DREEEEAM HOUSE!
"BARREL-BROWN" IS A FAVORITE.

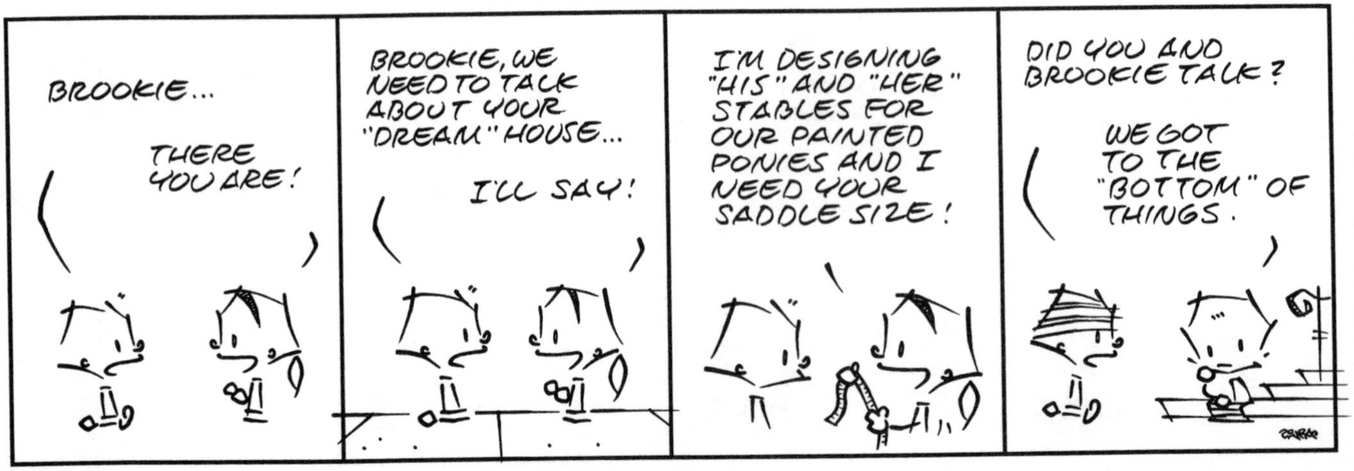
BROOKIE...
THERE YOU ARE!
BROOKIE, WE NEED TO TALK ABOUT YOUR "DREAM" HOUSE...
I'LL SAY!
I'M DESIGNING "HIS" AND "HER" STABLES FOR OUR PAINTED PONIES AND I NEED YOUR SADDLE SIZE!
DID YOU AND BROOKIE TALK?
WE GOT TO THE "BOTTOM" OF THINGS.

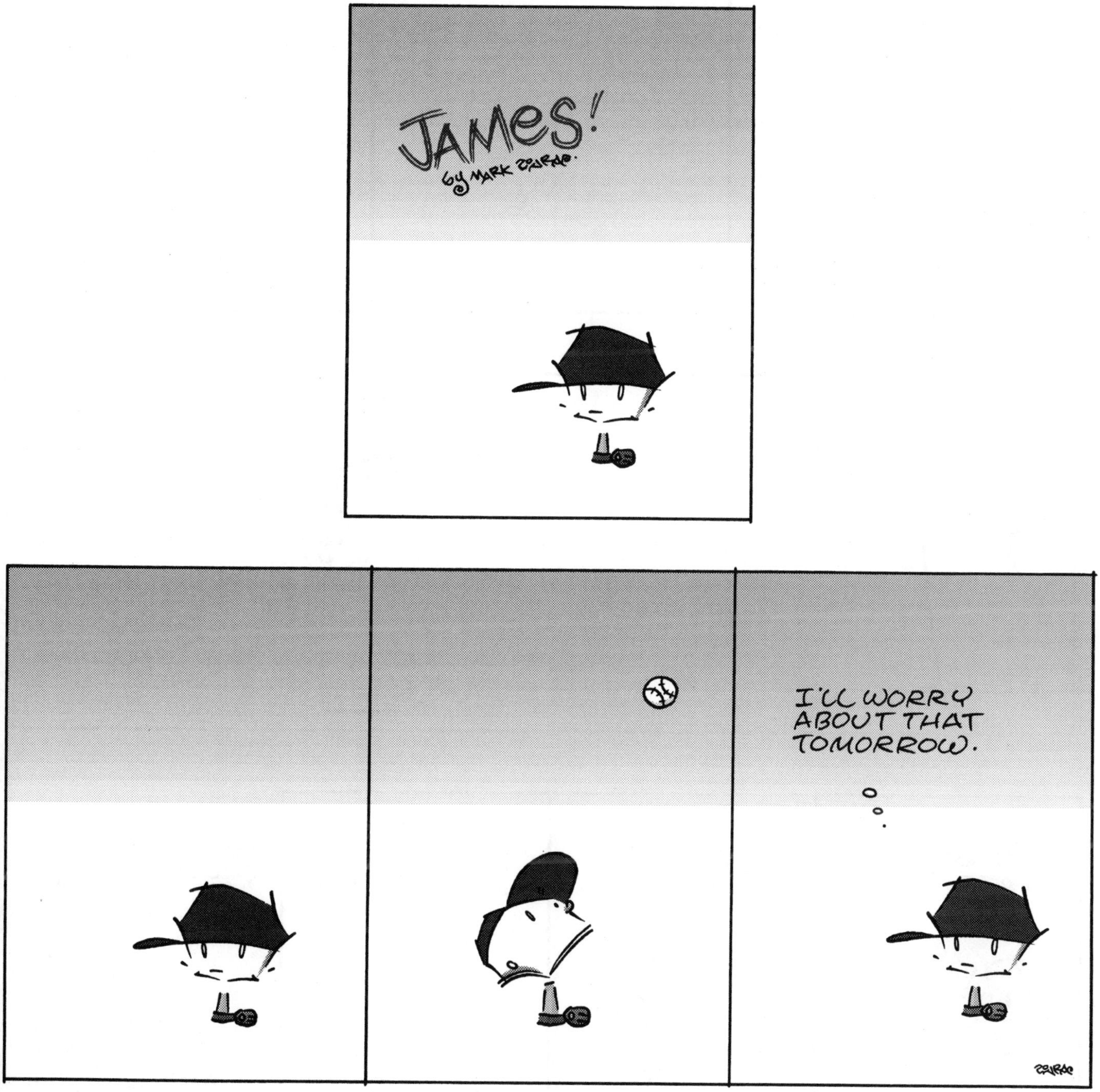
JAMES!
by MARK
I'LL WORRY ABOUT THAT TOMORROW.

YEARS PASS.

TH' WORLD TURNS.

WHAT'S IT ALL ABOUT?

PRESENT COMPANY EXCLUDED.

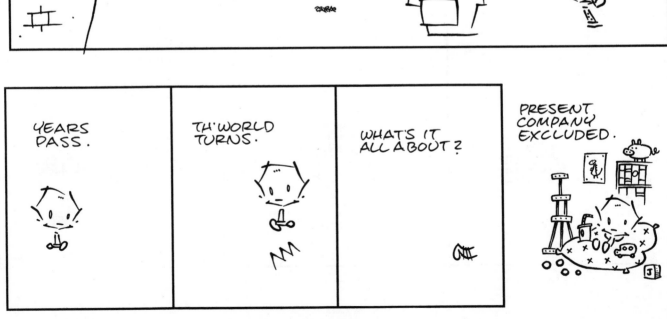

SPIN

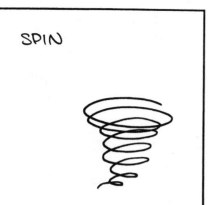

AND THE WORLD SPINS WITH YOU!

FROGS BE DANGEROUS!	FIRES BE DANGEROUS!	MEAN DIRTY DRAGONS...	THEY BE DANGER-OUS!!	MY SOURCES HAVE ASSURED ME.

"LET US CONSIDER THE WAY
IN WHICH WE SPEND OUR LIVES."

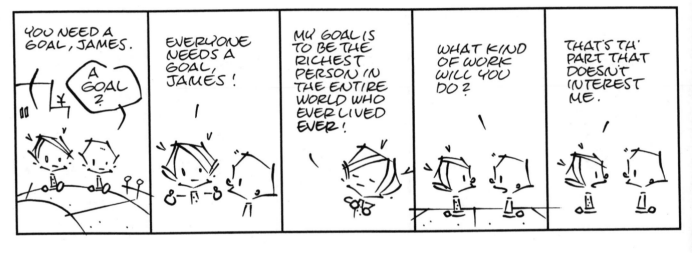

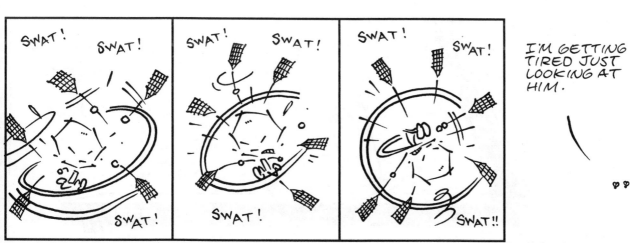

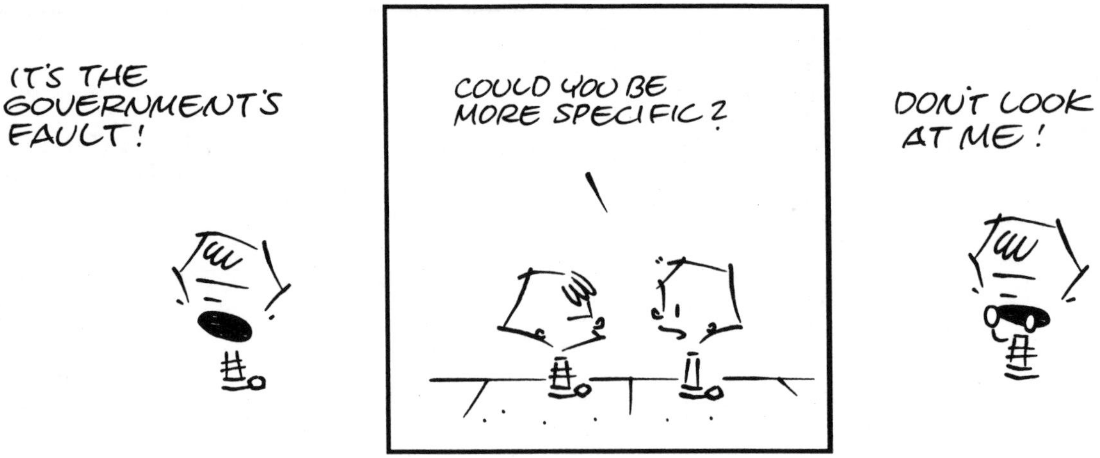
IT'S THE GOVERNMENT'S FAULT!
COULD YOU BE MORE SPECIFIC?
DON'T LOOK AT ME!

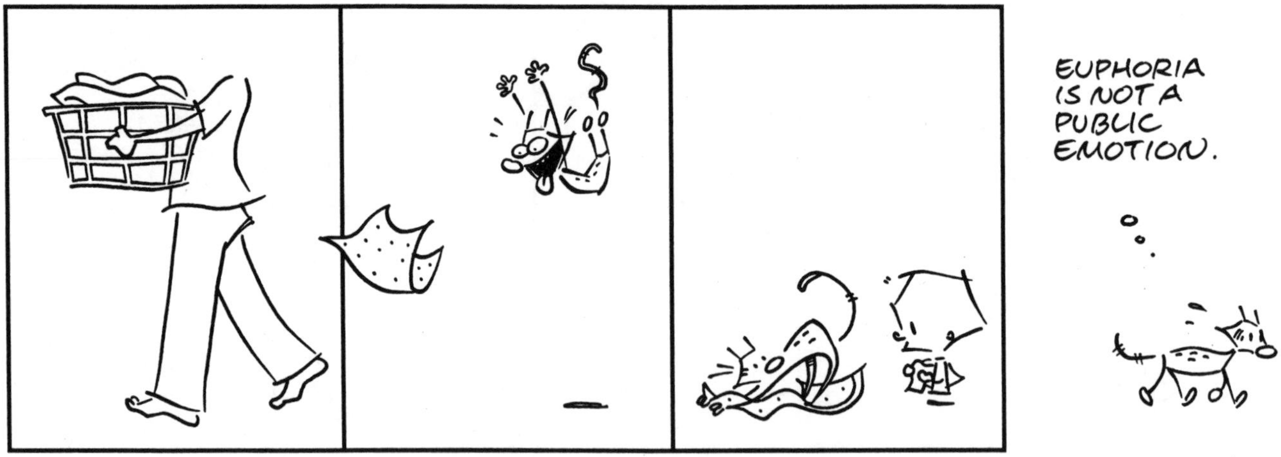
EUPHORIA IS NOT A PUBLIC EMOTION.

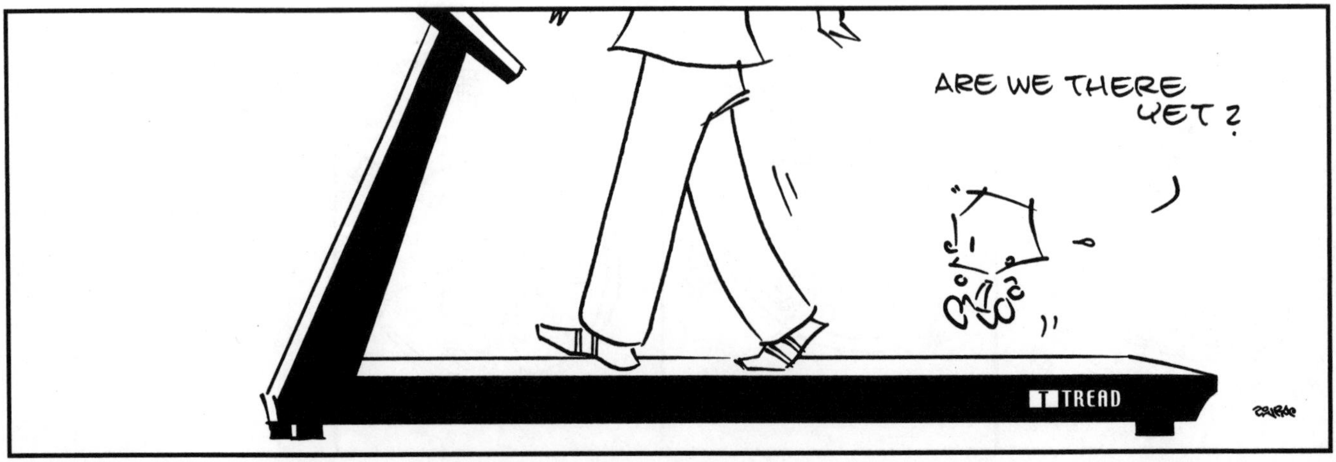
ARE WE THERE YET?
TREAD

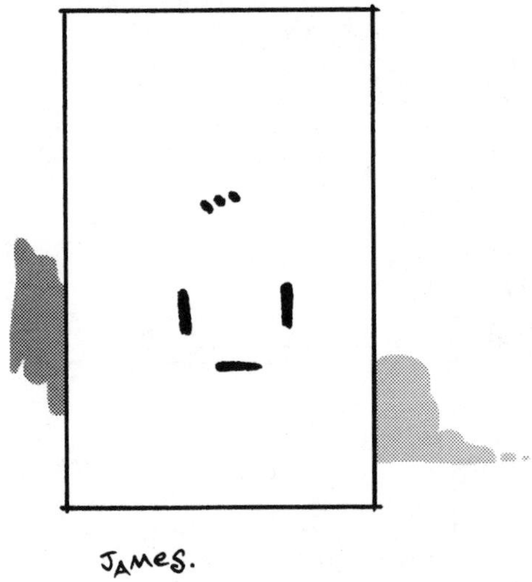

...
JAMES.

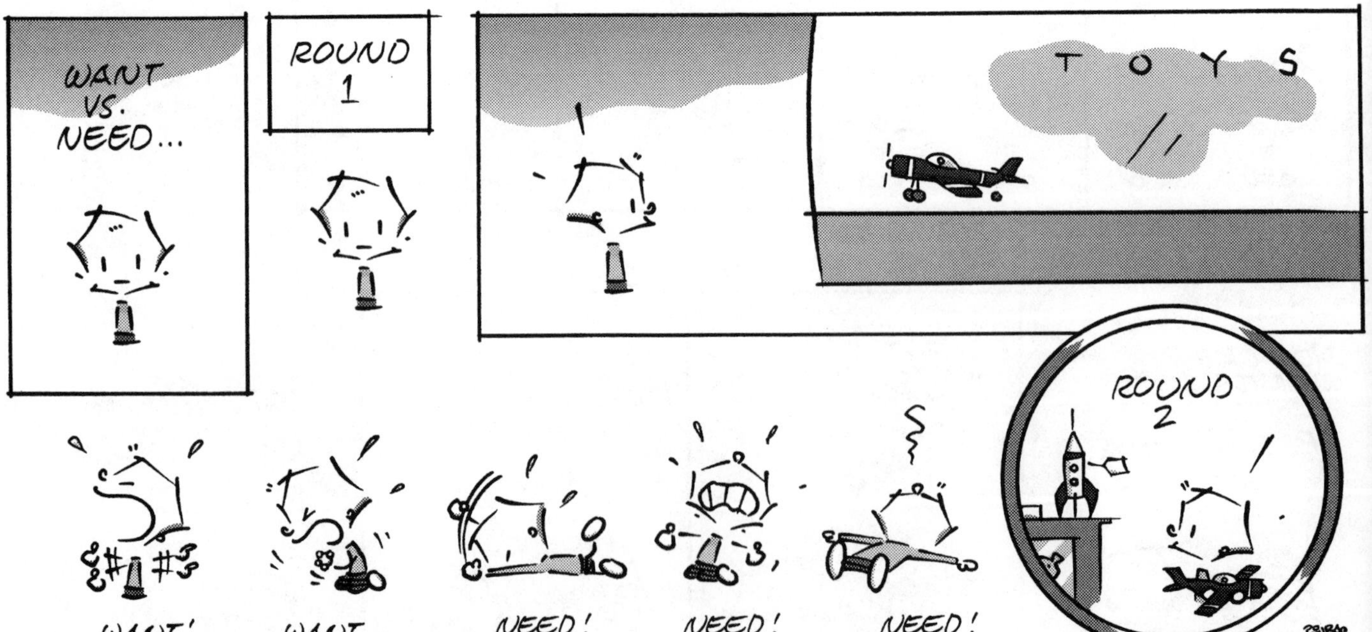

WANT VS. NEED...
ROUND 1
T O Y S
WANT!
WANT...
NEED!
NEED!
NEED!
ROUND 2

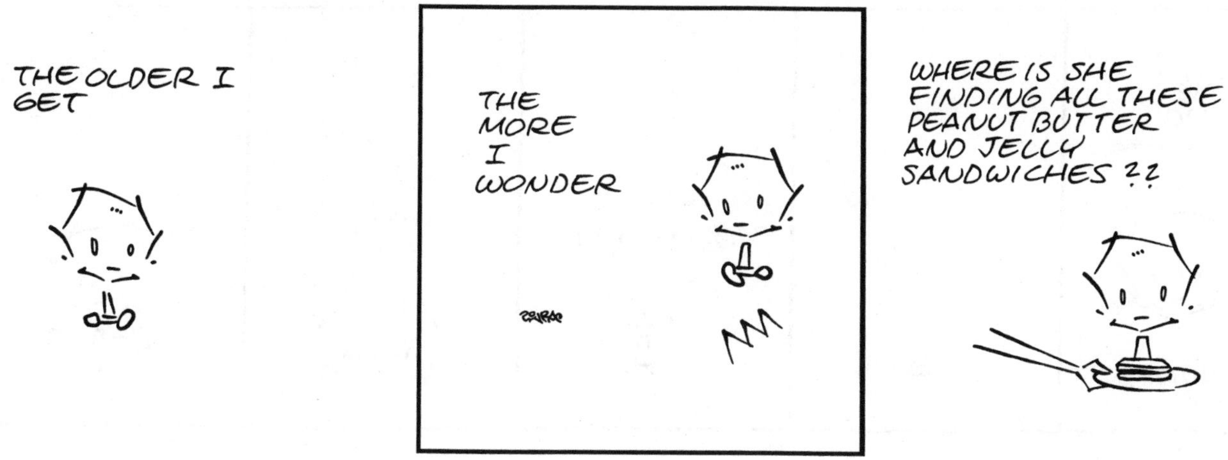
THE OLDER I GET
THE MORE I WONDER
WHERE IS SHE FINDING ALL THESE PEANUT BUTTER AND JELLY SANDWICHES ??

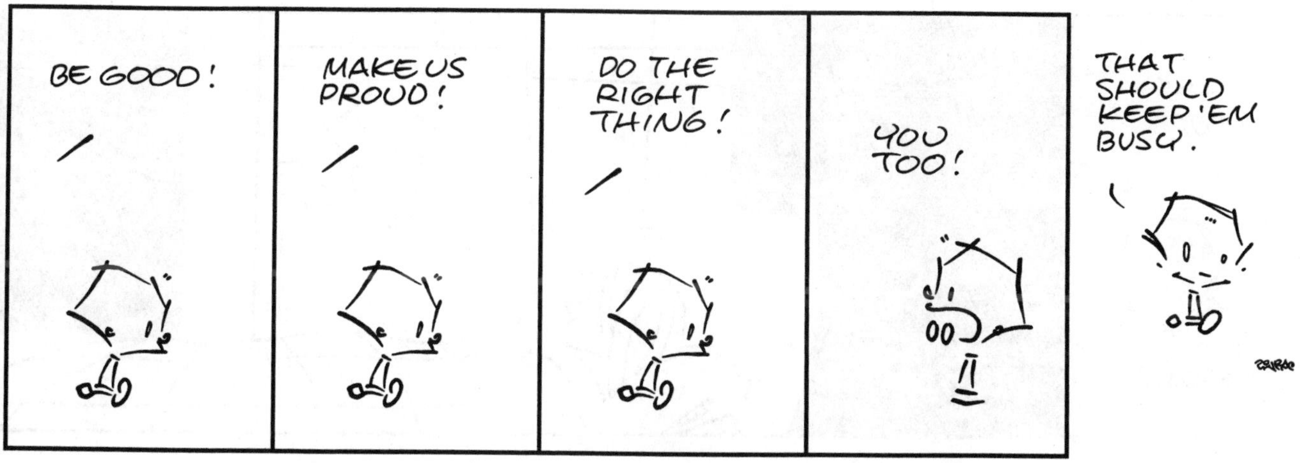
BE GOOD!
MAKE US PROUD!
DO THE RIGHT THING!
YOU TOO!
THAT SHOULD KEEP 'EM BUSY.

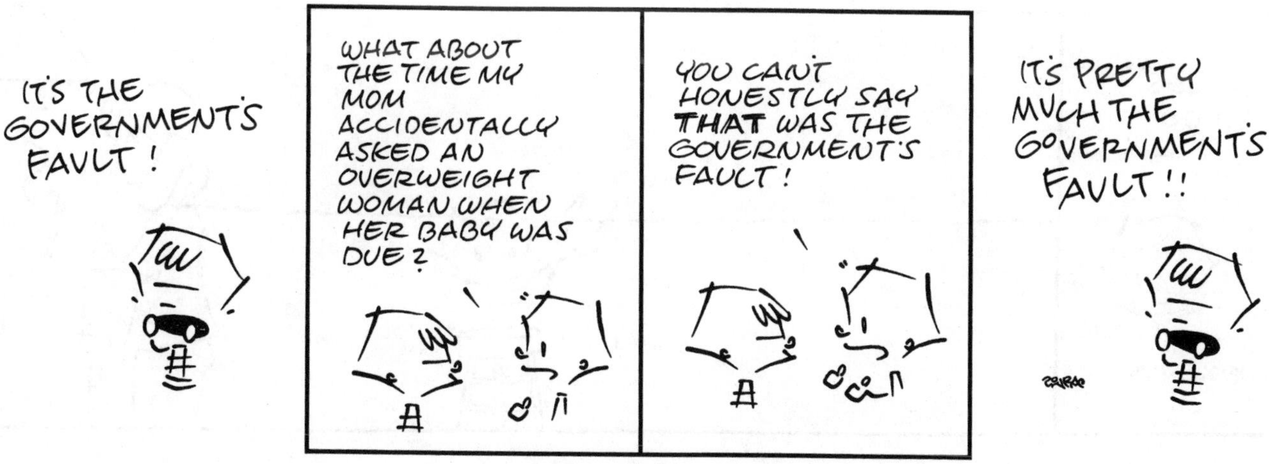
IT'S THE GOVERNMENT'S FAULT!
WHAT ABOUT THE TIME MY MOM ACCIDENTALLY ASKED AN OVERWEIGHT WOMAN WHEN HER BABY WAS DUE?
YOU CAN'T HONESTLY SAY THAT WAS THE GOVERNMENT'S FAULT!
IT'S PRETTY MUCH THE GOVERNMENT'S FAULT!!

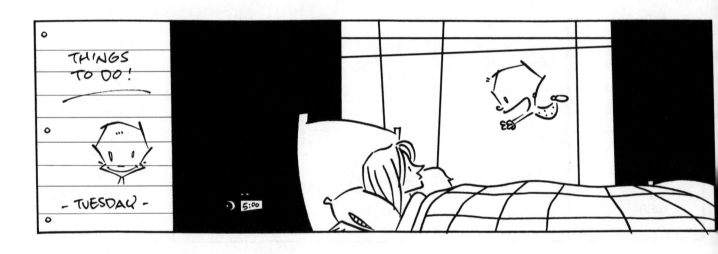

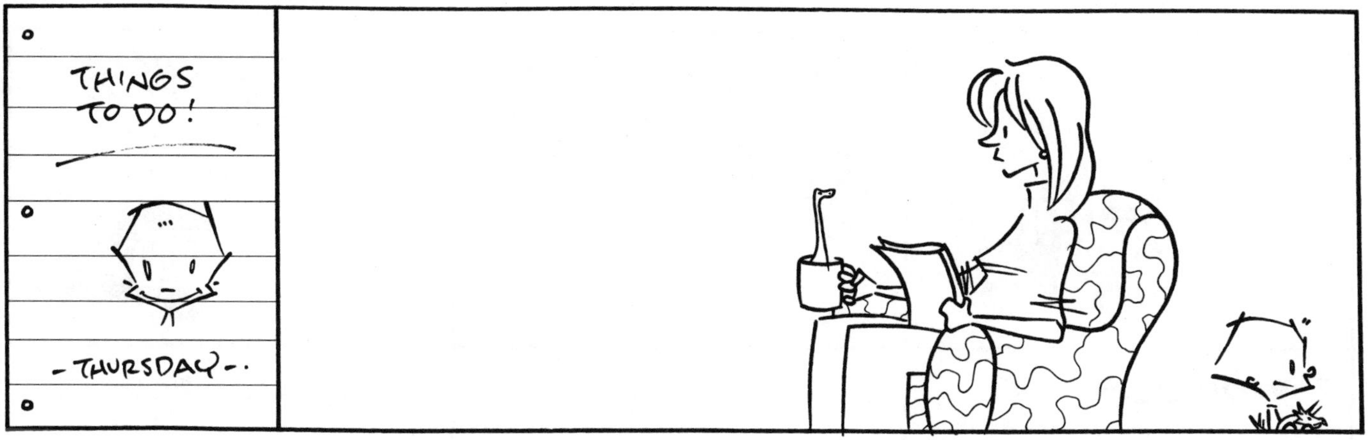
THINGS TO DO!
- THURSDAY - .

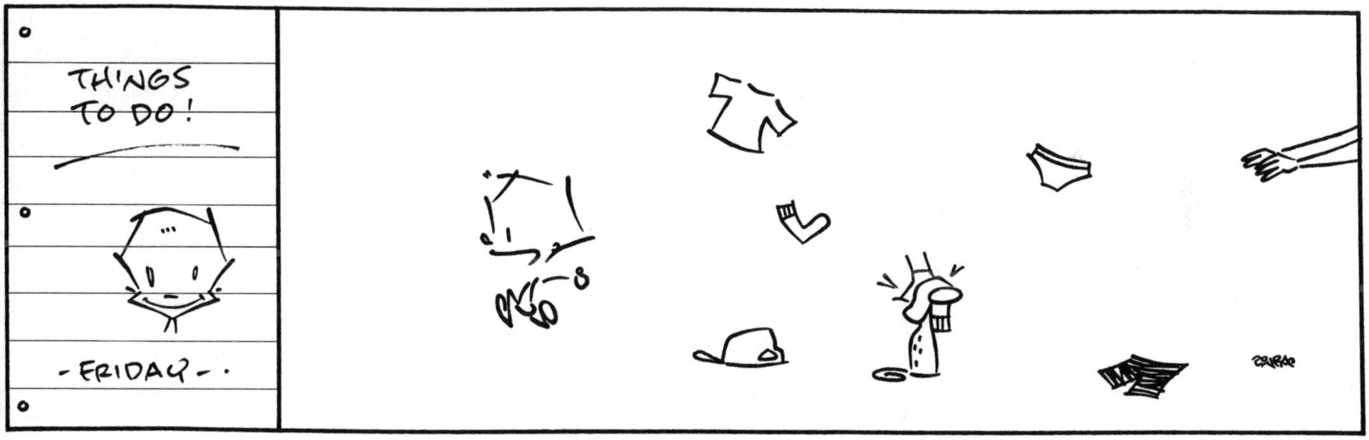
THINGS TO DO!
- FRIDAY - .

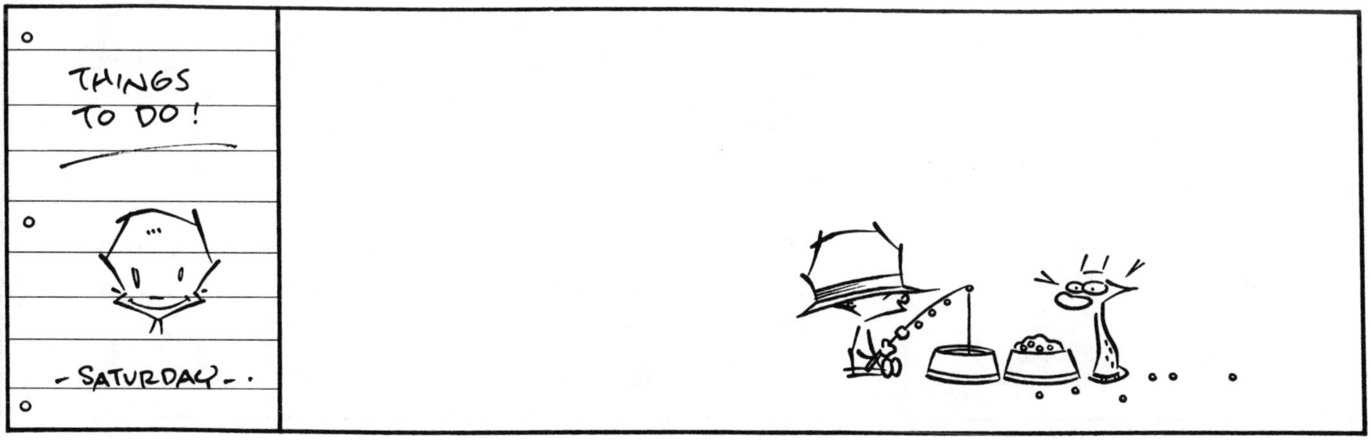
THINGS TO DO!
- SATURDAY - .

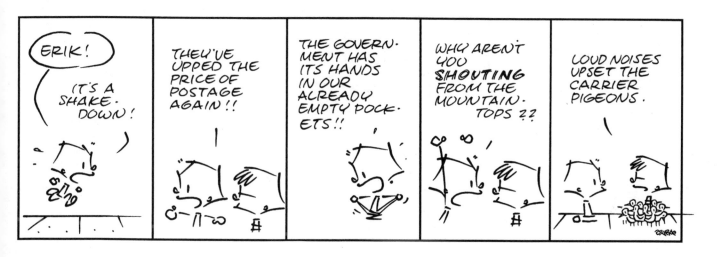

GET READY
FOR IT!!

FOR
WHAT?

THE DETAILS
ARE MURKY.

WHAT A RACKET!

DAD SNORES.

OUCH, THAT'S LOUD!

AND MOM SLEEPS THROUGH IT!

MARRIAGE IS A MIRACLE TO CONTEMPLATE.

THEY PREFER NOT TO THINK ABOUT IT.

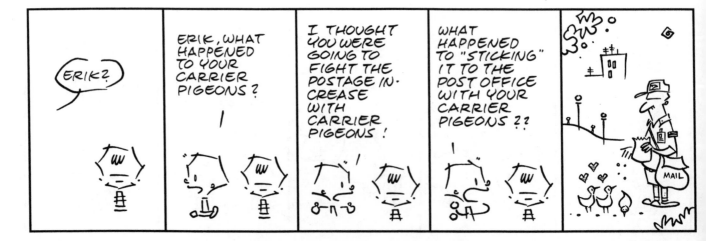

ERIK?

ERIK, WHAT HAPPENED TO YOUR CARRIER PIGEONS?

I THOUGHT YOU WERE GOING TO FIGHT THE POSTAGE INCREASE WITH CARRIER PIGEONS!

WHAT HAPPENED TO "STICKING" IT TO THE POST OFFICE WITH YOUR CARRIER PIGEONS??

MAIL

JAMES

SO YOU CAN HANG UPSIDE DOWN ON THE MONKEY BARS!

SO WHAT? **SO** WHAT??

I DON'T ANSWER QUESTIONS ON MY DAY OFF.

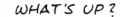

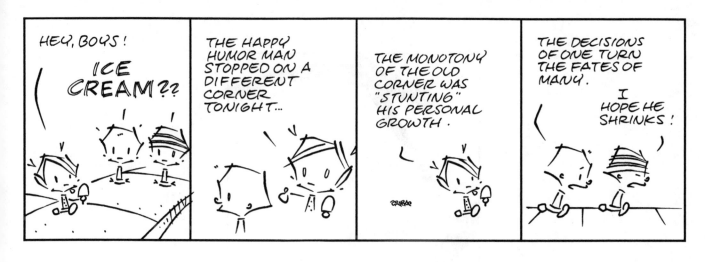

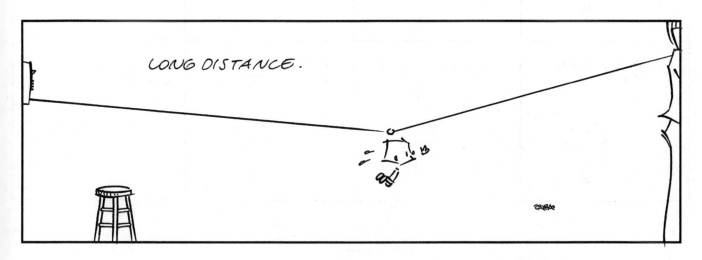

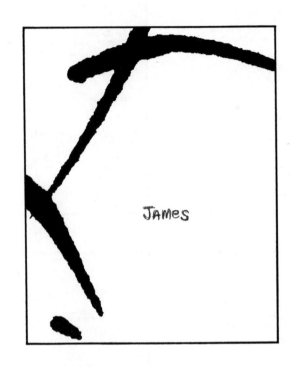

JAMES

YOU'RE "BORED"?	WHAT ABOUT YOUR TOYS?	YOUR BOOKS?	YOUR PIANO?
YOUR PUZZLES, BLOCKS	AND DRUMS?	**HOW** CAN YOU BE "BORED"??	IT'S A PERSONAL CHOICE.

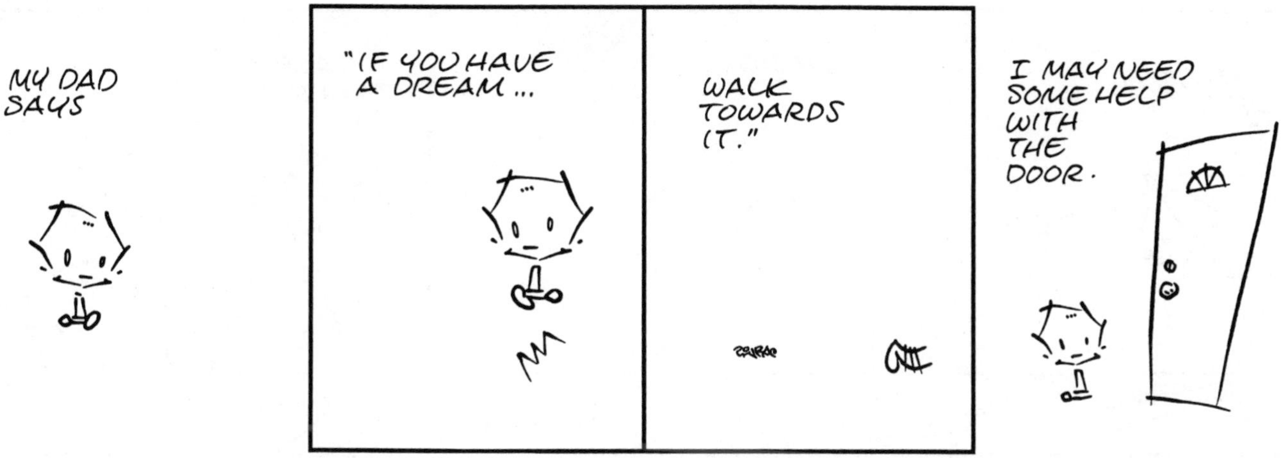
MY DAD SAYS
"IF YOU HAVE A DREAM ...
WALK TOWARDS IT."
I MAY NEED SOME HELP WITH THE DOOR.

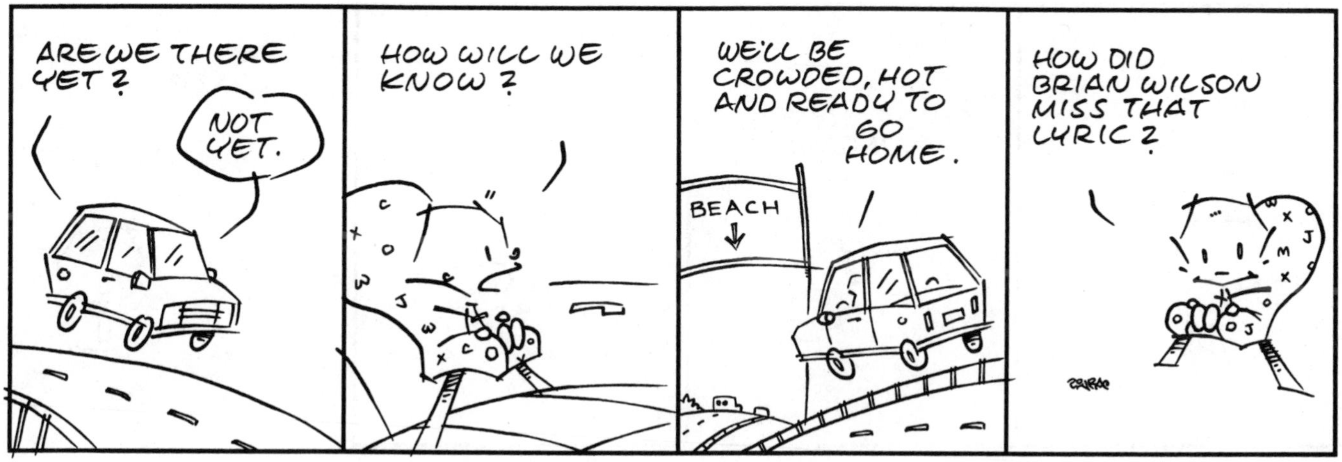
ARE WE THERE YET?
NOT YET.
HOW WILL WE KNOW?
WE'LL BE CROWDED, HOT AND READY TO GO HOME.
BEACH
HOW DID BRIAN WILSON MISS THAT LYRIC?

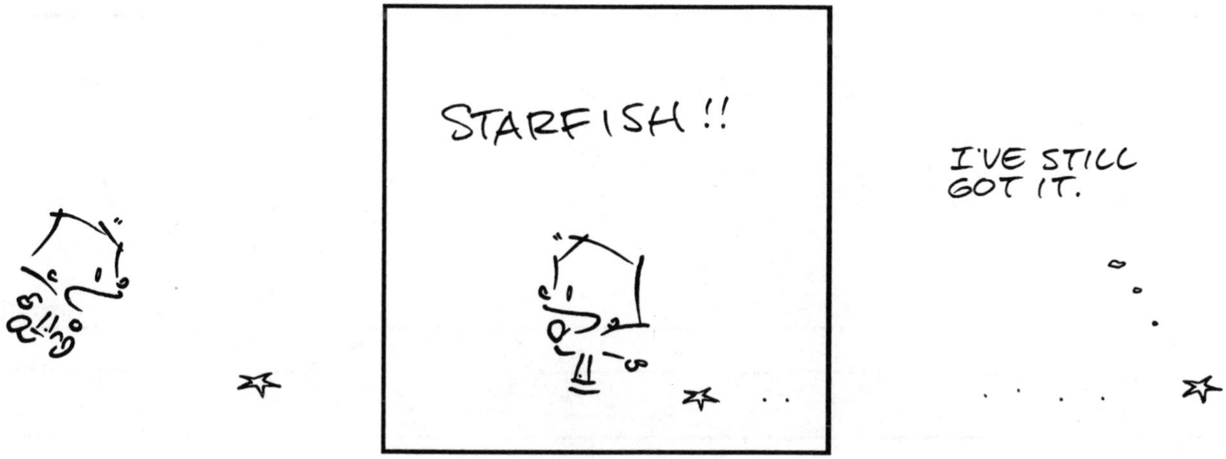
STARFISH!!
I'VE STILL GOT IT.

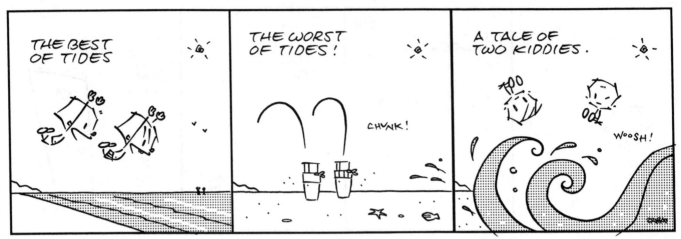

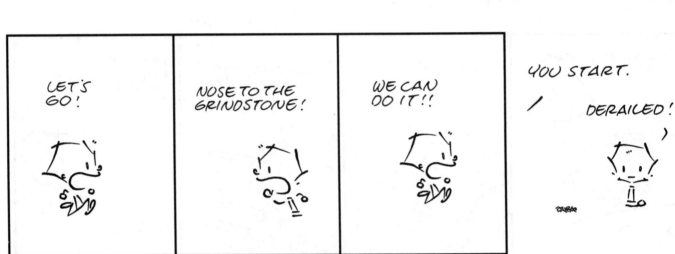

JAMES

AGAIN WITH THE MONKEY BARS ?? WHAT ARE YOU — TRYING TO MAKE THE REST OF US LOOK BAD ?

TRYING TO SET SOME KIND OF AN UPSIDE DOWN **WORLD** RECORD ?? IS THAT WHAT YOU'RE TRYING TO DO, JAMES ? IS IT ?? SHAME ON YOU, JAMES ! **SHAME** ON YOU !!!

IF MY LEGS CAN SLEEP THROUGH THAT, THEY CAN SLEEP THROUGH ANYTHING.

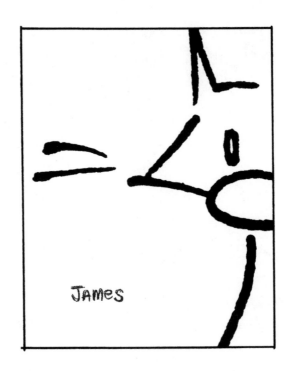

JAMES

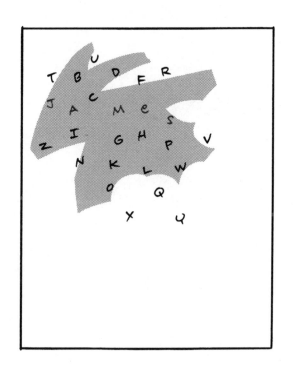

MULTIPLE CHOICE!

© ALL OF THE ABOVE.

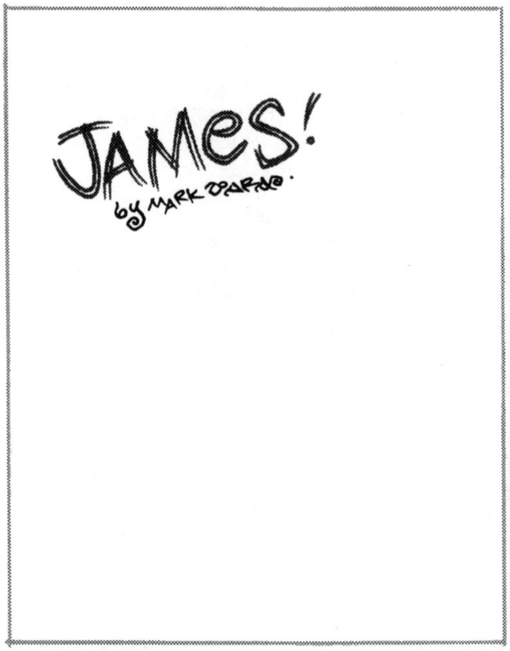
JAMES!
by MARK

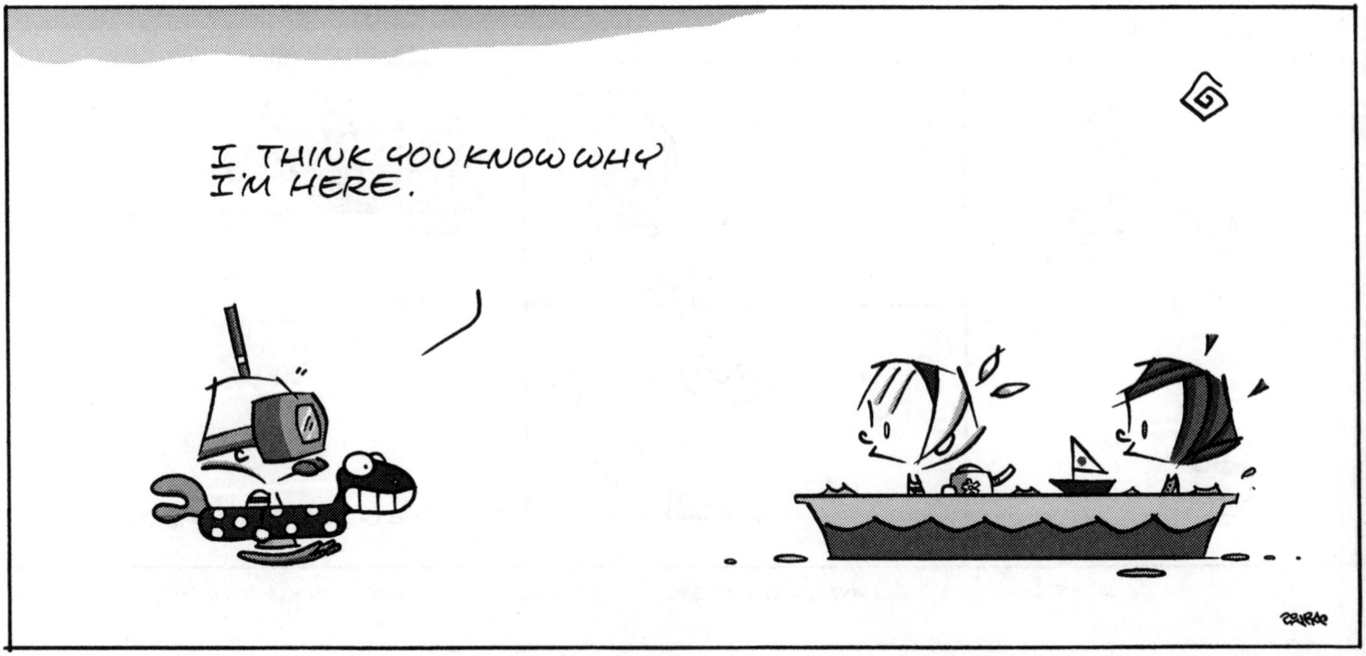
I THINK YOU KNOW WHY I'M HERE.

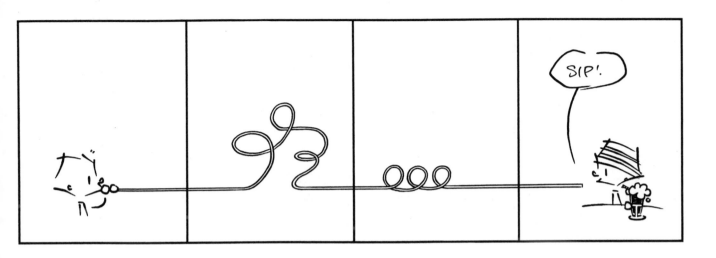

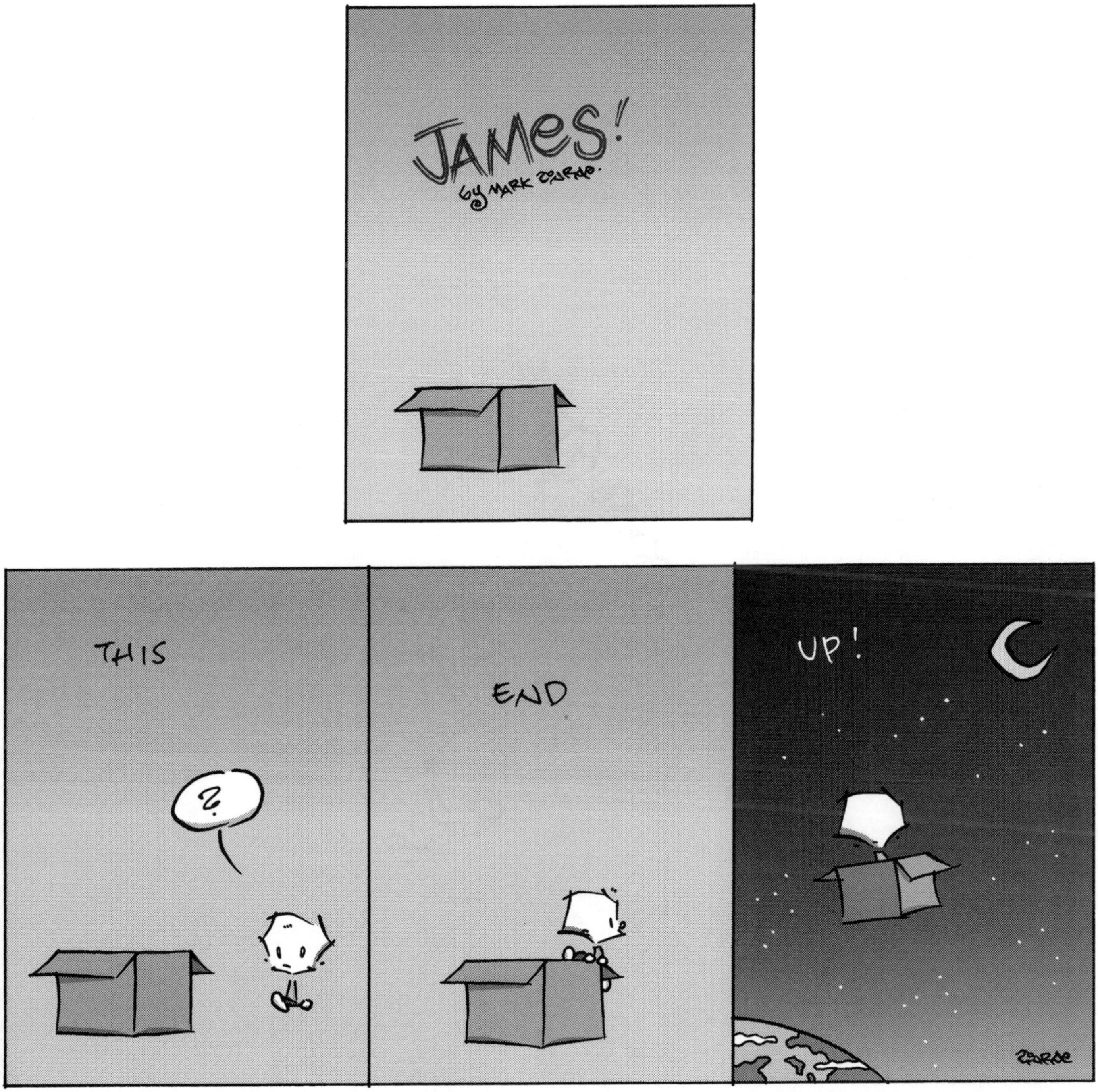
JAMES!
by MARK TONRA.
THIS
?
END
UP!